What people ar

The Tragedy o

T0265653

The Tragedy of Madagascar is a must read for anyone who cares about the fascinating, beguiling, maddening red island off the coast of Africa - or for anyone who wonders why so many forgotten, seemingly invisible people are trapped in poverty across the globe. With a sharp eye for detail, analysis, and storytelling, Adams is an expert guide who brings the island to life. There are few books about Madagascar, and this one will quickly become the go-to book to understand the island's history, its politics, and its depressing trajectory. A fascinating, well-written read.

Brian Klaas, Washington Post columnist and author of *The Despot's Accomplice* and *Corruptible: Who Gets Power & How It Changes Us*

Adams's book is incredibly insightful and will be valuable for Malagasy leaders, its people, and the international community. It is well-written and well-researched, provides an in-depth picture of modern Madagascar, and is a wonderful contribution to the historical literature of the country. It sheds new light on the progress of democracy in a developing country and the responsibilities of our leaders and the Western countries. A great read for anyone interested in Madagascar's past and its future.

Monja Roindefo Zafitsimivalo, Former Prime Minister of Madagascar

The South of Madagascar has been struggling for years to find enough water to feed all of the people in the region. In his new book about the island, Nathaniel Adams has written an important chapter about climate change in the Great South, one that beautifully tells the stories of the millions of people here trying to survive in an unforgiving land.

Vital Batubilema, UN World Food Program, Madagascar

The Tragedy of Madagascar

An Island Nation Confronts the 21st Century

The Tragedy of Madagascar

An Island Nation
Confronts the 21st Century

Nathaniel Adams

Winchester, UK
Washington, USA

JOHN HUNT PUBLISHING

First published by Chronos Books, 2022
Chronos Books is an imprint of John Hunt Publishing Ltd., No. 3 East St., Alresford,
Hampshire SO24 9EE, UK
office@jhpbooks.com
www.johnhuntpublishing.com
www.chronosbooks.com

For distributor details and how to order please visit the 'Ordering' section on our website.

ISBN: 978 1 78904 874 2
978 1 78904 875 9 (ebook)
Library of Congress Control Number: 2021913620

A CIP catalogue record for this book is available from the British Library.

Design: Stuart Davies

UK: Printed and bound by CPI Group (UK) Ltd, Croydon, CR0 4YY
Printed in North America by CPI GPS partners

We operate a distinctive and ethical publishing philosophy in
all areas of our business, from our global network of authors to
production and worldwide distribution.

Contents

To PS, TR, AP, KB, CG, MP, MM, and LS,
For your endless inspiration

And to my father,
For showing me the way

Acknowledgements

I would like to thank all of my friends and contacts in Madagascar and Paris who, through their kindness and encouragement – and in some cases, a lot of hard work – made this book possible. While I can't possibly name them all, here are a few who deserve special mention and to whom I remain deeply indebted:

Stephane Andrianavalona
Jean Yves and Hanta Ranarivelo
Tafitasoa Rasolofonjatovomalala
Patrick Rasamoela
Michael Samoela

Introduction

We shall not cease from exploration; and the end of all our exploring will be to arrive where we started and know the place for the first time.
-T.S. Eliot

We had waited for the General all day.

It was a warm day in Antananarivo and I stood with my translator, Michael, outside a government building swapping stories about life and politics in our respective countries. We were in the neighborhood known as "The 67," a poor section of the city settled mostly by coastal people, where we had arranged to meet a man who had been cryptically described to me as a senior member of the armed forces with vital information to share. Each time we called to check on his location the General would put us off, saying he would be there in 30 minutes, right after he finished mailing a package at the post office and running a couple of other errands. Day turned into night, and I told my translator I was leaving if he didn't show up by seven.

At ten minutes before seven, the General called and told us to meet him a few streets away, deeper into the heart of The 67. "This is strange," my translator said. Then it dawned on him. "I think he wants to meet you after dark, in a place where no one can see him with you."

We drove to the assigned street and Leon, my taxi driver, looked worried as he parked on a dimly let street and let us out. "Be careful with your bag here," he said, pointing to my backpack and showing me how to wear it in front rather than on my back. "Call me as soon as you're done." We walked down the main road and turned a corner onto a side street where the General, who I will call General X, had told us he would be. All

I could see were a few restaurants – shacks really, each with kerosene lamps illuminating a desolate interior. It was almost pitch dark now, but the street was busy with people I couldn't see. We stopped, and as my translator called the General to ask where he was I felt someone tug on my backpack, then a hand fishing in my pocket for my phone. I pushed them away and turned to my interpreter. He shrugged his shoulders, indicating no answer to his call. "It's not safe here," I said. "Let's go."

We started walking back toward the main road, but before we had gone a block the door to a black SUV swung open and a chauffeur stepped out, opening one of the back doors and gesturing toward the back seat in one motion. "He wants to talk in here," he said, motioning me inside the vehicle. I peered into the back seat and there was a round-faced man dressed in slacks and a blazer. "Come in, come in," he said. "I am General X." I got in with my translator and the chauffer walked off with a woman who had been in the front seat. "I'm sorry for the delay. I didn't feel comfortable talking to you in the daytime," the General said. "If anyone sees me talking to a white man there will be rumors, lots of rumors. I could get in serious trouble."

"I understand," I said. Madagascar had just gone through a presidential election, with countless accusations of corruption and foreign interference marring the result. Antananarivo itself was a hotbed of political intrigue, and General X, as a well-known member of the new president's entourage, was taking a risk even meeting with me. He asked to see my passport. "Very interesting," he said. "You have a tourist visa. If you're an American spy I guess you're under some very deep cover." We both laughed, I somewhat nervously. In the darkness of the car, I could hardly see him. I assured him I didn't work for any government and just wanted to hear his version of events that took place in 2009, when a *coup d'etat* ousted Marc Ravalomanana, the twice-elected president of Madagascar, and replaced him with a political upstart backed by the military.

"That was an interesting time," he said. After a few pleasantries, his jovial face took on a serious expression. "OK, give me five hundred dollars and I will tell you everything," he said. "I was an active participant in the change of power, and no one has really asked me to tell the story before. But it needs to be told. I just need some money to tell it." I looked at Michael and rolled my eyes. This had never been part of the plan. I explained to the General that I was here in Madagascar on my own, currently unemployed and on a tight budget. He relented, and after some haggling that would have made my Malagasy friends proud, we agreed on a much lower fee for his time.

He insisted on going to my hotel for the interview, and his driver and the woman who had left us when I entered the car returned upon a signal from the General. We navigated the dark, empty streets of the capital and the General spoke to the others in the car in their native language while I tried to decipher some meaning from their words. When we arrived at the street below the hotel we walked up one of the city's many staircases, the General huffing and puffing behind Michael and me. We walked into the lobby, now empty except for a young night watchman listening to music on his phone, and the General asked if we could sit in a far corner. We ordered bottles of beer and he settled back into his chair, looking relaxed for the first time since I had met him. He folded his hands in front of him and looked away for a moment, composing his thoughts. Then he turned back to me and spoke in a strong, clear voice.

"This is how it happened."

* * *

There are times in the life of every nation when order gives way to violence, political instability or constitutional crisis. In Western nations these civil conflicts are thankfully rare, and in most cases long behind us, but in the developing world they still occur with some frequency. Unfortunately for Madagascar, these events have been erupting with increasing regularity since 1972, although the violence has not been on a large scale. In 2009 a personal rivalry between two longstanding rivals split the country apart, resulting in a societal schism that would last another decade. In March of that year, Andry Rajoelina, the 34-year old mayor of Antananarivo, led often violent protests through the streets of the capital city and seized power with the help of dissident army officers, overthrowing the popular Marc Ravalomanana halfway into his second term. Calling Rajoelina's seizure of power unconstitutional and a *coup d'etat*, aid donors suspended non-emergency assistance, exacerbating the country's already extreme poverty. Rajoelina managed to stay in power for over four years through a combination of skillful maneuvering and outright deception, but the coup would stain his reputation until democracy was restored, and even then he remained a deeply divisive figure. Ravalomanana, for his part, was forced to wait nine years to try to regain the office he still believed was his. When the two men finally confronted each other again in 2018 for what was expected to be a final showdown, Rajoelina won a decisive victory that appeared to end, at long last, the political strife that had bedeviled the island for over almost 50 years.

The overthrow of Ravalomanana had a devastating impact on the economy of Madagascar and the island's development generally. More importantly from a political perspective, the events of February and March 2009 continue to divide the nation today. Rajoelina supporters claim their man bravely led a popular movement to replace a president so intoxicated by power he authorized the shooting of dozens of innocent people, while Ravalomanana supporters call his overthrow a military coup, pure and simple. Each side clings to its version of the truth like a talisman, and a typical Malagasy's view of the president today is largely shaped by what they believe happened in those crucial days. So what is the truth – was Ravalomanana a murderer or the last honest democrat in Madagascar, one who was simply overwhelmed by events? I interviewed several people to find out, starting with the General, a man who was an active participant in the coup, and thus in the nation's downward spiral into obloquy.

General X joined the army in 1980 and became a general in 2015. In 2009, during those fateful weeks leading up to Rajoelina's coup, he was a senior officer and led one of the assaults on the presidential palace that led to Ravalomanana's departure. He therefore enjoyed a front-row seat to the events leading up to the coup, and over the course of three hours, he told me a rambling story of division, dissension, and the moment when the crisis reached a point of no return for him and his fellow officers, compelling them to get involved. Sitting out on my hotel's patio that night he told many half-truths and some outright lies, but with such conviction and panache that I and my translator both became mesmerized. It was one version of the story that every Malagasy knows in one form or another, either as heroism or tragedy.

General X began with an assessment of Ravalomanana's rise, telling me that the former mayor was largely supported by the military when he was first elected president in 2002. But he squandered his popularity within a few years, the General said, and became seen as wholly corrupt. "He was a good president but he was too selfish. He tried to get all the business in the country for his companies, to monopolize the market. He profited from his position." This was a common justification for the coup that I heard many times, but the General added a twist to it when he suggested that Ravalomanana became resentful of Rajoelina when the latter became mayor of Antananarivo and, in effect, stole the limelight from him in the island's capital. "When Rajoelina became mayor he became so popular Marc could no longer control the capital, and this bothered him." There was also a conflict brewing within the military when Ravalomanana took over, he added. The troops that had supported former President Ratsiraka – mostly reservists who were viewed as unfaithful by Ravalomanana – were sent to prison by the new president. "Many soldiers didn't like Marc right away because of the way he treated those men."

Like most people, General X saw a steady increase in corruption after Ravalomanana was reelected in 2006. "Civil society became stifled and public land was sold to businesses for his own profit," he claimed. "So Rajoelina revolted. He led some of the protests himself and they grew bigger and bigger. Everyone knew the President was finished." This, I already knew, was revisionist history at its finest: while a successful coup may look inevitable with the benefit of hindsight, in the early days of Rajoelina's protests no one knew how they would end, and very few would have predicted a sudden overthrow.

We eventually got around to the violence of February 7, 2009, and the General, now into his second bottle of the local brew known affectionately as THB – Three Horses Beer – related his version of events that culminated in an extraordinary claim: the president not only ordered the killings of unarmed protesters but murdered many more people than previously reported. "The Prime Minister, not the mayor, led the final march on the presidential palace," he began, "so even he wanted an end to the regime. We in the army were told to be on high alert as the crowds got closer to the palace. We knew we might have to intervene if a battle broke out." And then the most damning charge: "Ravalomanana personally told the army to firmly defend the palace at whatever cost, and that the army should keep the protesters back from the palace even if they had to use force." This order was then repeated to the presidential guard on site at the palace. "The presidential guard received the order to fire. When they knew there was no other option, they started shooting." I asked him if he saw any of the 30 or 40 people murdered that day as his unit later tried to restore order. "Forty? Many more than 40 people were shot, but the army hid dozens of bodies to reduce the real number. Two hundred fifty people were wounded and more than 100 people died for sure. Many families never saw their loved ones after that day and they never got an explanation as to what happened. We were told to stay silent."

I asked him to explain the army's reaction to the violence in the days afterwards. He responded by basically claiming that he and his fellow soldiers felt a public duty to overthrow the man who had twice been elected president. They saw themselves as neutral arbiters in a conflict quickly spinning out of control but, through somewhat perverse logic, came to the conclusion that neutrality, in this case, demanded their support of "the people," meaning the throngs of protesters led by Rajoelina. He explained it this way:

"In Madagascar, the army is the last option to defend the people and the state. So the army attacked the presidential guard the next day to stop the bloodshed. The army has many more troops than the presidential guard and we were able to quickly encircle them. From that day on the people clearly supported the army in the standoff and when that became clear, Ravalomanana fled and the Army took power at CAPSAT [the central military base in Antananarivo]. Overnight we became the leaders of the country and reestablished public order. But by the next day the Army leaders felt out of place. We weren't supposed to have political power, you know. That is not our role. So the question became, who should we give the power to, now that order has been restored?"

This piqued my interest. Almost everyone knew the army had installed Rajoelina and I wanted to see if he would deny it.

Instead, he doubled down on his claims of impartiality.

"Some people think we planned to install Rajoelina from the beginning, but we had no relationship with him so that is simply not true. But we were conscious that because of the new political instability the public was in great danger and that we needed to act. We were not taking orders from anyone and we acted independently to restore order and ensure a smooth transition to whoever the next leader would be. Remember the situation we were facing: people now thought the outgoing president was a murderer. We knew that Rajoelina was a man supported by the people, especially the people protesting. Because the people supported Rajoelina, the army transferred power to him. He was the obvious choice."

I pressed him further on this. If the army was neutral why did they immediately hand power to one of the rival contestants for power? "Listen," he said. "The army follows rules, and we just want to have public order. Once we saw that the situation had calmed down and there was no more violence, we did the right thing and restored a civil government. By giving the government to Rajoelina we followed the will of the people."

This decision would have serious consequences, of course, not only for the resolution of the crisis in 2009 but, as many could have predicted, for the next several years as well. Rajoelina vowed to hold an election soon after executing his coup, but found one pretext after another to delay a vote. "Well, it's true that we gave him the power only temporarily, so that he could hold elections. But he kept it as long as possible!" Here the General feigned outrage, banging on the table and rattling the empty bottles in front of him. "We did not know he would do that, and like many people we were not happy about it. In fact, a few officers led by Colonel Charles [Andrianasoavina] revolted because of the length of time it was taking Rajoelina to hold an election. Others tried two of their own coups in fact but there was not enough support and Rajoelina put them in jail afterward."

Sure, I said, I know there were a few officers who tried to overthrow Rajoelina after his seizure of power, but most stood by him, knowing they would be rewarded by the new president for their support during the coup. And Rajoelina, in return, would do everything he could to keep them loyal to him during a highly chaotic transition. This the General did not dispute. "Of course Rajoelina felt beholden to the army for making him president. One of his first acts was to name a General, Camille Vital, as Prime Minister to thank us for the army's support. Also, the Vice Minister in charge of Foreign Affairs was another general. But I want to emphasize, this was not a *coup d'etat* because the army only acted to help people in danger, and we gave the power back to the people as soon as possible, not to Marc [Ravalomanana]. Remember that after the transition was over, people publicly thanked the army for what they had done. The people in Madagascar respect the army because we are trying to fight the lawlessness and insecurity that are such a problem here." He later acknowledged that corruption in the army is a problem just as it is in other key institutions on the island, but insisted that the military plays an overwhelmingly positive role in society.

And as for those army members who had been imprisoned when Ravalomanana became president in 2002 for their supposed disloyalty? The General proudly told me of his role in releasing twenty-five former generals after Rajoelina ordered them set free, in response to what the General called a public outcry for their liberation. A few political leaders who had opposed Ravalomanana were also released simultaneously. This was something else that endeared the army to the public, according to the General.

The night grew long, and as the General's litany of self-justifications continued I ended our interview by asking him what role the army saw for itself today. Having once crowned a king, or at least a president, would they hesitate to do so again? They had played no appreciable role in the two elections since the coup, in 2013 and 2018, and this return to normalcy had pleased the General. "In 2013, the Army would have supported whoever won. The same for 2018. We would not have acted to prevent Marc's candidate (Jena Louis Robinson) from taking power or Marc himself from returning. The army knows it must support the winner of our elections. And we are not involved in politics anymore; in fact, we are neutral now towards Rajoelina. He himself told us, told the whole country, to wait until December to evaluate him, and that is what everyone is doing. No one is protesting the president now, as you can see. He is still in his first year and we will all judge him later after he has had some time."

This man who had been so bombastic in his defense of the army's conduct during the coup ended with a surprisingly sober analysis of where Madagascar finds itself today. As a military man, public safety was his biggest concern: "We are not a full democracy yet. The story with democracy here is still unfolding, still developing. But Madagascar is not unique in that respect – in fact, we are just like many African countries. The biggest problem in Madagascar is the lack of security around the country. The second largest is the large numbers of unemployed youth, which is related to the first problem. In Madagascar the national police are charged with resolving this problem. But they can ask the Gendarmes and the Army for assistance, which we've done. Also, there is an urban/rural dimension or divide to the insecurity problem: we see kidnapping in the cities and attacks on the rural roads, the stealing of cattle elsewhere. So we need to create jobs, programs to get our youth participating in building the country – and we need financial assistance from abroad to do this."

* * *

There is no other place in the world quite like Madagascar. Most people know it's an island located somewhere off the southeast coast of Africa, and if those people have children they are probably familiar with the animated movies named after the island, but that's usually about it. Unless they happen to be French or are especially inclined toward world history, most people don't know it was a French colony for the better part of sixty years, much less that it was ruled by a largely stable monarchy for some two hundred years before that. All of my American friends are astounded to hear that Madagascar is the size of Texas and that over 25 million people live there. Those millions are almost entirely unknown to the people of the rest of the world, who, if they took the time to visit the Great Red Island – so named for the unique color of its red, lateritic soil – would immediately discover two things about them. First, the ethnic diversity of the Malagasy people is extraordinary, with 18 ethnic groups representing a unique Afro-Asian mix that resulted from the overlapping settlement from two continents. Second, a majority of those people are desperately poor, doing whatever they can to meet their basic needs each day. And even more diverse than its people is the island's biodiversity, already endangered to be sure, but still awe-inspiring for the spectrum of its national parks, white sand beaches, tropical rainforests and dozens of animal species that became extinct on the African mainland but survived on the large chunk of land that broke away from the continent millions of years ago. Madagascar is truly a jewel of an island.

Such untapped potential on the island makes General X's story even more disheartening. The General's narrative, while problematic in many respects, nonetheless captures perfectly the distance travelled from all of Madagascar's potential at independence to the political and economic basket case it unfortunately is today. An island of abundant natural resources and a young, industrious population has been systematically throttled by the chronic infighting and self-enrichment of its leaders, even as the rest of the world ignores it. Indeed, the General's recollection of the chaotic days of 2009 in Antananarivo highlighted several themes that still dominate Madagascar's political life today. First, the island has been paralyzed by chronic political instability, producing coups and other national crises that are becoming more frequent, not less. Four or five such crises, depending on who's counting, have engulfed the country since 1972, each time bringing the island's economy to a halt and forcing many sectors to rebuild from scratch. Second, the two-man rivalry between Ravalomanana and Rajoelina, now well into its second decade, has stifled any real development of mature political parties that cater to the interests of the people. While highly entertaining and an easy prop to understanding a nation's recent history, a political system dominated by two people over twenty years is not healthy for democracy. Third, the corruption that has become ubiquitous on the island and which people like the General engage in as a matter of course has siphoned off income from an already destitute population, who have become increasingly cynical about their leaders and the entire political process. Lastly, the ethnic distrust of people like the General who hails from the coastal provinces toward the Merina, the island's elite tribe located in the central highlands, holds the island back from the sense of national unity it needs to develop all of its various regions.

Madagascar has now been independent for sixty years. It was well situated in 1960 to succeed as a post-colonial state, and indeed, got off to a magnificent start under its first president. With the right leadership the country could have used that momentum and the sense of empowerment following independence to forge a robust democracy and an uncorrupt government. It could have lifted millions of people who were desperately poor out of poverty and into middle-class lifestyles similar to those on the neighboring island of Mauritius (the most democratic nation in Africa and one of the wealthiest). Its leaders could have prioritized the protection of its rainforests and otherwise preserved its unique natural environment. With the help of the international community, they could have proactively prepared the island for the onslaught of drought and other effects from climate change that are now beginning to be felt in various regions of the island. And the country could have curbed its once-rampant population growth and ended the simmering ethnic tensions that have plagued it for centuries.

If you know anything about Madagascar today you know that none of the possibilities raised in the preceding paragraph came true (except for the facts about Mauritius). Unfortunately, the island has made almost no progress in improving the lives of its citizens since 1960. Its political system is highly unstable, with coups and constitutional crises becoming disturbingly common and populism on the rise. Malagasy people are just as poor now as they were at independence, and there are millions more of them, as the population continues to grow at an alarming rate and with no end in sight. Meanwhile, the southern region of Madagascar is fast becoming a wasteland as crops dry up and shorelines recede due to climate change. Distrust among the regions and the capital city continues to hamper the island's sense of unity and economic development.

All of which makes Madagascar a profound exception to an unmistakable paradigm shift taking place around the world. With constant news reports of wars, pandemics, terrorism, poverty, crime and natural disasters, it's easy to forget that we actually live in an age of optimism, at least among those who study global trends for a living. Multiple books and articles by highly respected authors have been written in recent years lauding the progress made in the world across a broad spectrum of basic development categories – poverty, health, life span, war, human rights and democracy. With the sole exception of climate change, which everyone agrees is a major challenge, and perhaps the very recent erosion of democracy and the growth of economic inequality in some regions, most experts agree that human life across the world is getting better for billions of people. Even the Coronavirus pandemic is seen as a temporary setback on the inevitable march toward health and prosperity that awaits us.

Steven Pinker's bestselling book, *Enlightenment Now,* makes this case more forcefully and more broadly than any other. The values of the Enlightenment, he claims – namely reason, science and humanism – have brought unprecedented progress to the world over the past two centuries. In everything from the safety of long-distance travel to the reduced devastation of wars and advancements in public health, the world has made incredible strides. Despite the barrage of news reports bemoaning the state of the world and a focus on global crises, Pinker finds overwhelming evidence that things have actually gotten significantly better. "And here is a shocker," he writes. *"The world has made spectacular progress in every single measure of human well-being.* Here is a second shocker: *Almost no one knows about it."* [1]

Evidence of global progress, according to Pinker, can be found throughout a dozen or more categories, but a few stand out as emblematic of the vast improvements for basic human welfare. First, people are living longer, healthier and more prosperous lives. "Life expectancy across the world has risen from 30 to 71, and in the more fortunate countries to 81. The proportion of humanity living in extreme poverty has fallen from almost 90 percent to less than 10 percent, and within the lifetimes of most of the readers of this book it could approach zero. Catastrophic famine, never far away in most of human history, has vanished from most of the world, and undernourishment and stunting are in steady decline."[2]

Second, the world has become less violent and safer. "War between countries is obsolescent, and war within countries is absent from five-sixths of the world's surface. The proportion of people killed annually in wars is less than a quarter of what it was in the 1980s." Genocides, once common, now occur much less frequently. Meanwhile, Americans are half as likely to be murdered as they were two dozen years ago and, over the course of the 20th century, Americans became 96 percent less likely to be killed in a car accident. Life in poorer countries, he says, will also get safer as they continue to develop and get richer.

Third, societies have become more democratic and individual freedoms have expanded. "Two centuries ago," he writes, "a handful of countries, embracing one percent of the world's people, were democratic; today, two-thirds of the world's countries, embracing two-thirds of its countries, are. Not long ago half the world's countries had laws that discriminated against racial minorities; today more countries have policies that favor their minorities than policies that discriminate against them. At the turn of the 20th century, women could vote in just one country; today they vote in every country where men can vote save one."

All of this progress has inevitably contributed to human happiness, according to Pinker. Americans have more free time and disposable income than ever before, and "are using their leisure and disposable income to travel, spend time with their children, connect with loved ones, and sample the world's cuisine, knowledge and culture. As a result of these gifts, people have become happier." Pinker sees only two major problems the world has failed to adequately address: climate change and the threat of nuclear war. But even these he faces optimistically, writing that with "practical long-term agendas" now on the table, they are problems that can one day be solved.[3]

The evidence presented by Pinker is incontrovertible from a statistical point of view, and scholars who have predicted the coming decline of the human race now have to grapple with his mountain of facts pointing in the other direction. But what makes his argument unique is his belief that the intellectual values of the Enlightenment sparked the current wave of progress. Indeed, he writes, "The bulk of [his] book is devoted to defending those ideals in a distinctively 21st century way: with data. This evidence-based take on the Enlightenment project reveals that it was not a naïve hope. The Enlightenment has *worked* – perhaps the greatest story seldom told."[4]

Scholars of the developing world have now taken up these broad themes and applied them to their research on poor countries, with most of them reaching the same sunny conclusions. Steven Radelet's book, *The Great Surge,* examines the economic progress made in the Global South and finds overwhelming progress over the past few decades. Real progress for most developing countries began in the 1990s, he claims, in poverty, income, health and education. Most remarkably, the number of people living in extreme poverty (less than $1.25 per day), shrank from almost 2 billion in 1993 to just over 1 billion in 2011, meaning a billion people around the world have been lifted out of extreme poverty in just the last two decades. "After rising relentlessly from the beginning of human history," he writes, "the number of people living on less than $1 a day dropped by more than half in just eighteen years." And the percentage of people living in extreme poverty has been falling even faster, making the decline in extreme poverty "one of the most important achievements in global economic history."[5] Incomes for most families are now higher than at any time in history, and although income inequality has worsened within many Western countries, across the globe, income is more equal than it has been in centuries. But the surge in living standards goes beyond incomes, he writes. Far fewer people than ever go hungry, and the world now grows more food than it needs. Women have more opportunities, democracy has expanded, and basic human rights are more widely respected than ever before. What is most remarkable about this progress, he claims, is that such great strides have been made in so many areas at the same time. There have been spurts of progress in certain areas before, but "the simultaneous improvement in so many aspects of development is unprecedented."[6]

In contrast to Pinker's focus on the values of the Enlightenment, Radelet gives much more modern and specific reasons for the remarkable progress that erupted in the 1990s. First, the end of the Cold War ended the various civil wars in many developing countries and legitimized market-based economic systems and democracy. Second, globalization and the spread of new technologies provided key opportunities that allowed people to attain greater prosperity. And third, new leadership in developing countries themselves brought more effective institutions and smarter policies to those countries. Foreign aid, he notes, also had a "moderate positive impact" on economic progress. Collectively these forces produced a tidal wave of improvement in living standards across the globe, including in some of the poorest places on Earth.[7]

International human rights experts, focused as they are on human suffering, often depict the world as a grim, unjust place, but even their outlook is starting to change. Kathryn Sikkink, in *Evidence For Hope: Making Human Rights Work in the 21st Century*, finds remarkable advances made in global human rights over the past century and tells a mostly uplifting story. Progress has undeniably been made in human rights, she says, largely as a result of struggles fought by brave men and women to secure those rights. Those struggles led to new laws and institutions protecting greater and greater swathes of humanity. She cites lower incidences of genocide and famine, fewer war-related deaths for both combatants and civilians, and greater equality for women in many areas of study. "If I am more hopeful than others," she writes, "it is because I have seen dramatic improvements in some human rights in my lifetime, such as greater equality and opportunities for women and sexual minorities."[8] Overall, her analysis shows the record is far more positive than current pessimism might suggest, since there is less violence overall and fewer human rights violations than in the past.

Sikkink uses a provocative argument that not only places her firmly in the optimists' camp but exemplifies the paradigm shift in favor of progress now taking shape. Like the other new believers mentioned above, she believes that empirical comparisons over time are more useful than "comparisons to the ideal." For example, when looking at the number of undernourished people in the world, she notes that there were still 800 million of them in 2015, which sounds appalling, but is actually less than either the absolute number of undernourished people or the undernourished percentage of the world population in 1990.[9] We need to keep both sets of data in mind when thinking about undernourishment around the world, she believes. Her larger point is that rather than to continually lament the significant human rights challenges still remaining, we should focus on the positive overall trends and make sure the message of progress is heard just as loudly as the predictions of more calamity.

Prominent journalists are now bringing these claims regarding human progress to a wider audience. Nicholas Kristof of the *New York Times* has recently begun writing an annual piece at the end of each year explaining why the past year or the upcoming one will be "the best year ever." Like Pinker and others, he describes the progress made in fighting poverty and disease around the world and believes such advances will only continue. In the early 1980's he writes, 44% of all humans were living on less than about $2 per day, while fewer than 10% do so today, and by 2030 that number will be just 3-4%. Over three hundred thousand people access clean drinking water each day for the first time; meanwhile, the percentage of children dying before age 5 across the world declined from 27% in 1950 to 4% today. The last famine recognized by the World Food Program struck just part of one state in South Sudan and last for only a few months in 2017. And thanks to the incredible reductions in poverty in China in India, income inequality on a global level is steadily declining. "If you're depressed by the state of the world, let me toss out an idea: In the long arc of human history, 2019 has been the best year ever...Since modern humans emerged about 200,000 years ago, 2019 was probably the year in which children were least likely to die, adults were least likely to be illiterate and people were least likely to suffer excruciating and disfiguring diseases."[10]

Taken together, these books and articles paint an astonishing picture of success in combating some of the greatest scourges humanity has ever faced, including many that have been with us since the dawn of time. Indeed, after reading them one wonders whether we have a right to be upset about anything going on in the world today. Like virtually everyone else who has read them, I came away with a certain sense of relief that all is not lost, and with a hope that all of the trends described within them continue. And yet despite the carefully researched arguments from each of the authors cited above, I see three reasons why we should be cautious in trumpeting these gains so confidently.

First, while great progress has been made to date, there is some concern that much of it resulted from "once in a lifetime events" like the end of the Cold War and the economic transformations of the world's two most populous nations, India and China; with those gains now almost fully realized there is no certainty that the numbers of poverty and disease will inevitably continue to drop. The gains we've made can therefore be seen as more tenuous than they at first appear.

Never mind the stray asteroid hitting the Earth or the threat of artificially intelligent systems eventually destroying humanity; the threats to global peace and prosperity are much closer at hand. A major war between two or more powerful countries or a global health pandemic would have immediate calamitous repercussions, while the longer-term threats of climate change and unchecked population growth could make life deadly or intolerably miserable for untold billions of people.

All of this became unmistakably clearer in 2020 when the Coronavirus struck virtually every corner of the globe with such terrible force. As it spread outward from China to North America and Europe, eventually reaching Africa, Madagascar and other developing nations cowered in fear of the havoc a pandemic would cause given their fragile health systems. All of the economic gains touted by Radelet and others threatened to be wiped out in a matter of months. In the midst of the crisis, experts began predicting that for the first time since 1998 global poverty would increase, with the World Bank estimating that as many as 60 million people would be pushed into extreme poverty as a result of the pandemic. The UN has recently warned that the world is facing its worst food crisis in 50 years, and that at least half a billion people, for a total of 2 billion, could slip into destitution by the end of 2020.[11] The number of people living on less than $1.90 a day, which had been falling steadily since 1990, is now sure to rise again, and in some areas like sub-Saharan Africa the impacts could result in poverty levels similar to those from 30 years ago. A key UN resolution committing the world to eliminating all poverty and hunger and providing universal access to education by 2030 may now be "a pipe dream."[12]

In Africa, the economic and social disruptions of the Coronavirus are battering millions of workers who had only recently seen their incomes begin to rise. The World Bank estimates that sub-Saharan Africa will see its first economic recession in 25 years in 2020, with nearly half of all jobs lost across the continent. From Kenya to Nigeria to Rwanda, Covid-19 threatens to push tens of millions of people in Africa into extreme poverty. But beyond that, it's also undoing decades of progress on a great African achievement: the growth of its middle class. These new voices for modernization have been critical to the continent's recent growth by using their newfound status to push for democratic reforms, better schools and health care. The number of middle class Africans has in fact tripled over the past 30 years, but 8 million of them, now facing a loss of steady income for the first time since achieving middle-class status, could be forced into poverty because of the virus and its economic fallout.[13]

Meanwhile, other diseases once thought to be on their way out have experienced a resurgence in Africa, one of the unintended consequences of millions of people taking the necessary precautions to avoid Covid-19. Immunizations, which have prevented 35 million deaths around the world from vaccine-preventable illnesses just over the last 20 years, are now viewed as too risky to seek out in many parts of the world. In the Spring of 2020, for example, when the World Health Organization and UNICEF warned the pandemic could spread quickly if children gathered in groups to line up for shots, many countries suspended inoculation programs. The arrival of vaccines and health workers also slowed significantly. As a result, diptheria, cholera, poliovirus, and measles have all flared, to the point where nearly 200 million people were at risk of missing immunizations against these diseases in 2020. Measles, a far more contagious disease than Covid-19, could actually end up killing more people than the Coronavirus.[14]

Second, while the Coronavirus may prove to be a speedbump temporarily slowing the spread of human progress, climate change is likely to serve as a permanent check on human improvement. Indeed, global warming is so terrifying in large part because once its effects become serious, there is no going back. The consequences of climate change will be so severe that any optimism about the future must be tenuous. As David Wallace-Wells has written, "There is no good thing in the world that will be made more abundant, or spread more widely, by global warming. The list of bad things that will proliferate is innumerable." This will inevitably change how we view the field of world history. What was once understood as an inexorable march from barbarism to civilization, enlightenment and wealth will be retold as something quite different: a race to achieve previously unthinkable standards of living that depended upon spewing heat-trapping gases into the atmosphere in quantities so obscene as to render much of the planet uninhabitable. Ours and preceding generations will look even more foolish to future readers when it is pointed out that we had all the knowledge and tools at our disposal to avoid most of the damage.[15]

The worst case scenario from climate change would reverse nearly all of the human progress made during the past two centuries. But as Wallace-Wells eloquently confirms, it will not take worst case outcomes to produce effects harmful enough to "shake the casual sense that as time marches forward, life improves ineluctably."

"Those ravages are likely to begin arriving quickly: new coastlines retreating from drowned cities; destabilizing societies disgorging millions of refugees into neighboring ones already feeling the pinch of resource depletion; the last several hundred years, which many saw as a simple line of progress and growing prosperity, rendered instead as a prelude to mass climate suffering...But if the planet reaches three or for our five degrees of warming, the world will be convulsed with human suffering at such a scale – so many million refugees, half again as many wars, droughts and famines, and economic growth made impossible on so much of the planet – that its citizens will have difficulty regarding the recent past as a course of progress or even a phase in a cycle, or in fact anything but a true and substantial reversal."[16]

Finally, some regions of the world, most notably sub-Saharan Africa, still have such alarming development challenges ahead of them that to talk of great progress there almost seems callous, even borderline offensive. While China and India have been responsible for much if not most of the development gains to date, Africa has seen much less progress across a range of categories. The number of people living in extreme poverty and the number of undernourished people in sub-Saharan Africa continued to rise through 2010, although the percentages are falling. Income inequality has skyrocketed across the continent, causing some to question whether the rise in incomes is only making the region more unequal.[17] Several studies have found that sub-Saharan Africa lagged behind the other developing regions in meeting global development goals. And a few countries in Africa seem to be making no progress at all.

* * *

All of which brings us back to Madagascar. Madagascar is one of the poorest countries in the world today, with a per capita GDP of less than $400 in 2016 and a staggering rate of poverty. The past two decades have been lost years for this island nation, with very little improvement in the lives of its people. We know that because progress in development can now be measured and compared, thanks to the Millennium Development Goals (MDGs) established by the United Nations in 2000 as a way of charting progress across the developing world. With the MDGs, the UN identified eight goals that it hoped to achieve by 2015, in a myriad of categories ranging from poverty reduction to public health and equal opportunities for women. Upon their completion in 2015 the UN hailed the results of the MDGs as "the most successful anti-poverty movement in history," for all the reasons enumerated by the optimists cited above. But Madagascar showed very little progress in most categories and none in others, including the most important ones. The first MDG, the most important of all of them, was "to eradicate extreme poverty and hunger." One target of this goal was to reduce extreme poverty by half from 1990-2015. Globally, the goal was met well in advance of the 2015 deadline (declining from 47% to 14%). Madagascar, however, not only failed to make progress toward a 50% reduction, *it actually saw an increase in extreme poverty*. In 1993, 67.1% of the population was living on less than $1.25 per day; in 2010 that number was over 82% and in 2015 it was believed to be still close to 80%. According to the World Bank, per capita GDP, which has never been above $600, actually declined between 2000-10, and has continued to fall since then, in large part due to high population growth and two political crises during that period.[18]

A similar target under this goal was to halve by 2015 the percentage of people suffering from hunger in 1990. The goal was just missed globally, declining from 23.3% to 12.9%, but again, *Madagascar actually saw an increase in undernourishment*, from 27.3% to 33% of its people. The total number of undernourished people on the island also increased from 3.3 million to 8 million. The World Bank reported that an incredible 62% of the people in Madagascar were still living on less than the cost to purchase 2100 calories of food a day in 2013, and thus hardly able to survive above a starvation level. UNICEF found that half of all children under the age of five suffer from chronic malnutrition, one of the highest rates in the world.

Its results with the other MDGs were mixed. The country fell short of reaching universal primary school enrollment and the World Bank found that Madagascar now has the world's fifth highest number of out-of-school children in the world.

Furthermore, its success in other metrics used to judge a country's advancement into the modern world is also discouraging; for example, the rate of access to electricity in Madagascar is one of the lowest on the planet, at only 13%.

The failure to make any progress in reducing extreme poverty or hunger when almost the entire rest of the world was doing exactly that is a damning indictment of Madagascar's political class. But as we'll see in Chapter 2, the political system itself has been plagued by such chronic instability as to render its government largely ineffective. Its democracy – to the extent one can call it that - is perilously fragile, with the specter of a military coup in 2009 still haunting the country. Its human rights record remains bleak, with pretrial detentions and police corruption a fact of life and over a million people in the south one step away from famine.[19] Moreover, Madagascar has sadly done virtually nothing to prepare for the demographic disaster that awaits it at mid-century; nor has it come up with any strategy for dealing with the effects of climate change that will also begin to ravage its people and its economy in the next few decades. Its population continues to soar, its economy is unable to cope, and the number of Malagasy living a precarious existence continues to rise. Meanwhile, drought in the south of the countries is pushing many villagers to relocate or take up banditry, while reducing the overall food supply. By any meaningful measure, therefore, post-independence Madagascar is clearly not a success story.

Its capital city, Antananarivo, is a woeful case in point. High in the central plateaus, at an elevation of 4,200 feet, Tana was once a charming city with a bustling downtown area ringed by lovely green and brown hills. It was relatively safe, even at night, and high up in those hills it almost felt like a small town. Now every guide book will tell you Tana is a place to be skipped if not avoided (although there are some great restaurants). The capital has become notoriously polluted, and an afternoon spent choking on the smog and fumes rising from every downtown street and vehicle will make you sick. It's safe enough during the day, but when I asked my taxi driver about walking around at night he didn't even reply, preferring to show me what would happen by drawing his hand, palm down, across his throat. Dozens of homeless children lie on the streets with no parent in sight.

And while everyone says the traffic in their city is a nightmare, Antananarivo is on another level, not just because of all the cars and buses on the street but because of the mass of humanity spilling out from the sidewalks, which can no longer begin to contain them. Tana's population has gone from 1 million people in 1990 to 3.2 million in 2019, and the city is simply overwhelmed.

And yet there is nothing inevitable about Madagascar's downward slide, and economists are often puzzled when confronted with the depressing statistics cascading out of the country. The 2009 crisis played a role, to be sure, but the real mystery surrounding the great island's development may be its long-term decline, traceable almost as far back as independence. With per capita GDP falling since 1960 the average Malagasy's standard of living has declined as well, and few countries, even including those in sub-Saharan Africa, have witnessed such poor results over time.[20] It hasn't been one slow, inexorable, decline, of course; Madagascar has embarked on a growth spurt on several occasions. But each time it showed signs of an economic takeoff, the resurgence ended a few years later in a major political crisis. This happened in the early 1970s, the 1990s, the early 2000s and again in 2009.[21] And while the long downward spiral is obvious to anyone looking at Madagascar's history, what increasingly concerns experts tracking its development is the increasing frequency of the crises. This troubling development has led some political economists to identify a uniquely Malagasy paradox, centered around a confounding link between economic growth and political instability. Each time the country takes a step forward, something quickly happens that causes it to take three steps back.[22]

So while the larger trend across the world today is clearly toward peace, health and a reduction in poverty and disease, there remain places like the great island of Madagascar where progress is stagnant, and may even be heading in the opposite direction. The international community should not lose sight of those countries or regions still falling behind. Just as important, we should try to understand why they are failing and what risks their failure poses to other similarly situated countries. And let's think about what failure in 10 or 20 countries would mean for a world in which everyone else is making steady advances. Because if Madagascar – a quasi-democracy that suffers from no war, no terrorism, no border disputes, no violent ethnic conflict and no economic sanctions – can't keep up with the rest of the world, then perhaps we should check our faith in the inevitability of global progress.

* * *

It gives me no pleasure to write this book, for Madagascar is a country I love more than any other except my own. I first traveled there some 25 years ago as part of a student exchange program, mostly on a whim, and have been returning periodically ever since. It was my sophomore year at Georgetown and I was looking for a French-speaking county in which to spend half of the next year. I originally chose Paris, but one day I got a message from an advisor for the semester abroad program asking me to see him the next day. Something's wrong, I thought. When I arrived at his office at the appointed hour the advisor, a genial, gray-haired man in his sixties told me the Paris program had been cancelled due to ongoing strikes and protests that threatened to shut down the capital for weeks if not longer. I should therefore consider other options.

"We have a well-established program in Brussels that I think you would you love," he said.

"Belgium?" I said incredulously, and perhaps a little too loudly. I had my heart set on going to Paris, and Brussels just sounded like a dull substitute. I think he sensed my disappointment, because before I knew it he had pulled out a map of some place that was clearly not Europe.

"Well, we also have a few affiliated programs in French Africa," he said.

"Really?" I asked. "Like where?"

"Like Cameroon," he said, and pointed it out on the map. "They speak French there." I hesitated, and he began to draw his finger across the waist of Africa, stopping at a large island just off the coast, in the Indian Ocean. "Or Madagascar." I must have looked interested, because he began to tell me about it. "It's a bit exotic, but they recently democratized and I've heard they're very welcoming of foreigners."

Some important decisions I've made after careful deliberation and some I've made on the spot. Looking back now, I'd say each method was about equally effective. For some reason I can't explain, I saw that man's finger tapping on Madagascar and knew I was destined for that mysterious, footprint-shaped island with the unforgettable name.

"That sounds great," I said, "I'll go there."

"Well, surely you'll want a few days to do some research on it and talk to your parents before you make a final decision," he said. "Why don't come back on Monday and we'll..."

"No, no," I said. "I don't need any more time. I'll go to Madagascar. You can sign me up now."

It turned out to be an incredible experience. Over the course of four months I saw a nation that had recently held its first democratic election but was devastated by crippling poverty, weak institutions and a low rate of education. I lived with a wonderful host family and made dozens of Malagasy friends, who were as kind and generous to me as any friends I've ever had. I traveled around the whole island – by car, by bus, by ship, and by plane – and saw one of the most beautiful countries in the world before it became an ecotourist destination – indeed, before it had much tourist infrastructure at all. I followed its progress, or lack thereof, from afar, returning each decade to visit people I knew and to try to relive that first experience all over again (which is, of course, impossible). What I saw and heard about over the years was a nation in trouble.

So I decided to return to Madagascar in 2019 and write about its problems firsthand. While I'm relying on some social science research to illuminate my story, I prefer to look at the island through the eyes of a spectrum of individuals who represent all that is great and tragic about the island. During almost nine months of often desultory travel throughout this sometimes enchanting, occasionally maddening country I was fortunate enough to interview politicians, economists, teachers, village leaders, entrepreneurs and farmers. What I hope is that after listening to this kaleidoscope of voices the reader will see the country in living color, and experience its remarkable potential and endless frustrations almost as intimately as I did.

It would be impossible to understand the twenty-first century dynamics of any country without first understanding its past, so the next few chapters will give a brief history of the island, starting with the rival kingdoms that sprung up in various regions, then turning to the drama and violence of French colonialism and the missed opportunities of Madagascar's first sixty years of independence. All of this will culminate in the rise of the President himself, someone who has ridden the populist wave, now spreading through the developing world almost as fast as the Coronavirus, all the way to the top. It was President Rajoelina, more than any other individual, who shaped the contours of modern Madagascar with his brazen seizure of power in 2009, and who continues to shape it today.

If he were the president of a larger (or European) nation he might be discussed in the same sentence as Putin, Orban and Duterte, but as he only leads Madagascar he is merely one of the most controversial presidents the world has never heard of. With the weakness of the country's institutions and civil society now on full display, it is no exaggeration to say that the future of Madagascar rests on his success or failure. Later chapters will examine the lack of economic opportunity stultifying a generation of young Malagasy now entering the workforce, the rapid and unsustainable rise of the island's population, and the coming climate crisis in the south of the island.

But first, let's go back to the General for a moment. When we finished the interview it was around midnight, and as we stood out on the terrace of my hotel saying goodnight I could see the normally chaotic city beneath us pitch dark and eerily quiet. The General left through the iron gate leading to the staircase that would take him back down to his car, and I began to gather my things and head upstairs. But as I heard the gate close and saw the General disappear from view, I felt someone approaching me over my right shoulder. I turned around and saw the hotel concierge, now free of his headphones, standing next to me. He was a young man with his long hair tied back into a knot behind his head and facial features that could have been mistaken for Malaysian or Indonesian, and though it was dark I could see him looking at me with a troubled expression. He was clearly agitated, and as he began to speak tears came into his eyes. This conversation would come back to me time and again as I traveled throughout the island and tried to understand the divisions among its people.

"*Monsieur Adams,*" he said, "I was pretending to listen to music but I heard your entire conversation with that man. It was almost all lies! I know what happened that day. It was nothing like what that man said. You must talk to one of Ravalomanana's people to get the real story."

I tried to calm him down but, having begun, he couldn't stop now. "You can't let the world think our president was a murderer," he said. "You must find out the truth!"

I promised him I would try.

Chapter 1

Discovery and the First Kingdoms

These Austronesians, with their Austronesia language and modified Austronesian culture, were already established on Madagascar by the time it was first visited by Europeans, in 1500. This strikes me as the single most astonishing fact of human geography for the entire world ... How on earth could prehistoric people of Borneo, presumably voyaging in boats without maps or compasses, end up in Madagascar?
- Jared Diamond, *Guns, Germs, and Steel*

They came first by the dozens, then in waves. Setting out from Borneo and Sumatra in their outrigger canoes and later, in larger twin hulled outriggers, they had no idea that the island of Madagascar, some 4000 miles to the west, even existed. They may have been driven out by waves of migrants to modern day Indonesia or by religious persecution, or they may have decided to make use of their seafaring talents to expand their trade to wider spheres. A direct route from Southeast Asia to Madagascar is possible, or they and their descendants may have taken a circuitous route, settling first on Ceylon and the Maldives, then moving across the Arabian Sea to Socotra and eventually along the coast of modern day Tanzania and Kenya. There they would have introduced their crops from Indonesia – coconuts, breadfruit, yams, bananas – which quickly replaced hunting and gathering as the main way of life along the East African coast. At some point after the first century AD they would have undertaken further exploratory journeys further south, first to the Comoros islands, and soon thereafter, perhaps around the middle of the fourth or fifth century AD, landed on Madagascar. What they found there must have awed them.

The island now known as Madagascar was named by no less a personage than Marco Polo, the famous Venetian explorer. Passing through Arabia on his way home from China in 1294, he wrote a description of "Madeigaskar" based on stories he heard from other travelers. The only problem was that he had confused the great island off the east coast of Africa with the bustling port of Mogadishu on the African coast, so none of the things he described were true of the real Madagascar. Besides getting the name wrong, he wrote of lions, giraffes, camels and huge flying birds on his mythical island that lifted elephants off the ground and dropped them to their deaths from a great height. The island was a source of indescribable wealth in his telling, full of gold, ivory and jewels.

And yet if none of those animals existed on Madagascar when the first settlers arrived, they did find a land wholly unlike anything else in the world at that time. Having separated from Africa millions of years ago, Madagascar's flora and fauna had developed independently from that of its much larger neighbor, such that thousands of species that became extinct in Africa survived in Madagascar. If they found no lions or camels, these settlers certainly would have seen giant lemurs and tortoises, and Polo's giant elephant-crushing bird was probably an exaggeration of the *Aepyornis maximus*, a flightless, ostrich-like bird that stood almost 10 feet tall and laid eggs 12 inches long and 9 inches wide – the equivalent of 150 hens' eggs – and which must have been a primary source of protein for the proto-Malagasy.

These first Malagasy settled on the western coast of the island across from Africa, and gradually made their way north and south until they had formed a ring of settlements around the island, from the fine natural harbor at Diego Suarez in the north to the more hospitable climate along the east coast and even the thorny desert in the south. By the end of the first millennium, whether by choice or through expulsion, a few communities had sprung up inland, pushing all the way to the high plateaus in the center of the island. The first Arab traders arrived on the coasts around the same time, and although their impact today has been largely forgotten, for five hundred years they played a significant role in the island's development, introducing tools, utensils, cloth, glass beads and porcelain to the island, in exchange for Malagasy staples like beef, rice and honey. They also brought the slave trade to Madagascar, at first importing slaves from Africa to Madagascar but later carrying them in both directions.[1] Slavery had existed for centuries on the west coast, but this was the first time an external trade in human beings was established on the island, a practice that would haunt Madagascar through the ages, as it did so many African territories.

By 1500 the population of the unique Afro-Indonesian people of Madagascar had grown exponentially to almost all parts of the island but remained divided into small tribes or clans without anything close to a single political authority. Two groups, however – the Merina and the Sakalava – were beginning to coalesce into larger tribes that would, in a few centuries, rule all but the wild southern regions between them. It was also around 1500 that the first Europeans arrived, resulting in an epic clash of civilizations that, through cooperation and conquest over five centuries, gave rise to the modern Malagasy state.

The record of the first European visits to the island is one of utter failure. The Portuguese came first, of course, sailing around the Cape of Good Hope in their caravels on their way to the Spice Islands. Vasco da Gama led the first fleet to India in 1498 but did not seek out the large island across from Mozambique, known to Arabs as the Island of the Moon. Neither did the second Portuguese fleet, which left for India in 1499; but when four of their five ships were sunk by a tremendous storm near the Cape, the fifth ship, captained by Diogo Dias, was driven around the Cape and further east. Dias made landfall on August

10, 1500 on what he first assumed was Mozambique, but what he quickly gathered was a large island, which he named Sao Lorenco. When news of Dias's discovery reached Portugal the court realized that this must be Marco Polo's Madagascar, and it duly appeared on a Portuguese map in 1502.[2]

After some deliberation Portugal concluded that the island had little to interest in them in the way of gold, spices, or anything else worthy of a diversion from India and the Spice Islands, but as it was on their way to the East they lost hundreds of shipwrecked sailors there, including 600 men in 1527 alone.[3] Most of them probably died of disease or were killed by the Malagasy, but enough returned to Lisbon to keep alive the rumors and possibilities of Madagascar in Portugal and throughout Europe. These early Portugal explorers were soon followed by French sailors in the 16th century. After a few exploratory visits, however, King Francis I, in serious financial difficulty, issued a decree forbidding any of his subjects from visiting the lands claimed by the Portuguese in exchange for the King of Portugal's agreement to cancel substantial debts owed to him by Francis, and that was the end of French voyages into the Indian Ocean for over 50 years.

The Dutch then found their way to the great island, but when hundreds of their men died on Madagascar in 1601 during the first few voyages, they opted to base their operations in the neighboring island of Mauritius, which had only been discovered by the Portuguese a century earlier and remained uninhabited until the second Dutch expedition landed there in 1598. The Dutch named this neighboring island after Maurice, the Prince of Orange. A Dutch settlement was later reported in Madagascar near the Bay of Antongil in 1645, but this too was abandoned in favor of a lighter presence on the island that would bring them supplies and slaves to Mauritius while avoiding the dangers inherent to a settlement on Madagascar.

Then it was England's turn, with East India Company fleets

stopping at St. Augustine's Bay on the southwest coast of the island as early as 1607 and thereafter making almost annual visits to either coast of Madagascar on their journeys to and from India. A pattern of trading then began with the natives; in most cases relations with the Malgasy were fine, but they endured enough hostile receptions to always keep the visitors wary. The first plans for an English settlement came under Charles I, and the first expedition arrived in St. Augustine's Bay in 1645 with 144 men, women and children. Like previous expeditions, however, the English settlers were decimated by disease and warfare, and the remaining settlers left the island after only a year. A second attempt was made on the more hospitable offshore island of Nosy Be in 1649, but the timing of that venture coincided with the rise of the fearsome Sakalava tribe and it too lasted only a short while.

After such a dismal record it is hard to imagine any other nation becoming eager to visit Madagascar, but the French settlement at Ft. Dauphin became the closest thing to a real colonial presence in Madagascar until the 19th century. In 1642 Cardinal Richelieu granted a charter to the *Societe Francaise de L'Orient*, which sent a small party to Madagascar to establish a settlement in the southeast of the island. The settlers arrived in September of that year and declared the entire island a possession of France, constructing an initial fort at San Luce before moving the colony to a peninsula further south, which proved to be a healthier and more defensible location. The party named the settlement Ft. Dauphin after the dauphin prince of France, who by that time was no longer a prince but had ascended to the throne as King Louis XIV. If it did not prosper, the colony at least held its own for the next twenty years, at which point the young king began to take a more avid interest in Madagascar. He granted a royal charter to the new French East India Company in 1664 and provided it with much greater resources than previous companies had enjoyed. Over the next few years thousands of additional settlers arrived at the fort.[4]

With no clear policy and increasing distrust between the settlers and natives, the directors of the East India Company faced a quandary as to whether to forge ahead with the settlement or give up. After five years the company, like others, decided to quit Madagascar and focus its efforts on India, with its rights to the island reverting to Louis XIV, who remained reluctant to give up on the colony that had been named after him. When the king sent an emissary to report on the state of the colony, however, the envoy not only recommended that the colony be abandoned at once but also returned to France with all but 200 of the remaining settlers, who were left to fend for themselves amid a hostile population. The colony's ultimate demise then became the stuff of legend.

Fifteen teenage French girls had been sent by Louis XIV in October 1672 from an orphanage in France to Bourbon (Reunion) to become brides for the settlers on that island, which was now looking like a far better option for a colony. After a short stay on Madagascar, the ship bearing the fifteen girls set sail for Bourbon, only to be shipwrecked almost immediately after leaving Ft. Dauphin. The girls, fearful of further calamities, begged to be married to some of the settlers at the fort rather than risk any further hazards on another attempt to reach Bourbon. The French Major in command at the fort, La Breteche, agreed, and they all found willing husbands, but the Malagasy women who were already married to the settlers were not pleased, to put it mildly. The men attempted to divorce their Malagasy wives by returning them to their fathers and saying, "Thank you for this woman," as was the local custom. The Malagasy women, however, reported this betrayal to local Malagasy warriors, who had been looking for any excuse to rid the area of its French presence. In August 1674, in the middle of the French marriage ceremonies, half of the colonists were massacred, including all but one of the girls. When another French ship arrived the remainder of the colonists made their escape, but not before thirty years of effort to build a colony had ended in ignominy.

Or perhaps not. The debacle at Ft. Dauphin cannot be put down as a complete disaster. Though it would take them another two centuries, this first settlement sparked French interest in the Mascarene Islands that would last until the present day. The failure at Ft. Dauphin led to the colonization of Bourbon (now Reunion) and later Mauritius, which was colonized and renamed Ile de France after the Dutch abandoned that island. These new possessions ensured continued French interest in Madagascar as a source of supplies for its more prosperous nearby colonies, and once in control of the Mascarenes, it became much easier for France to establish trading posts on the east coast of Madagascar. Reunion soon became the base for French territorial ambitions in Madagascar after Mauritius was lost to Britain in the 19th century. The beginnings of a colony on the great island can be said to have started then.[5]

* * *

The massacre of the French settlers ended European attempts to colonize the island for nearly a century, but it coincided with the rise of the two greatest indigenous kingdoms ever to appear in Madagascar. By the end of the 17th century the Merina in the high plateaus and the Sakalava on the west coast were both growing in strength. Because of its enormous impact on the western half of the island, some historians consider the rise of the Sakalava to be perhaps the single most important political revolution in the history of Madagascar. As a warrior tribe they combined military strength with religious authority and commercial acumen, benefiting from major population movements from other parts of the island looking for protection. Building an empire based on cattle and slaves, they built one of their kingdoms, known as the Boina, into the most powerful monarchy in Madagascar during the 17th century.[6] The Sakalava extended their authority to the north and reached the height of their power in the middle of the 18th century before entering a period of gradual decline. They used their position on the west coast of the island to their advantage, making wider contacts with the outside world than the rest of the Malagasy tribes. The Boina king Andriantoakafo extended his kingdom north as far as Nosy Be, and by the time the kingdom eventually passed to Queen Ravahiny, the first of the great Sakalava queens, the Sakalava were received on equal terms by the Merina, as evidenced by the queen's official visit to their expanding kingdom on the central plateau.[7]

The Merina were emerging as a formidable power of their own by this time, but because of the concentration of their population in the interior of the island they were still largely unknown to Europeans. When Baron Benyowsky, a Polish-Hungarian count acting on behalf of France, had a map of Madagascar prepared in 1776, it showed an empty space in the middle, evidencing the fact that to this point the Europeans' knowledge of the island was limited to the coasts. The next year he sent an envoy, Nicolas Mayeur, on a secret mission into the interior to investigate possible trading opportunities. On his return to the coast Mayeur wrote a report that concluded with news that startled its readers in Paris: "The Europeans who have frequented the island of Madagascar and who read these memoirs, will have difficulty in persuading themselves that in the interior of this great island entirely surrounded by savage peoples there is more enlightenment, more industry and a more active administration than on the coasts where the inhabitants are in constant relations with foreigners."[8]

These interior highlanders were of course the Merina, who were lighter skinned and whose physical features were more Asian than those of the coastal tribes. Merina political power had been slowly growing for centuries after establishing their first settlements in the highlands shortly before 1000 AD.

Thereafter, rapid population growth ensued from major waves of immigration, probably from Sumatra and perhaps later from Java, and intensive rice cultivation. The highlands became the main source of slaves for export from the island's northwest coast by the 17th century in exchange for small quantities of silver and pottery.[9] The first kings of the modern Merina line appeared in the 16th century, when a succession crisis over the rightful heir to a sitting queen was decided in favor of her elder son and her younger son was put to death. (The assassination of rivals unfortunately became a tradition in Madagascar as a way to ensure stability – not always successfully – upon the death of a ruler). The Merina kingdom grew throughout the 17th century to encompass the entire central region that became known as Imerina, roughly the area within a radius of 20-25 miles of Antananarivo. It soon eclipsed even the Sakalava kingdom as the most powerful on the island, although by the 18th century the Sakalava would regain their previous status as they used their control of trade along the west coast to import firearms.[10]

Even with its systematic assassination of rivals, dynastic succession became a chronic problem for the Merina, just as it had been for the Sakalava. After King Andriamasinavalona's death around 1710, the Merina split up into four kingdoms, with war soon breaking out between the two most powerful, based in Antananarivo and Ambohimanga, and lasting for most of the 18th century. In 1787, however, a new king was installed in Ambohimanga that would shape the destiny of the Merina forever. He took the name Andrianampoinimerina ("The Prince in the heart of Imerina"), and over the next seven years, through alliances and conquests, he reunited the Merina into the most dominant tribe of Madagascar.

Andrianampoinimerina ruled from 1778-1809 and came to power by killing his uncle, the king of the hill settlement of Ambohimanga. His rule marked an important break with the minor kings who had ruled Imerina for centuries and constituted a more sophisticated form of government than had previously been seen anywhere on the island. When he died in 1809 he had made Antananarivo, then with 25,000 inhabitants, the capital of the Merina kingdom, and the kingdom's only serious rivals were the Sakalava and a few other tribes along the east and west coasts who controlled some of the foreign trade. His conquests did not come easily, at least not at first. From 1792-1796, Andrianampoinimerina attacked the rival town of Antananarivo three times before subduing it, and could have been content with that conquest. But he proceeded to conquer the rest of Imerina, at times peacefully using threats or signing treaties, and at other times through force. He later expanded his kingdom's frontiers further to the east, where he defeated a large tribe known as the Bezanozano, and to the south, where he defeated an equally large tribe known as the Betsileo. Thus in little more than a decade Andrianampoinimerina had extended his control from his fief of a few square miles in Ambohimanga to all the inhabited areas of the high plateaus (roughly the size of New Jersey).[11]

Andrianampoinimerina then set about creating a highly efficient state. At the center was the king himself – a semi-divine figure who represented the all-important link to the ancestors and owned all the land in the kingdom. Some tracts of land were parceled out to individuals akin to feudal lords who ruled over a village or two. The king instituted a rigid class structure with strict rules about intermarriage. At the top were the nobles, followed by the middle classes (the "hova" and the freed slaves), and at the bottom were those still bound by slavery. Agriculture and especially rice cultivation became the basis for the kingdom's economy, and rice developed a mystical place at the center of Merina culture. ("Rice and I are one," Andrianampoinimerina famously declared). With plentiful livestock, expanding agricultural fields and wood available from the forests of conquered tribes, the Merina became self-sufficient in everything except weapons, which they learned to acquire from the coast in exchange for slaves captured during military expeditions. Toward the end of Andrianampoinimerina's reign, an average of 1500-1800 slaves were exported per year, mostly to French traders who shipped them to plantations on Mauritius and Bourbon (Reunion).[12] As a final act of authority he ordered the killing of various family members who could have prevented his son Radama from ascending to the throne upon his death. As will be seen, the Merina from his day gradually became the elite tribe of the island, possessing more education and skills than any other, which aroused no small amount of jealousy and resentment among the other 17 tribes.

While the Merina and Sakalava grew in strength and the European powers focused on other territories, another notorious group carved out a small part of the island for its own purposes for about 40 years at the end of the 17th and the beginning of the 18th century. Madagascar in general and one of its offshore islands, Ile St. Marie, in particular, became the greatest pirate refuge in the world during this time. Their main hunting grounds were around the southern coast of India and the entrance to the Red Sea, where they hoped to intercept ships from Muslim India on the way to Mecca. Madagascar offered them a ready supply of meat, fish, and rice, and there were thousands of inlets in which to escape from pursuing ships. The extensive beaches of the island were perfect for storing their ships and cargo for long stretches if necessary. With no other European presence on the island there was no organized effort to control or outlaw them. And the natives along the east coast were organized into small clans that posed no great danger if the pirates treated them with respect and paid them small tribute.

The first pirates, mostly English, refrained from attacking European ships, but they soon decided not to limit themselves, especially after the British East Indian Company began taking the threat of piracy more seriously and devoting considerable resources to ending it. Later pirates accordingly became more ruthless, even attacking ships from their own nation. Some of them become spectacularly wealthy while living or hiding out on Madagascar, as evidenced by one expedition led by a pirate named Taylor:

> Returning from the Malabar coast, where they captured several India prizes but had some narrow escapes from fleets of armed East Indiamen, [Taylor and his crew] called in at Bourbon at April 8, 1721. Here they found an answer to a pirate's prayer – a Portuguese ship disabled and helpless after a violent storm and carrying the Portuguese Viceroy of Goa and a fabulous treasure principally in diamonds, which alone were worth three or four million dollars. With this enormous booty they sailed to Ile St. Marie where the share-out yielded something in the region of [over one million dollars per man in modern terms], including 42 small diamonds each, or the equivalent in larger stones. This was more than enough to persuade many of them to retire and settle in Madagascar. The others got ready to sail with Taylor on another venture to the Red Sea. But news of a strong British naval squadron rounding the Cape with instructions to hunt down the pirates caused them to alter their plans. In December 1722 they split up, some going back to Madagascar to settle there, and the rest under Taylor returning to the West Indies.[13]

Eventually the pirates left and Madagascar became the scene of more traditional European interest. More specifically, French possessions around the island began to form a noose around the neck of Madagascar, one that would loosen and tighten intermittently over the next 150 years. Toward the middle of the 18th century sovereignty along the east coast was threatened by French trading interests based on the islands of Bourbon and Mauritius. Ile St. Marie, the island off the northeast coast of Madagascar, became their first target. French plantations on Bourbon and Mauritius needed regular supplies of food and slaves to keep them productive, and the northeast coast of Madagascar supplied all these commodities. Ile St. Marie soon became an ideal offshore base for the trade. The French Indian company appointed an agent, Guillaume Gosse, to negotiate a treaty with Queen Bety, the ruler of the island, for the transfer of the island's sovereignty to France, and this was successfully concluded in July 1750. However, in September of that year the islanders rose and killed Gosse and fourteen French men after a dispute with the natives unwisely led them to desecrate the tomb of Bety's father, the former king. The governor of Ile de France responded by burning a few villages on the coast of the mainland, and sent a French corporal, Jean-Onesime Filet, to Ile St. Marie to restore order. Filet not only did this with great success, he also married Queen Bety, further cementing French control of the island.

France then tried to colonize the main island again, this time in almost laughable fashion. In 1772 the previously mentioned Baron Benyowsky, the Polish-Hungarian count, escaped capture by the Russians for some dubious crime and found his way to Mauritius, from which he sailed to Paris and somehow managed to get an audience with the French king and present an extravagant plan for a French colony on Madagascar. (Another attempted colony at Ft. Dauphin had just failed again in 1771 after less than three years). For reasons that escape modern historians, the French government agreed to entrust Benyowsky with his desired mission, and Benyowsky left in 1774 with a company of troops to start his colony. Within two years most of the settlers had again died in the attempt, and an investigation landed Benyowski back in France to appeal to the new King, Louis XVI, for more funds and another chance. Now fully aware of his incompetence, France denied Benyowsky's bid to return to Madagascar, but this only led him to Vienna and then to England to "offer" Madagascar to each of them. After all European powers had rejected him, he finally secured private backing in the United States and sailed back to Madagascar from Baltimore in 1785. Once there he quickly seized a small trading post and tried to persuade the local chiefs to drive out the French traders, now his sworn enemies. By now irate, French officials sent a small military detachment to arrest Benyowsky, eventually killing him in an assault on his fort in May 1786.[14]

Even without a formal colony, French trading posts had increased in size and significance on the mainland of Madagascar with the steady expansion of their settlements on Ile St. Marie and Bourbon. Specifically, France used its base at Ile St. Marie to establish several posts on the east coast of the island by 1800, principally at Tamatave and Foulpointe. At Foulpointe, a handful of official agents bought cattle and rice on behalf of the French authorities on the Mascarenes, while 22 independent traders conducted a thriving business in slaves. As mentioned earlier, however, until the end of the 18th century European knowledge of Madagascar remained limited to the coasts. In addition, the northern coast of the island, with its fine natural harbor at Diego Suarez, was still unexplored by Europeans, and the Antankarana tribe in that area (the "People of the Rocks") had little contact with the rest of Madagascar or outsiders. Other than Mayeur's visit very few if any European expeditions had managed to climb onto the high plateaus. And this remained the situation for the first decades of the 19th century, with France content for the time being to watch its coastal settlements grow.

As French settlements and trading posts encroached onto Madagascar it fell to Andrianimpoinimerina's son and heir to the throne, Radama I, to try to extend Merina rule over the rest of the island. Taking power upon his father's death in 1810 at age 17 and ruling until his own death just 18 years later, Radama, along with his father, is considered the most successful of all the

Merina kings and queens. With the help of European powers, he modernized his country through the institution of a system of formal education and the formation of a professional army, while also ending the slave trade on the island. He forged an alliance with Britain that kept French territorial designs at bay for over half a century, and he expanded his father's domain even further, almost succeeding in unifying the island under one ruler for the first time. Geopolitics were shifting just as Radama became king. Britain was moving closer to its defeat of France in the Napoleonic Wars, which would have major implications for Madagascar. In December 1810 France capitulated to the British in the Indian Ocean and Britain took control of Mauritius, with Robert Farquhar appointed its new Governor. Not wasting any time, Farquhar oversaw the expulsion of the French from the mainland of Madagascar the next year. In May 1814 Britain and France signed the Treaty of Paris, which ended their long war but led to immediate confusion concerning Madagascar and almost turned the island into a British possession. The treaty, while ceding to Britain "the Isle of France [Mauritius] and its dependencies, especially Rodriguez and the Seychelles," restored Bourbon (Reunion) to France. There was no mention of Madagascar, however, and Farquhar used this oversight and the ambiguity of the word "especially" to argue that there were other dependencies now belonging to Britain besides the two named. Strengthening his argument were the facts that the French trading posts had been dependencies of Mauritius, and that a plain reading of the treaty only required that Bourbon be handed back to France. Farquhar therefore decided to interpret the treaty as giving Madagascar to Britain, and proceeded to act as its governor.

France protested vigorously, and London was too pleased with the other terms of the treaty to start a new dispute with its erstwhile enemy. Farquhar was ordered to renounce any British claim to Madagascar and allow the French to reclaim their former territories along the coast. Thus ended any British attempt to colonize the island, although its influence would endure there. Still, it's interesting to contemplate what might have happened had the Foreign Office backed the Governor's claim and if Madagascar had eventually become a British, rather than a French, colony.

Farquhar was a persistent fellow, however, and decided that if he was temporarily forbidden from extending British sovereignty to the great island he could still exert enough influence through what came to be called 'informal empire' to perhaps allow things to break Britain's way in the future. He soon devised a plan to establish an alliance with the rising Merina state he had heard so much about from recent visitors to the island. He would help the young King Radama extend his kingdom throughout the island and by doing so keep British influence ahead of that of France, who would be kept to a few isolated outposts along the coast or prevented from returning at all. And he would use this newly purchased British influence to end the slave trade on Madagascar (it had been abolished by Britain in 1807) by persuading Radama to end the trade in his kingdom and, eventually, throughout the island.

The Governor sent an official mission to Antananarivo in October 1817 under Sergeant James Hastie to negotiate a treaty with the king. Radama, however, would only agree to abolish the export of slaves if Britain agreed to provide him with the equivalent, in arms and money, of what would have been his proceeds from the slave trade. Eventually, the two sides reached an agreement and a treaty was signed. Radama agreed to prohibit the export of slaves (anyone caught doing so was forced to become a slave!); in return he would receive annual deliveries of 1,000 dollars in gold, 1,000 dollars in silver, 100 barrels of gunpowder, 100 English muskets, 400 soldier's uniforms, 12 sergeants' swords, and sundry other supplies. The treaty also recognized Radama as "King of Madagascar," something he insisted upon and which may have been his ultimate objective. For its part, Britain obtained its goals of suppressing the slave trade and excluding French influence from the island.[15]

Not everything in Radama's court was pleasant to British sensibilities, and despite his admiration for the king Sergeant Hastie also witnessed the cruelty and backwardness of his regime. The treatment of people suspected of serious crimes, for example, was utterly barbaric. The presumption of innocence did not apply here: these unfortunate souls were either dismembered until they confessed, or more commonly, forced to swallow poison derived from the fruit of the *tangena* shrub – mixed with three pieces of chicken skin and rice – to see if they would vomit it back up. If all three pieces of chicken skin came back whole, the accused was considered innocent, but still might die from the poison. If not, they were found guilty and usually executed. Also, any infants born on certain days throughout the year designated as unlucky were sacrificed. These practices lasted for most of the rest of the century despite regular British efforts to end them.[16]

By 1820, Britain had trained the Merina army into a formidable military force, as was its charge under the terms of the treaty. It was now time for the two great kingdoms of Madagascar, who had been circling each other for over a century, to meet on the battlefield. From 1820-24, Radama personally led his troops into battle against the Sakalava, where they fought to a draw until Merina suzerainty was recognized, and along the northeast coast, where the Antankarana, Tsimihety, Sihanaka and Antemor tribes also recognized Radama's authority. After fourteen years on the throne, the young king was the unchallenged ruler of almost all of Madagascar. The desolate plains of the southwest remained outside his control, as did most of the Bara tribe's territory in the south. Merina rule never extended into certain areas of the Sakalava kingdoms, and even in areas where it did extend Radama's authority was never complete; for example, in 1825 one of the Sakalava kingdoms rose up and massacred all the Merina garrisons in the area. But Merina power had clearly surpassed any other on the island and no other chief could challenge his claim to be king of Madagascar.[17]

Radama's legacy was to be more than martial, however. Along with the expansion of his kingdom he also welcomed the London Missionary Society into Madagascar as part of his alliance with Britain, a decision that would have profound implications for the highlands and for Merina power. The missionaries opened their first school in 1820 with three students. By 1822, they had expanded their operations into three fields: scholastic education, some early vocational training, and the study of the Malagasy language, which led to preparation of the first English-Malagasy dictionary and the translation of the Bible. School attendance increased when the missionaries began to use Malagasy as the language of instruction and to train Malagasy teachers at a "Central School" in Antananarivo to serve in neighboring villages, thus allaying inherent suspicion of foreign teachers among the Malagasy. Enrollment increased to 2,000 by 1824, by which time the missionaries also made remarkable progress in producing a written (Roman) alphabet.

Radama never truly embraced Christianity himself, however, and the missionaries often got the impression he was tolerating their religious sermons solely to maintain their other services. "In general, the promise of Heaven and the threat of Hell made less than the usual impact in a people deeply imbued with the idea of survival after death in the family tombs, with the spirits of ancestors presiding over daily life," according to one historian.[18]

Radama died in July 1828 at the age of 36, very likely as a result of alcoholism. A full-blow succession crisis ensued. Before dying he had expressed a wish for his daughter Raketeka to become queen and marry his nephew Rakotobe, who could both be trusted to continue his general policies and continue to support Christianity. Traditionalist officers in Radama's court who opposed Christianity's growing influence on their country had different ideas, however. The king's death was kept secret until August 1, when the officers announced that Radama's eldest wife would assume power and take the name Queen Ranavalona. A few who dared to object that this usurpation ran directly counter to the king's plans were instantly speared to death. And so all of Radama's efforts to modernize Madagascar were instantly set back by another generation at least. Yet his formidable legacy remains: in less than 20 years he had ended the export of slaves, introduced formal education to his country, formed a standing army and almost completed the unification of the island. It's hard to say what he would have done if he had lived another 30 years – traditionalist forces may have overcome his modernization efforts and reliance on Christianity, or his reforms may have endured.[19]

The installation of Queen Ranavalona I on the throne was the first military coup on the island, but it would not be the last. And it proved to have disastrous consequences for Madagascar, as the Queen's 33-year rule quickly descended into what can only be described as a reign of terror. While she wielded great power, her reign in fact marked the end of personal despotic rule by the Merina kings; from now an oligarchy drawn mainly from the Hova middle class would exercise disproportionate power over the monarch.[20] And to meet the unprecedented situation now facing the nobles – that of a ruling queen as opposed to a king – a new post was created: the queen's guardian, who would of course be a man and who was also expected to be her official lover. The post was usually combined with that of commander in chief or prime minister. One of the eventual prime ministers, Rainilairivony, would go on to become even more powerful than the queens he supposedly served.

The Queen wasted no time in changing Radama's policies.

Toward the end of 1828, the Queen informed the British agent in Antananarivo that she no longer wished to receive the arms and materials called for under the British treaty, although she would refrain from resuming the export of slaves. Next, the French marshal under Radama, a man named Robin, was expelled, and the British General Brady, who had done so much to build up the Malagasy army, soon retired. The schools established by missionaries were allowed to reopen religious services but, at the same time, the queen began to revise traditional practices like the trial by *tangena*. Her temporary accommodation with Christianity may have been tactical: after Radama's death France began to reoccupy some of their trading stations on the east coast (later evacuated with the July Revolution in Paris and the rise to power of Louis-Phillipe), and the Queen probably wanted to stay on good terms with the British to balance French power. She also decreed that Radama's order limiting any European's stay on the island to ten years and a day be strictly enforced.

But the Queen soon reversed course and became unremittingly hostile towards Christianity, an uncompromising stance that would last until her death. Her hostility began when a fundamentalist Malagasy preacher marched on the capital one day with 200 followers, purportedly to meet with the Queen and advocate for the end of slavery, war and work. The unfortunate preacher made the mistake of telling her that no one should be a slave since all humans were created equal. When she inquired whether such equality included herself and the slaves she imported from Mozambique, he replied affirmatively, whereupon she placed the preacher and three of his chief followers in a rice pit, poured boiling water on top of them and filled the pit with earth. Seventeen other followers were placed on trial by *tangena*, after which eight were executed. On March 1, 1835, she issued the proclamation that would become her legacy, one forbidding Christian practices and ordering a strict adherence to ancestral customs. The missionaries in Antananarivo were not ordered to leave, but seeing no point in staying, all but two of them soon departed. In 1837 the first Malagasy Christian martyr was speared to death, followed by many more.[21]

Madagascar now entered the darkest period of Queen Ranavalona's reign, and indeed of its entire history. The persecution of Christians continued but many thousands of other, nonreligious Malagasy were also tortured or died under the *tangena* ordeal. Ranavalona revived the sacrificing of children born on unlucky days and expanded the death penalty for minor offenses. A few military expeditions were sent to expand the queen's territory but never met with much success, in part because of a decline in the army's competence following Radama's death. Closure of the missionary schools ended formal education for the great majority of the people. While the exporting of slaves did not resume, the internal slave trade in Madagascar, which had continued under Radama, was still common at slave markets throughout the island. Exports of slaves from the northwest areas of the island not under Merina control also resumed. With so much suffering on the island the population of Madagascar from all causes – slavery, execution, torture – may have declined by as much as a million people during the Queen's reign.[22]

While most of the previously influential Europeans fell out of favor with the Queen and left the island, a few new arrivals managed to win her trust. The first of several notable Frenchmen to gain privileged access to the Queen's court was Jean Laborde, who arrived in the capital in the 1830s and became a trusted adviser to the Queen. Among many projects he built a huge industrial complex 50 miles outside of Antananarivo that began producing the island's first manufactured goods on a large scale. He also constructed the Queen's Palace, known as the *Rova*. The industrial facility greatly reduced the queen's reliance on foreign imports and thus allowed her to deal with the Europeans from a position of greater strength. For many years all European visitors to Madagascar were subject only to their own nation's laws, but the Queen decided to change that. After she informed the French resident in Antananarivo that all aspects of Malagasy law would henceforth apply to them, a brief skirmish took place in 1845 between the French navy and certain Malagasy tribes along the east coast; this caused her to end all foreign trade and order the expulsion of all foreign traders, something no other Merina ruler had done. France and Britain each decided against a punitive expedition but refused to admit any guilt or pay the fine requested by Ranavalona, so for a period of years Malagasy ports were closed to all but the Americans, who managed to avoided the Queen's wrath and enjoyed a monopoly in trade and a favored position at court during this time.

Despite her ruthless obsession with stamping out the last remnants of Christianity on the island, the Queen never quite succeeded. In 1849 she decided to try again. One inauspicious day she ordered that 2,000 Christian worshippers be rounded up and brought to trial. Most were simply ordered to pay a fine, but in a warning to the rest of the faith, fourteen of them (including six women) were hurled to their deaths over a 500 foot precipice near the Queen's Palace (still known as Ampamarinana, "The Place of the Hurling"), while four were burned alive. And yet Christian worship continued, behind closed doors or at secret meeting places.

The British government of Mauritius eventually came up with the funds to pay the large fine demanded by the Queen, and trade was restored in 1853. But 1857 became the darkest year yet on the island, after robberies and petty thefts continued to occur in the capital despite the harsh punishments instituted by the Queen. Ranavalona's answer to the rise in crime was to give all thieves and criminals a choice: come forward and receive a light sentence, or wait to be denounced for your crimes by your fellow citizens and face execution. Of those who chose the latter, dozens were eventually plunged into boiling water, burned alive or speared to death. Others, including over 1,200 cattle stealers and other serious criminals, were placed in chains and tied by iron collars in groups of six and sent to remote locations to die, "the survivors carrying the irons of the dead until the last one expired."[23]

This could not go on forever. Perhaps not surprisingly, in 1857 a group led by supporters of the Queen's son, Prince Rakoto, began plotting a coup against the Queen, which apparently involved at least the knowledge if not the encouragement of some prominent Europeans in Antananarivo. Also not surprisingly, their plans to overthrow the Queen were discovered and reported to the Queen, and four prominent Europeans were banished from the island, followed by a fifth who left soon thereafter of his own accord. Tension reigned in the capital for the next few years until, to the great relief of the coup plotters, the Queen died in August 1861, and one of the most brutal reigns anywhere in Africa mercifully came to an end. Curiously, during the French colonial period that followed, some Malagasy nationalists tried to resurrect the Queen's reputation as a strong ruler and a defender of ancient traditions who valiantly tried to defy British and French ambitions to occupy more of the island; but this aspect of her legacy would be small consolation to the tens of thousands of Malagasy who suffered repression, persecution or death at her hands.

* * *

Another succession crisis ensued upon the Queen's death, but this time the modernists present in the royal court held off the traditionalists and proclaimed the Queen's favorite son, Prince Rakoto, as King Radama II. The new king reversed most of the queen's policies almost immediately: the death penalty was henceforth abolished, he decreed, and the *tangena* ordeal was forbidden. Moreover, forced labor was reduced and an amnesty was granted for Christianity and minor crimes. The amnesty was soon extended to captives from the Sakalava and other tribes, and a new era of peace swept over the island. Trade was resumed with the Europeans and the longstanding 10% duty on imports and exports was abolished. Radama II announced that freedom of religion would once again prevail and invited the missionaries back to Madagascar to teach and resume their other activities. Lurking behind the new calm that descended on the country was an intensification of the British-French rivalry over Madagascar, however, as each nation tried to curry favor with the new king. Radama II appeared to be favorably disposed to each of them. In 1862, both countries signed treaties with Radama II that gave their citizens wide trading privileges and the right to own property on the island, in return for recognition of Radama as King of Madagascar.

And yet palace intrigues never stopped swirling. The ink on the new treaties was barely dry when a plot was formed by Radama's Chief Minister and others to assassinate the king. Once again, traditionalist officers who felt threatened by the king's pro-European stance and embrace of the missionaries had prevailed to overthrow an enlightened ruler. Radama II was assassinated in May 1863 by strangling (to avoid the shedding of royal blood), but for years rumors persisted that he had survived the botched attempt and was planning a return to the throne. The Prime Minister then decided to put the king's widow on the throne and marry her himself – she became known as Queen Rasoherina. The royal couple quickly reinstituted the death penalty, although freedom of religion continued and the *tangena* ordeal was still abolished. In fact, most of Radama II's progressive policies remained in place.

There would no respite from crises in foreign relations

for the new queen, however. In some ways she brought them on herself when she announced that the treaties with Britain and France would have to be modified, and that the trading concessions contained within them were no longer valid. Britain accepted her decrees, but France insisted on various rights established under the treaty signed with Radama II, eventually demanding an indemnity of 1.2 million francs as compensation for expenses incurred by French private interests that had been active in Madagascar. The dispute was left unresolved when, in July 1864, the Queen replaced the chief minister with a man named Rainilaiarivony ("Father of Rilaiarivony"), who would serve as Prime Minister and royal consort – and act as the real power behind the throne – for the next 30 years. He did his best to stave off the French threat to the island during his years in office, but given the imbalance in military power between the two nations he never had a chance in succeeding.

The uncertain status of the foreign treaties was Rainilaiarivony's first order of business. Madagascar signed a new treaty with Britain in June 1865, but France insisted on prior payment of the indemnity before she would agree to anything. The Queen finally consented, but in a heartwarming display of patriotism the Malagasy people requested to pay a share themselves, and a collection was duly taken up among the Merina and beyond. After much effort the full amount was finally collected in silver dollars and sent to the French agent at Tamatave. As promised, a treaty was signed with France in August 1868, although the right of French citizens to own property on the island remained ambiguous.

Queen Rasoherina died in 1868 and Rainilaiarivony announced her cousin as successor to the throne as Queen Ranavalona II, after a brief attempt was made to install an avowedly Christian prince as king instead. Historians agree that Rainilaiarivony intervened and chose a queen rather than a king simply to assure the continuation of his own power, which was consolidated when he married her.[24] But the near-success of the so-called "Christian Plot" caused him to join the growing cultural shift in favor of Christianity and improbably become the leader of Madagascar's Christians. The new queen undoubtedly pushed him in this direction as well. She ordered the palace idols, stones and trinkets, which had figured so prominently in the monarchy's decisions for decades, removed from her coronation ceremony and replaced with a Christian Bible. She and Rainilaiarivony were married in accordance with the rites of the Christian church – but only after he divorced his wife, who had borne him 16 children. The queen's conversion to Christianity and her replacement of the idols was too much for the idol-keepers, however, who marched on the palace in September 1869 to demand their restoration. The queen responded by burning the idols and demanding that the people do the same with theirs. The idol-keepers were not heard from again.

The queen extended Radama II's warm embrace of the missionaries, and during her reign they thrived as never before. The London Missionary Society's success in Madagascar was greater than that in all of its other missions combined. In 1890 they had over 1,200 churches, 59,000 member and 248,000 adherents, mostly in Imerina. In 1880 the Prime Minister, by now a self-proclaimed true believer in the faith, decreed that all children over age seven must attend school. But since the state continued to rely entirely on the missionaries to provide all of the education called for in his edict, as well as the schools themselves, this effectively left the missionaries in charge of the island's education. By 1894, there were 137,000 children in Protestant mission schools, along with 27,000 in French Catholic mission schools, in each case mostly in the highlands.[25]

Rainilaiarivony also attempted to reform the administration of justice, promulgating a new legal code in 1881, which was later used by the French during the colonial period. The new code was altogether more humane than its predecessor and by 1868 had reduced the number of crimes punishable by death from 18 to 12. It also repeated the prohibition on the importation of slaves, although the most effective measure against the external slave trade had already been taken several years earlier when the African or "Mozambique" slaves had been freed. The new prohibition virtually ended the external slave trade, but internal slavery involving solely Malagasy slaves continued right up to the French occupation.[26] The Prime Minister also did his best to establish ministries to deal with routine governmental matters, but after so many years of despotic micromanagement the ministers he appointed were often reluctant to take measures into their own hands. He reformed the military in 1879 by reintroducing compulsory military service, and the country soon had a standing army again of 30,000 soldiers. Finally, he extended Merina rule to the Bara territory to the south of the capital, largely through peaceful measures like prisoner releases and generous payments for supplies. The very south and west of the country remained beyond Merina control.

Thus on balance Rainilaiarivony introduced some much needed reforms to Madagascar, but the threat of foreign occupation of the island worried him endlessly. As his government resumed trade and other contacts with Britain and France in the second half of the 19th century, one of the two great powers was bound to try to acquire Madagascar for itself. And it would probably be France, he reasoned. Except for Farquhar's short-lived attempt to claim the island for Mauritius, the British had never shown any interest in annexing Madagascar. France, on the other hand, had been much more aggressive, at various times claiming sovereignty over parts or the whole of the island, and had already annexed the small offshore islands of Nosy Be and Ile Sainte Marie. Rainilaiarivony thus decided on a foreign policy that favored the British, who were only too happy to be embraced by the government of such a large and promising territory.

The opening of the Suez Canal changed the future of Madagascar irrevocably, however. Up until the Canal opened in 1869, the fastest route to Britain's prized colony in India was around the Cape of Good Hope, which made Madagascar's location vitally important. Under no circumstance would London have stood by and watched her chief rival, France, acquire the great island in the middle of the sea lanes to the Raj. But with the opening of the Suez Canal, which cut the distance from Europe to India by over 6,000 miles, Madagascar became strategically insignificant. Meanwhile, France's ignominious defeat in the Franco-Prussian War in 1870 had weakened her, but not irreparably, and she was quick to recover. If anything, that defeat only increased France's desire to avenge the country's disgrace through the acquisition of a great colony like Madagascar.[27]

In May 1881, after a minor dispute arose over an incident in the Comoros, France began to press its advantage. In addition to the humiliation of its defeat against Prussia, the unstable governments of France's Third Republic had turned to an aggressive policy overseas to compensate for recurring problems at home. They were also under pressure from the *colons* in Reunion to acquire Madagascar as a possible solution to mounting economic problems and overpopulation on Reunion. Baudais, the French commissioner to Madagascar, insisted that Rainilairivony recognize French sovereignty over the northwest coast of the island based on treaties obtained from local chiefs by French naval officers between 1840-42. These claims rested on obviously shaky legal ground, as the Franco-Malagasy treaty of 1868 had explicitly recognized the queen as sovereign of the whole island, but France was looking for any pretext to take control of Madagascar, and this was the best it could find.

When the dispute over the northwest coast became a crisis, Rainilaiarivony sent a delegation to Europe and the United States in late 1882 to try to resolve it. An offer by Madagascar to neutralize the northwest area of the island was rejected by

France, whose public now supported an even tougher stance on Madagascar after the recent British occupation of Egypt. An offer by Lord Granville in London to mediate the dispute was similarly rejected by France. The United States, for its part, ratified the 1881 treaty that recognized Queen Ranavalona II as ruler of the whole island but could do no more.

No longer interested in compromise, France soon resorted to more robust military action. In May 1883 French ships shelled two Malagasy posts on the west coast, followed by a bombardment of the city of Majunga, which they then occupied. Baudais sent an ultimatum to the Queen, demanding recognition of a French protectorate over a certain portion of northern Madagascar, the repeal of Article 85 of the 1881 code prohibiting the sale of land to foreigners, and a new indemnity of one million francs to satisfy the claims of French nationals, including Jean LaBorde. The Queen refused and gave a stirring and defiant speech to her brethren in the capital, whereupon France bombed and occupied the east coast city of Tamatave in June.[28]

Queen Ranavalona II died in July 1883. Rainilaiarivony chose a 22-year-old princess to be Queen Ranavalona III and then married her, his third royal wife in 20 years. The war with France had bogged down into a stalemate, with the French entrenched in Majunga and Tamatave but unable to advance further. In December 1884 they seized the harbor of Diego Suarez, but their position along the coasts still did not threaten the government in Antananarivo. After another year both sides were ready for peace, and in December 1885 they signed a treaty which seemed to be a boon for France: the right to occupy Diego, a huge indemnity of 10 million francs, the right of French citizens to lease property on the island for an indefinite duration, and the appointment of a French Resident in the capital who would henceforth oversee Madagascar's foreign relations. The treaty did not require the Queen to give up any territory in the north (other than French occupation rights in

Diego) and recognized her internal sovereignty over the whole island. Some of the treaty terms were anathema to the nobles in Antananarivo, however, forcing Rainilaiarivony to go back to the French envoys and seek a further interpretation of those terms in Madagascar's favor. He sent a letter of clarification dated January 1886 – an amendment of sorts – which the French representatives then signed. The French government in Paris, however, did not feel bound by the letter and proceeded to ratify the treaty without any mention of it, which would lead to some confusion later.

Britain then reentered the scene, though only in a commercial capacity. Article 9 of the new treaty with France stipulated that French troops would remain in Tamatave until the ten million franc indemnity was paid, so Rainilaiarivony had great incentive to pay it as soon as possible. To do so he secured a loan in June 1886 with a British bank for $4 million dollars, to be secured by the bank's involvement in Madagascar's collection of customs duties. The French were incensed, realizing the advantage this would give Britain over the island's affairs, and forced Madagascar to accept instead a loan from the *Comptoir d'Escompte de Paris* for 15 million francs, with that bank now assuming control of the island's customs revenues. The Malagasy were also prohibited from buying arms with the loan, presumably since they might use them one day against France.

France was satisfied with this arrangement, but only temporarily. They needed Britain out of the way before they could succeed in their larger designs for Madagascar. Having secured the Suez Canal, Britain now turned its attention to the headwaters of the Nile, fearing that an enemy power established there could threaten British control of Egypt. As a first step to the penetration of Uganda they sought control of Zanzibar, and to get it they signed a treaty in July 1890 with Germany, the most active power on that island, that ceded Heligoland (a small island in the North Sea) to Germany in exchange for

German recognition of a British protectorate over Zanzibar. But in his haste to consummate the agreement with Germany, Lord Salisbury had forgotten about an earlier treaty – the Anglo-German Convention of 1862 – that guaranteed the independence of Zanzibar. France exploited this oversight immediately, protesting that as an adherent to the earlier treaty she should have been consulted on any change to Zanzibar's status. Lord Salisbury admitted he had forgotten the 1862 Convention and searched for some concession to France to make the problem go away. Not long after this debacle, in a treaty signed in August 1890, Britain recognized a French protectorate over Madagascar in return for France's acquiescence in the British protectorate over Zanzibar. Despite some criticism of the government's action in London, support for Britain's global strategy prevailed and the whole matter was soon forgotten. The Foreign Office in London lamely explained that they had merely recognized the existing state of affairs after Madagascar's agreement to grant a de facto protectorate over the island to France in their treaty of 1886. With some justification, the affair is still remembered in Madagascar as the British Betrayal.[29]

* * *

France now had its protectorate over the great island. Yet according to some historians Madagascar was in 1895 more advanced than most of the other African countries when they achieved their independence from colonial rule sixty or seventy years later. Madagascar by this time was far from an uncivilized place, at least not in the capital of Antananarivo. Education and enlightenment had already begun to take hold there, albeit with some European help. In the public sphere, government work was efficiently carried out by various departments headed by bureaucratic ministers. The advancement toward a more sophisticated culture was largely the work of the missionaries who had by then been in Madagascar for over half a century; but the rapid spread, at least in the plateau area, of primary education, Christianity and medical services were by now carried out almost exclusively by Malagasy, and this made the island remarkable.[30]

On the other hand, there were some serious problems on the island when France took control. Slavery still existed within Madagascar, and since government work was unpaid, corruption began to increase throughout the island as ministers and other functionaries looked for other sources of income. The decline in Rainilairivony's energy began to show as he aged, and the daily barrage of diplomatic and military headaches that besieged him left him with fewer resources for managing the state; meanwhile, law and order also suffered, with increased banditry and raids into Merina territory by the fearsome Sakalava. All of these factors conspired to present additional pretexts for French intervention.

The dispute with France persisted even after their protectorate was established. Rainilairivony used the letter agreement he believed formed an integral part of the 1886 treaty to take back some of the area south of Diego Suarez that France felt it was entitled to. He also continued to import weapons from shipments along Madagascar's long, ungovernable coastline. In essence, the Prime Minister had refused to accept the French protectorate on the terms demanded by France, which left Paris with no choice but to impose one by military means. When a French envoy arrived in October 1894 and presented a new draft treaty as an ultimatum that neutered Malagasy sovereignty even further, Rainilairivony rejected it and both sides prepared for war. In November the French National Assembly voted a special credit of 65 million francs for military intervention in Madagascar. General Jacques Duchesne, a veteran of the Franco-Prussian War, was put in charge of 658 officers and 14,773 men, the latter including 3,800 troops from West Africa and Sakalava territory.[31]

The French campaign began with the bombing and occupation of Tamatave in December 1894. General Duchesne then wisely chose to advance from the northwest, the French Navy shelling Majunga in January 1895 and the advance guard of the army arriving there in February. The push to the capital began, but only after the brief battle of Marovoay, where hundreds of crocodiles crawled onto the battlefield to drag corpses and wounded men into the river nearby (perhaps the General should have known better – the name of the town means "Many Crocodiles"). Meanwhile, the Merina army proved to be no match for French firearms and discipline, and patriotic morale in the capital turned out to be surprisingly low. The defiance and unity of the Malagasy people, it seemed, had been eroded by some recent harsh exactions of the monarchy, along with corruption and nepotism drifting from the royal palace. The French Army, for its part, suffered few battle casualties to this point but malaria and dysentery had begun to take a heavy toll. The decision to use the Lefebvre wagon to carry supplies rather than mules or human porters meant that a road had to be built in high heat, further weakening them. At last, however, the road to Antananarivo lay open, and Duchesne sent an advance column to travel the final 100 miles and take the capital. The queen gave one more defiant speech exhorting the town's defense, but the final assault took place on September 30 with little resistance. French military casualties were negligible – only 20 dead and 100 wounded – but almost 6,000 died from disease.

On October 1, 1895, Duchesne entered the capital and signed a treaty with the queen's representatives establishing a French protectorate, this time for sure. It gave the French Resident-General full control over the island's internal and external affairs and the right to station as many troops on the island as France wanted. The queen remained on the throne for the time being, and France's initial plan was to rule the island through the handful of Malagasy ministers already in place, but Rainilairivony was dismissed immediately. These plans had to be scrapped in late 1895, however, when an uprising began throughout the island, targeting both the French, for their occupation of the island, and the Merina, as revenge for their high-handed treatment of the other tribes during the monarchy. France now realized, perhaps for the first time, both how difficult the Malagasy would be as colonial subjects and how unpopular the Merina regime still was throughout the rest of the island. By the middle of 1896 the rebels, known as the *menalamba* ("red lamba") for their distinctive dress, had taken control of most of the central province. It quickly morphed into a purely nationalist, anti-French insurgency as time went on.[32]

The rebellion in Madagascar only strengthened the hardliners in Paris who wanted more control over the island than a protectorate afforded, and in August 1896 the French Parliament formally declared the annexation of Madagascar as a French colony. At the same time it declared the abolition of slavery on the island. Parliament then sent General Joseph Gallieni to Madagascar in September with two objectives: first, to crush the Malagasy rebellion with an iron fist, and then to make Madagascar properly French, in part by humbling the Merina (which would also undermine Britain, the tribe's longstanding allies). As a show of authority, one of Gallieni's first acts was to conduct a summary trial of a government minister and an uncle of the queen for subversion; the trial later proved to be a political act by Gallieni to discourage the Malagasy from attempting any further revolt, and for the time being the attempt at humiliation had its intended effect.

In February 1897, Gallieni formally abolished the monarchy and sent the queen into exile. The prime minister's post was also abolished, and Gallieni became the first Governor-General of Madagascar. By the end of 1897, backed by 7,000 troops (only 1500 European), Gallieni had pacified all the territory previously controlled by the Merina. He then turned to the rest of the island, unifying it under one authority for the first time in the island's history. His use of "the oil spot method" – the tactic of steadily expanding a secure zone to larger and larger areas – to pacify parts of the southeast, nearly all the south and much of the west formerly controlled by the Sakalava became legendary in the annals of counterinsurgency doctrine. When he left in 1905, French pacification was complete but had inevitably come at the cost of many Malagasy lives.

With Madagascar now firmly under French control, Gallieni began to construct a functioning colonial administration. Twenty provinces were formed across the island, establishing the practice of the *"politiques des races,"* under which each ethnic group was administered separately and under its own chiefs, replicating the British policy of 'divide and rule' pioneered in India. Gallieni decided to keep the 1881 Penal Code in place for the Malagasy people (with a separate code for Europeans, of course). The imposition of law and order, as well as an efficient colonial government, came as somewhat of a relief to a beleaguered Malagasy population, as did various infrastructure projects undertaken by the French, such as the construction of new roads (especially from Antananarivo to Tamatave), modern port facilities, extended telegraph services, and the beginnings of the first railway. Less welcome was the colonial economy, which reserved imports to France and excluded cheaper goods from other countries through the institution of high tariffs, causing higher prices for the Malagasy. A French Parliament decree in 1900 requiring all colonies to be self-sufficient (i.e., to pay for themselves) caused Gallieni to resort to forced labor to make ends meet in the colony, which provoked outrage in Madagascar and even in some circles in France. Also unpopular were substantial land grants he awarded to French *colons* and various French companies.[33]

Gallieni was a remarkable administrator who went on to great fame in World War I. His legacy in Madagascar remains controversial, however. He was the first person – Malagasy or French – to establish a unified Malagasy state throughout the whole island, and he established the economic and administrative framework for the colony that Madagascar continued to use when it became independent in 1960. But his establishment of the *"politiques des races"* was intended to reinforce tribal divisions and stymie any sense of nationhood, while his crushing of the island's post-protectorate rebellion and his temporary resort to forced labor diminish his accomplishments considerably.[34]

* * *

After the traumatic years of conquest, rebellion and pacification under Gallieni, Madagascar settled down into a more peaceful existence as a French colony – at least for a while. The island's recent experience of nascent statehood and the comparatively advanced state of education produced a people unwilling to submit to colonial rule very easily, a rebellious sentiment that expressed itself earlier than in other colonies in Africa. France was obviously well aware of the clear contradiction between her commitment to liberty, equality and fraternity and her new dominance over millions of subject peoples. And her historic belief in the civilizing power of French culture led Paris to adopt a policy of assimilation of its colonial peoples as extensions of metropolitan France. But assimilation was opposed by French *colons* and traders, so it was always applied in a halfhearted way, in Madagascar and elsewhere.[35]

One area where French colonialism failed was in education. For a time after its annexation France began closing schools, both for budgetary reasons and as an easy way to separate church from state, a longstanding French goal. Later, as educational standards declined in the coastal areas, the administration was forced to scrap the *politiques des races* and appointed Merina officials to important positions in the provinces. While the mixing of tribes may have soothed ethnic divisions on the island temporarily, in the long run it only united the coastal peoples in their resentment toward their erstwhile rulers. French administrators never really attempted to bridge the resentments between the major tribes of the island, and the coastal–highland divide remains one of the unresolvable conflicts in Madagascar today.

Malagasy nationalism in response to French rule began in Antananarivo. The provinces, ever-fearful of a Merina return to power, were in no hurry to throw out their colonial masters. The Merina, of course, had every reason to regain their former status and power, and their higher levels of education and contact with French intellectual trends encouraged their nationalist aspirations. In reaction to their struggle the Merina faced a French colonial apparatus that was split into factions: there was an undeniable tension between the *colons*, who wanted no concessions made to the natives, and the colonial administrators who often had to reconcile official policy with the aggressive demands of the settlers. In the early 1920s, the first nationalists set up newspapers in the capital denouncing the abuses of colonialism and advocating assimilation of Madagascar as a full department of France with full citizenship for the Malagasy. But by the end of the decade, after harsh colonial laws prohibited anything that "might harm the prestige of France" or "provoke hatred of the French government," they had abandoned assimilation in favor of full independence.[36]

World War II impacted Madagascar significantly, as it did virtually every part of the world. The fall of France in June 1940 forced a critical decision on French officials on the island. At first they responded to De Gaulle's call to support the Free French, but the British bombing of the French fleet at Mers el Kebir caused them to reverse course and support the newly installed Vichy regime. Madagascar suffered as a result, as the British imposed an almost total blockade of the island through its control of the seas. The island was basically self-sufficient in food staples, but lack of money for oil, spare parts and road repairs caused substantial hardship.

Strategic interest in the island then revived for the first time since the opening of the Suez Canal. With the Canal now closed due to the Axis powers' control of the Mediterranean, Madagascar's position along the route to the Middle East and India regained its previous importance, especially when Japan entered the war in December 1941. In response, De Gaulle proposed a military operation to Churchill to restore the Free French on the island; Churchill eventually agreed to it but then made it a purely British operation, keeping De Gaulle in the dark until it had already begun. German records later showed the Japanese were planning to establish bases on the island in March 1942 to attack shipping along the Cape, but their plans were vetoed by Hitler. Nevertheless, if Britain had not acted there is a good chance the Japanese would have tried to occupy the island at a later date. Churchill's stratagem, codenamed Operation Ironclad, began on May 5, 1942, to capture Diego Suarez, which quickly fell to the British. The French Governor Armand Leon Annet refused to relinquish control over Madagascar, however, forcing the British to take it by force. Churchill was soon persuaded that, in addition to seizing Diego Suarez, firm control over the island would require capturing all of its ports, so British troops landed at Majunga and Tamatave in preparation for an assault on the capital, which took place in November. The Malagasy showed no inclination to fight the British and deserted the battle in droves. As with Diego, Britain took Antananarivo without much difficulty and soon handed the island over to the Free French, who never quite forgave them for the surprise attack on one of their colonies.

The end of the war ushered in a period of intense nationalism, but a conference held by Free French leaders in 1944 in the Central African capital of Brazzaville dashed any hopes of independence. Instead, France decided on a policy of complete assimilation, with the abolition of the inferior legal code for colonial people and limited representation for them in both the French Constituent Assembly and the subsequent French Parliament. Madagascar was allocated four seats in the Assembly, two for Frenchmen and two for Malagasy. While it pushed off any talk of independence it thus did allow for some limited democratic activity on the island. The first real political party, MDRM, was established in 1946 before France had fully regained control over its colony; it quickly began to advocate for immediate independence within the French Union. The Malagsy became French citizens under the new French constitution of 1946, but nationalist sentiment on the island only increased, and the next year a revolt erupted that would shake the French colonial state in Madagascar to its foundations.

On March 29, 1947, thousands of armed rebels attacked military posts, administrative centers and French settlers in a coordinated attack across much of the country. The rebellion soon fizzled out, however, in part because the south and west of the country had remained aloof, and because PADESM, the political party representing the coasts and the principal rival of the MDRM, had declined to take part. While its leaders hoped it would take on the character of a national rebellion, the revolt soon morphed into a regional insurgency located primarily in the provinces of Tamatave and Fianarantsoa. Still, by the end of 1947, the rebellion had spread to a third of the countryside. France sent large military reinforcements and, reinstituting Gallieni's oil spot method, finally defeated the rebels in March 1949 after a brutal pacification campaign.

It is hard to overstate the importance of the 1947 rebellion in Malagasy history. Hampered by its fractured leadership and vague political goals, the insurgency failed to dislodge France from the island, but two years of warfare and 89,000 Malagasy deaths (out of a population of just four million) mostly from disease and starvation, had a slow but profound effect on colonialism's demise on the island. In the immediate term, hundreds of the nationalist party's (MDRM's) leaders were subsequently arrested, with three prominent leaders subjected to a show trial during which some of the defendants were tortured. Many were sentenced to death or hard labor, although these sentences were later reduced to house arrest. The movement's three principal leaders (Joseph Raseta, Joseph Ravoahangy and Jacques Rabemananjara) remained in exile in France until independence in 1960. More broadly, the failure of the rebellion and the harsh measures used to suppress it crushed the MDRM and led to bitterness not only between France and Madagascar but also between nationalists and other groups on the island that had not supported the revolt. Any hopes of early independence were thus put on hold, to be renewed and redeemed only a decade later.[37]

As for France, Max Hastings has noted how the brutal suppression of Malagasy nationalism became a template for how to suppress other native populations in its empire, especially in Southeast Asia:

Successive revolving door governments of the [French] Fourth Republic proved feeble in everything save a willingness to deploy force in France's overseas possessions, with a ruthlessness seldom matched by the Soviets. Following a 1945 Muslim revolt in Algeria in which a hundred Europeans were killed, an estimated 25,000 people were slaughtered by French troops. After a March 1947 rebellion in Madagascar, where 37,000 *colons* lorded it over 4.2 million black subjects, the army killed 90,000 people. Only in the enervating climate of a world that had exhausted its stock of moral courage could the creation of such mountains of corpses by a European power have passed with such little remark. Algeria and Madagascar provide important context for the matching bloodshed that descended upon Indochina.[38]

The story of Malagasy independence becomes far less dramatic after the 1947 rebellion. Over the decade of the 1950s, the island saw an expansion of the voting franchise and greater autonomy within the French Union. The views of Malagasy political parties ranged from conservatives who wanted no change in the status quo to those advocating outright independence, with a small majority in the middle who wanted gradual autonomy or independence in some continued association with France. As nationalist sentiment on the island continued to build, events in France also began to favor greater autonomy for its overseas territories, especially after their defeat at Dien Bien Phu and the loss of Indochina. In the midst of the Algerian Crisis France gave all of its colonies the choice between immediate independence and a new constitution, which would mean greater autonomy within a newly formed French Community. In 1958 Madagascar (and every other colony except Guinea) voted to remain in that federation, which represented greater self-rule in some areas but still left France in control over the island's foreign affairs and its defense and economic policies.

This temporarily quelled nationalist sentiment, but only briefly, and within two years support for full independence had won out. Malagasy representatives met with French colonial officials in Paris and reached an agreement early in 1960 that Madagascar would become a fully independent nation within the French Community. A Malagasy army was established, but France would retain control of the naval base at Diego Suarez and have the right to station troops on the island. Madagascar stayed in the Franc zone under a mutually beneficial trade system with France. These arrangements gave France considerable influence over the new nation, but for the first time they were not imposed on Madagascar; the new President of Madagascar, Philibert Tsiranana, accepted them as necessary accommodations until the country became truly self-sufficient.[39] The main point is that in a matter of ten years, the island had gone from a suppressed colony firmly under the yoke of France to a newly independent state, and this had all happened peacefully. The people of the island had shown that the rebellion of 1947 was not in vain, the French Tricolor had come down, and Madagascar was free.

The colonial period then ended. According to Mervyn Brown, it will appear as a "brief interlude in the development of the Malagasy nation," for in some respects the country was still the same after 65 years of colonial rule. The sheer size of the island limited the effectiveness of French efforts to modernize or Europeanize the country. Indeed, away from the main towns life went on as if the French had never been there. But in other areas the colonial period had a profound effect on the island. An educational system produced Malagasy professionals ready to run the state administration system left behind by the French. A sense of nationhood now existed, even as the divide between the highlanders and the coastal tribes remained. So too did a modern trading economy, now based on exports of key items like coffee, vanilla and sugar, in addition to the traditional subsistence economy. A basic infrastructure of ports, railways, roads – and now airfields – dotted the island. Madagascar was thus very different in 1960 than it had been in 1895; but the difference was arguably not as great as in other African countries, where in many cases the colonial project midwifed a new country and imposed one common language out of many. In Madagascar the end of colonialism led to a recovery of independence rather than its birth, according to Brown. In the end the French presence may have been less of a rupture to the island than the rise and expansion of the Merina in the 19th century, and the mistrust among the regions, resulting in part from that rupture and in part from deliberate French policies that followed, still loomed ominously over the new nation in 1960.[40]

Chapter 2

The Coup

Democracy is never a thing done. Democracy is always something that a nation must be doing.
– Archibald MacLeish

One warm autumn afternoon, as the work day ended in Antananarivo and thousands of people flooded into the streets to head home, I met a friend for a beer. He had called me the night before and told me he wanted to introduce me to some of his friends. You'll like them, he told me, they're interesting. I joined him the next day on a main street above the downtown neighborhood of Analakely, and before I could say a word he signaled me to follow him onto an unmarked side street, where the sounds of the city quickly fell to a hush. He led me through a maze of increasingly narrow paths between tall brick buildings, some of them crumbling or chipping paint and leaning to one side. We stepped inside a doorway to meet a relative of his, an aunt or grandmother who spoke to me in broken French and invited me back for dinner the next week, before my friend tugged at my sleeve and our journey continued. We descended further into this urban oblivion until, eventually, we rounded a corner and found ourselves in a small courtyard, where a dimly lit bar spilled out onto a rectangle of cracked pavement. From inside the bar, the distinctive sound of someone singing karaoke wafted out to us like some cheap parody.

The scene was this. Two dozen people in their twenties and thirties. A couple of picnic tables outside and a small karaoke bar inside, with a lone bartender selling beer and skewers of barbecued meat. Neon lights flashing in all corners of the place. Everyone smoking, some of them singing and dancing.

My friend introduced me to one of his friends named Hubert, a young man with his head shaved and a professional air, which I attributed mostly to the fact that he was wearing a tie. As I met more people and the night got later, the conversation eventually turned to politics, with decidedly negative attitudes expressed toward the current president, Andry Rajoelina. It was mostly the typical rantings of the young and inexperienced, but at some point the talk turned from the airing of grievances to a plan for action. We only have two years to plan this, one of them said. Everything will change when we take over, another proclaimed. It suddenly dawned on me that I had stumbled on the makings of a plot to overthrow the government.

Hubert drew me aside. A garrulous man in his mid-thirties, he was the natural leader of this cabal. He told me he had three thousand students ready to march through the streets and demand the president's resignation on a moment's notice. When I expressed skepticism over these claims he grew defiant and insisted on the loyalty of his alleged supporters. "One of them is sitting right over there," he said, pointing to a young woman sipping a beer. She waved and confirmed what Hubert had just said. "Me and all my friends, we're ready to march," she told me.

Hubert called over another man who he claimed would provide any logistical support required for the coup. This man, also in his early thirties, was heavier and wore jeans and a white t-shirt. "I own a trucking company here in Tana," he said. "We have twenty-five trucks that haul gravel and carry supplies all across the city. I've also got ten buses that operate here. When we launch the revolution next year, we'll turn all of our vehicles over to the people, and they'll have whatever they need. We'll block traffic in certain areas and deliver food, water and supplies for however long it takes."

Three thousand students and an army of trucks wasn't a bad start if you wanted to stage a demonstration over some municipal failing like rising food prices or recurrent power outages, but it seemed to me a woefully inadequate nucleus for launching a coup, especially against a former coup leader himself who was known to be on constant alert for threats to his rule. It also wasn't clear to me if the goal was to reinstall Ravalomanana or simply overthrow Rajoelina and start over. But it's not every day you get to hear the secret plans of a revolution, so I gathered Hubert and his two lieutenants around me and proceeded to glean as much information as I could.

"So the uprising will start in 2021?"

"Yes," they said in unison.

"Why then?"

"Because that's how long it will take for people in Tana to see what a failure the new president is, and how much better the country was with Marc," the young woman, whose name was Nataly, told me.

"People aren't mad enough yet," Hubert said. "But in two years they will be."

"And in 2021 you'll give the signal and thousands of young people will march through the streets and force Rajoelina to step down?"

"Yes. Three thousand will turn into ten thousand, then twenty ..."

"And all of your trucks will be out there to support them?" I asked the bigger guy in the white t-shirt.

"Yes, we'll send them to all the key points in the city, bringing people, supplies, food, whatever we need to support the movement. We'll also block traffic where we need to."

"Will you have military support?"

"We're working on that. The president has paid off all the top officers so they won't leave him, but we think there are some junior officers who will join us as soon as they understand what's happening."

"You'll need money though, won't you, to start a revolution?"

They looked at each other guiltily, then Hubert turned to me. "That's actually what we wanted to talk to you about."

"Me?"

"Yes. You're an American, right?"

I nodded slowly.

"You know lots of people there, right?" Nataly asked me.

"We were thinking you could raise the money for us," Hubert said quickly.

I started thinking of the Facebook message I would send out to all of my friends and acquaintances, explaining how I needed each of them to send $1,000 to support a cause very close to their hearts – the upcoming revolution in Madagascar to overthrow the current president and reinstall his predecessor, who had just lost an election by double digits. I wanted to laugh, but when I looked at the earnest faces of the would-be revolutionaries in front of me, I decided to take a different tack.

"Look," I said, "By 2021 Rajoelina will only have two years left in his term, right?"

"Yes. So?"

"Why don't you just wait two years, organize and campaign for someone better, and beat him in the next election?"

Total silence followed. The three Bolsheviks in front of me looked at one another in disbelief.

"You mean *democratically*?" Nataly finally said.

"Yes."

"You really don't know how things work here, do you?" the big guy said.

"The president would never let Marc win the next election against him," Hubert explained. "He just wouldn't. The democratic way always loses here."

It was not so much the force of their arguments but their disdain for mine that surprised me. I was clearly outnumbered in this group – alone, really – in my undiminished faith in the democratic experiment that had washed over the globe, and especially in my part of the world, during the past two centuries. I felt my Western bias in favor of democracy rise up between us like an invisible moat. All of the values I had grown up with – the belief in representative government, the importance of majority rule and minority rights, the sanctity of elections – suddenly felt like the naïve assumptions of an idealist whose theories have already been tried and rejected. In this age of creeping authoritarianism, never had I felt so out of place, so behind the times. Never had I felt like such an anachronism.

This being Madagascar, where almost all foreigners are treated with respect, the group made a perfunctory effort to find common ground with me on whether a coup was ultimately warranted. At last Hubert suppressed a smile and winked at the other two. "You know what, that's what we'll do, we'll just wait until the next election and make sure we win. You're probably right." Hearing him say that made me think I had somehow contributed to the future stability of a place I had come to think of as a second home. My good deed for the day, as it were. At that moment a friend of Nataly's walked over and tapped her on the shoulder. It was her turn to sing karaoke. So the conspiracy stopped there, at least for that night, but not before the guy with the trucks and the buses pulled me aside and told me to keep in touch.

"Just come back in 2021," he said. "You might get to see some history. Tell all your friends in America to come too. Or they can just watch it on Facebook."

As I walked home that night I wondered what had led so many young people in Antananarivo to contemplate open rebellion against their government for the second time in a generation. The cynicism about elections that had become prevalent in many parts of the country didn't emerge from a void, I knew. When Madagascar finally broke free of French control there were scenes of jubilation, fueled not only by a feeling that the Malagasy had just accomplished something historic but by a belief that their beautiful island, blessed with so many natural resources and now free to chart its own course, had a bright future ahead of it. That bright future had dimmed considerably over the years. I didn't yet understand all the antecedents, but I knew that something must have gone terribly wrong in the last 60 years.

* * *

The optimism palpable at the time of independence proved to be justified. For over a decade, Madagascar was the scene of peace and internal stability that proved so elusive elsewhere in postcolonial Africa, and the country became known as The Happy Island. President Philibert Tsiranana skillfully managed the first ten years of independence with a mix of strength, through the dominance of his PSD party, and conciliation, by appeasing most of his political rivals. Internal order came not by repression but under the conditions of democracy, accompanied by the rule of law, free speech and a free press.[1] It was no accident, however, that leaders of the dominant ethnic group – the Merina – were largely absent from the halls of power during the first independence regime. After decades of repressing nationalist movements led by the Merina against their colonial rule, France was not about to hand the country over to them, and had quietly ensured a different outcome. But Tsiranana would still have to contend with the recrudescence of Merina power throughout his term, a movement which threatened to turn against him if he veered into any kind of anti-Merina alliance with the coastal tribes.[2]

Tsiranana acted to defuse the threat posed by the exiled MDRM leaders by personally bringing them back in his plane and taking credit for their return. The Merina, for their part, were bought off with senior posts in the administration and diplomatic service. The 1960 legislative elections returned a huge victory for the PSD, and with such dominance there was some talk of a one-party state, but Tsiranana preferred to retain at least the trappings of a multiparty democracy. The capital remained a stronghold of the opposition party – the AKFM – and the country's press freedoms allowed newspapers to criticize the government at will. Curiously, as there were many female doctors, lawyers and teachers in Madagascar, there were no women in the PSD's leadership, and there would not be a woman in the National Assembly until 1964.

Tsiranana was a fervent anti-communist, and socialism in Madagascar was always pragmatic, an ideology focused on improving the living standards of the people, with central planning coming only in the context of a mixed economy. He opposed the introduction of heavy industry and resisted expropriating any foreign firms, recognizing that Madagascar needed foreign capital to develop. Thus with hardly any industrial base and very modest exploitable mineral deposits, agriculture remained by far the most important sector of the economy in the decade after independence.

Madagascar's foreign policy in these years was characterized by anti-Communism and the priority of economic development. Fear of Communist invasion or subversion was the main reason Tsiranana allowed – indeed welcomed – the continued stationing of French troops on the island, and why he aligned himself with the West for economic aid and national defense. Tsiranana never established diplomatic relations with the Soviets, for example, and while he joined the OAU as a matter of course he had no time for the leftist speeches of Nasser and Nkrumah (Madagascar's self-identity as an African nation has always been relatively weak). His foreign policy predictably led to charges of complicity with American imperialism, but these had little political effect in a country focused on internal development.

With no external enemies and a feeling of unity resulting

from the common culture and language (albeit with persistent Merina/coastal divisions), it was easy to see why Madagascar was the envy of many African nations during this era. Its per capita income of $80 in 1960 ranked Madagascar as one of the 20 poorest countries in the world, but it did not appear that way. Many peasants had their own house and a small plot of land on which to cultivate rice. Basic requirements of food, clothing and shelter were met with relatively small exceptions. And political stability seemed assured, with PSD popularity reaching its peak in 1967, a year when GDP growth still outpaced the growth of its population. In 1970 Madagascar was even removed from the list of the world's poorest countries as its economy continued to show signs of modest improvement.[3]

Then, out of nowhere, a Marxist revolution. Cracks in Tsiranana's rule had begun to show a few years earlier, but no one anticipated the sudden storm of a socialist dictatorship in 1972. Perhaps they should have. As a growing peasant population started leaving rural areas for the cities in search of work, the economy could not keep pace, especially as an increase in university education began to produce more graduates also looking for jobs. But the major factor may have been a resurgent nationalism, as many Malagasy realized that despite their independence France still retained an inordinate amount of influence over the government and Malagasy life in general. In the eyes of many on the island, independent Madagascar had shown itself unwilling or unable to truly break free from France. By 1972, foreigners still controlled nine-tenths of the modern economy, and 90% of those assets were still owned by French citizens. In addition, Madagascar's unpublished military agreement with France from 1960 required regular intelligence exchanges about subversion and other political developments on the island, and called for periodic Franco-Malagasy military training programs to prepare for a hypothetical Communist uprising. France continued to share the naval base at Diego

Suarez and station hundreds of air force and military personnel on the island.[4]

Moreover, many important positions across the country were still filled by Frenchmen, despite the fact that Malagasy were qualified to perform them. One reason the Tsiranana administration hesitated to turn to native professionals was because, in most cases, Merina would have filled those positions, bringing coastal resentments back to the fore. Therefore it was the Malagasy government and not France who chose to retain French advisors throughout the island during this period. A considerable degree of French involvement after independence was to be expected, given their large aid and investment flows; but, in the end, the failure to make a case to the public for a temporary reliance on foreign involvement contributed to the fall of the regime.[5]

Modern historians have come up with two common explanations for Madagascar's unwillingness or inability to shed the rudiments of French influence during the 1960s. First, some argue that before turning over power France successfully organized and manipulated a fledgling political party (the PSD) to do its bidding in exchange for independence – to the point that all efforts at true decolonization were stymied. Others contend that the coastal tribes feared a resurgence of Merina dominance of the island in the wake of France's departure so much that they actually preferred to keep a modicum of French influence on the island as an antidote to unrestrained Merina power. Under the latter scenario, the pro-Western foreign policy of Tsiranana reflected an overriding domestic preoccupation – to reinforce barriers against the Merina. Both explanations hold merit and indeed need not be seen as mutually exclusive.[6]

With tensions mounting for the first time since independence it did not take long for violence to erupt. In April 1971, up to 100 armed men in the south of the island attacked police stations and other government buildings to protest the lack of economic opportunity in the region, with the largest attack at Ampanihy. The attackers were brutally cut down, with unofficial reports of 1000 dead and thousands more wounded. This attack was a precursor to a true revolution the next year, when thousands of students gathered in the *Avenue de l'Independence* in the capital to protest the lack of reforms in education and the continued dependence on France. When the government responded with force, killing several students, a general strike was called by trade unions and church organizations that brought over 100,000 people into the streets. In September 1972, a new constitution was put to a referendum; Tsiranana urged a "No" vote, but when it passed overwhelmingly he resigned and Gabriel Ramanantsoa became head of state with a mandate of five years. The *cotiers* accepted the rise of this Merina stalwart because of his professional reputation, but were acutely aware of the threat of Merina dominance again.[7]

The new government knew its first priority had to be to answer nationalist calls for real independence. Didier Ratsiraka, the new foreign minister, took over the renegotiation of the cooperation agreement with France in 1973. When it was signed Madagascar left the Franc zone and France handed over all of its military bases, accepting its displacement gracefully and continuing to provide foreign aid at a high level. Ratsiraka also pulled off a complete reorientation of the country's foreign policy, ending its agreements with South Africa and Israel and establishing relations with Communist China, the USSR, North Korea and Eastern Europe. Madagascar also joined the radical wing of the OAU for the first time.

More violence was to come, however. Ramanantsoa resigned in February 1975 in favor of Richard Ratsimandrava, but just six days into his tenure he was assassinated along with two of his bodyguards. A military junta of eighteen officers took charge, calling themselves the Directorate, and the nation was riveted for the next few months by the trial of those deemed responsible for the murders. By June, Ratsiraka had outmaneuvered everyone and was elected as supreme leader of the country at age 38 by a two-thirds majority in the Directorate, which was then disbanded. His *cotier* origins and support for decentralization gave him enough coastal support, while his reputation as an intellectual and his search for a new foreign policy brought him the requisite backing from Antananarivo and the AKFM.[8]

Madagascar then entered into a period of revolutionary socialism, which was disastrous. Perhaps only Queen Ranavalona's reign of terror had been worse, and many of the country's problems in the 21st century can be traced back to Ratsiraka's rule. His first acts were to rename the country the Democratic Republic of Madagascar and immediately nationalize the banks, insurance companies, major port and oil refineries, and the main shipping company on the island. In a series of radio broadcasts to the nation in August 1975 he fulminated on everything from the lessons of history to his theories of socialism, which were then published as the "Little Red Book." Another key component of his rule was nationalism, expressed through condemnations of French influence to his Malagasy audience and rants about anti-imperialism abroad. The principles of his Socialist Charter were presented to the people in the form of a new constitution, which was remarkable both for the pride of place it gave to socialism and for the unprecedented power given to the President – even more than in other socialist countries. Elections would be held by universal suffrage, but only socialist candidates could run. The Constitution was approved in December 1975 and Ratsiraka officially became president in January 1976.[9]

Madagascar was not alone among African states in taking the leap into revolutionary socialism during this time, as the Ethiopian revolution in 1975 and the looming Marxist takeovers in Mozambique and Angola showed. But Malagasy culture, based on its reverence for the ancestors, was still a profoundly traditional society, and in the end there was little appetite for Ratsiraka's policies. The most obviously revolutionary part of his program was his foreign policy, which was officially non-aligned but in practice pro-Soviet. The Communist camp he sought to join lacked the necessary resources to support him, however, and the country's primary aid donors continued to be Western nations, particularly France. Economic policy also followed socialist models, at least initially. More nationalizations followed, both in the sugar industry and several import-export companies. But in a notable departure from socialist doctrine, Ratsiraka, despite his best wishes, never achieved a one-party state. Many left-wing parties refused to give up their independence and forced him to form his own party, AREMA, which became part of a socialist coalition known as the FNDR.

Within three years of launching his revolution the economy reshaped by Ratsiraka was in shambles. Foreign debt had ballooned to over $1 billion and the President was forced to appeal to the International Monetary Fund for help. In June 1980 the island entered into its first standby agreement with the International Monetary Fund (IMF). The government blamed its problems on the second oil price shock of the late 1970s, but most observers recognized that internal policies were more to blame. The massive borrowing and investment plan, contrary to the doctrine of self-reliance enshrined in the Little Red Book, distorted Madagascar's agricultural economy and brought little in return except more debt. Fixing low prices for staple foods caused producers to grow less, so that even rice had to be imported. Ratsiraka tried to maintain his socialist policies in the face of all the evidence, but continued reliance on the IMF and other aid donors – coupled with the conditionality that came with their loans – eventually pushed him in the other direction. He signed a new agreement with the IMF in 1982 and at regular intervals thereafter, essentially embracing market economics and holding on as a socialist in name only. He eventually became a favorite of Western aid donors and foreign aid reached $330 million by 1985.[10]

With so much schizophrenia coming from the presidential palace, unrest began to spread among the Malagsy people. Sporadic violence became more serious in the 1980s, with serious rioting in Diego Suarez, Tulear and other west coast towns. Groups of *dahalo* (bandits) appeared for the first time since the beginning of the century, at first stealing cattle but then attacking and robbing travelers along the highways. Growing unemployment and the beginnings of a large-scale movement of rural dwellers into the cities caused a rise in urban crime. The universities became hotbeds of agitation, both against the regime and the quality of education: Ratsiraka expanded the university system to the provinces, but with so many more students suddenly attending college, standards inevitably declined.

In January 1982, Ratsiraka stood for election against another Marxist candidate and won handily. His opponent, Monja Joana, cited electoral fraud and rioting ensued; Joana was arrested and imprisoned for eight months. The country's secret police (the DGID), led by the president's brother-in-law, became a symbol of abuse and provided another reason for protests against Ratsiraka's authority. Meanwhile, the country's economic outlook did not improve, with external public debt more than tripling from 1982-85 and then doubling in the next two years to reach more than $2.6 billion, more than total GDP. During most of the 1980s GDP stagnated or declined so that, with population increasing relentlessly at more than 3% per year, GDP per capita fell by 25% from 1980-87. The effects on all classes were severe, but on the poor they became unbearable. In a country where food had always been abundant and affordable, supplies of many basic items, even rice, became prohibitively expensive due to inflation. Urban poverty became widespread, with child beggars appearing for the first time and homeless families occupying garbage dumps.[11]

Ratsiraka responded to the growing calls for his resignation by instituting press censorship and banning political parties outside the FNDR. By the late 1980s, his goal was merely survival, based on keeping the opposition divided and maintaining the support – or at least neutrality – of the army. He was re-elected in 1989 but with just 62% of the vote, which, given his tight control of the country, was telling. The end of the Soviet Union and the transition to multi-party democracy in much of Africa showed the tide clearly moving against him. In successive negotiations with the IMF, Ratsiraka had been forced to reverse most of his economic policies. Domestic pressure now pushed him to make changes in politics and human rights, and he agreed to lift the ban on political parties in March 1990. He then hosted French President Francois Mitterand and agreed to compensate French companies that had been nationalized and allow France to use the naval base at Diego Suarez once again. He even hosted his erstwhile nemesis, South African President F.W. de Klerk.

With the Soviet Union preoccupied with the implosion of its Eurasian empire, Madagascar's leaders began quietly turning back toward the French, mostly out of necessity. The Franco-Malagasy relationship had never really disappeared even when anti-Western rhetoric from Antananarivo reached its height, and France had remained the island's largest trading partner, accounting for 25-30% of Madagascar's exports and imports by the early 1990s. The problem for Ratsiraka was that, after spending so much political capital rejecting Madagascar's relationship with France and reorienting the country's foreign policy to the East, the sudden collapse of the Soviet Union left the great island somewhere in geopolitical limbo. Meanwhile, his radical changes in foreign policy and the nation's crushing debt had left the majority of Malagasy people destitute.[12]

By the end of the decade Ratsiraka had reversed all of his former policies, foreign and domestic, though he refused to remove references to socialism in the Constitution. The economy began to show signs of life, achieving 4.9% growth in 1989 followed by a 3.5% rise in 1990. But it was too little, too late, and with his presidency unraveling amid growing unrest the Council of Churches, based in Antananarivo, now attempted to forge a solution. They called for a convention in August 1990 that created a movement known as *Forces Vives* (FV) to discuss solutions to the country's political and economic problems. In June 1991 FV called for a general strike that led to daily anti-government demonstrations of 100,000 or more. In July they announced the formation of their own transitional government, and for a time no one was sure who was in charge. In August twenty demonstrators were killed at a demonstration in Majunga; France then suspended aid and called for Ratsiraka's resignation. The army remained neutral and the stalemate continued into September and October, with rival governments each purporting to rule. Most aid donors suspended assistance pending a resolution. In the south, a lack of rain caused famine and migration to other areas. Finally, in October, Ratsiraka agreed to share power while a road map to democratic rule was drafted and implemented.

The transition to democracy was swift. Another constitution, one that significantly reduced the power of the president, was approved by the Malagasy people in August 1992 in a referendum. This was followed by the first peaceful democratic transfer of power in Madagascar's history, when Albert Zafy defeated Ratsiraka easily in both the first and second rounds of voting in late 1992 - early 1993. Turnout in the first round was a fairly high 74%, an encouraging sign for those who had labored so hard to end one-man rule. This completed the process initiated by the churches three years earlier, and a seemingly impregnable dictatorship was overthrown and replaced with something resembling Western-style democracy. To everyone's credit, the transition occurred mostly peacefully, with no overt interference by the army and in accordance with the constitution.[13]

The only question at the time was whether it could last. Revolutionary socialism seemed to be a thing of the past, but could Madagascar build a real democracy for the 21st century? When the new President Zafy passed a constitutional referendum in 1995 giving him increased presidential powers, thus undoing the restrictions from the 1992 constitution, it looked as if another leader had been tempted to reach for more power. Sure enough, his administration quickly lost public support, and the President was impeached in July 1996 after an economic decline and accusations of corruption in his office. The High Constitutional Court (HCC) upheld his impeachment but ruled that he could still stand for new elections scheduled for later that year. Perhaps inevitably amid such chaos, sectors of the population began clamoring for a stronger hand, and Ratsiraka was called out of retirement to run against him. In a second-round runoff between the two men Ratsiraka won an improbable victory with 50.7% of the vote. Zafy took 49.3% and lost by only 45,000 votes; he later claimed he had won but had somehow been swindled by the HCC.

Ratsiraka's second stint in office was an improvement over his first term but ultimately ended in another failure. At least he was careful enough not to mention socialism again, which by now had become thoroughly discredited on the island and, indeed, throughout much of the world. His second term was highlighted by a constitutional amendment passed in March 1998 by his AREMA party that greatly strengthened the powers of the presidency. It allowed him to dissolve the National Assembly and appoint the Prime Minister without the Assembly's agreement. It also provided for significant decentralization, with the provinces gaining greater autonomy. Members of the opposition, including ex-President Zafy, tried to impeach him in February 1998 for his decentralizing reforms and his efforts to increase his powers at the expense of the National Assembly. Only sixty deputies voted for impeachment, well short of the 92 required. Nevertheless, by 2001 Ratsiraka had become widely unpopular again.

* * *

New leaders burst onto the scene with regularity in Madagascar. Perhaps that's true everywhere, but it seems to be even more so on this island, where young men in their mid- or even early thirties become famous politicians overnight before giving way to someone even more dynamic and fading, in most cases, back into relative obscurity. Ratsiraka is himself a fine example of this sudden rise, having vaulted to the head of his country at such a young age in the 1970s; unlike others he found ways to remain near the center of power for almost twenty years, albeit through the occasional use of force. In 2001, another leader took center stage in the nation's political consciousness, and for the first time it was someone from the Merina tribe and a native Tananarivian. But like so many others before and after him, his rise would never be assured until a debilitating national crisis had passed.

Marc Ravalomanana's rags-to-riches story is inspiring in a country with so little social mobility. Born into a Merina farming family outside of the capital, he spent his early twenties selling yogurt in the streets of Antananarivo off the back of his bicycle. He worked hard enough to earn a modest living, and perhaps most yogurt salesman would have been content with that life. But "Marc," as his millions of fans on the island still call him, dreamed of something more, and with the encouragement of his Protestant church he applied for and secured a loan from the World Bank to build his own factory. A charismatic man with a keen business acumen, Ravalomanana soon expanded his yogurt business into a veritable empire, eventually becoming one of the richest men in Madagascar. At age 32 he became founder and CEO of the vast dairy conglomerate TIKO and used some of the profits from that business to launch other successful companies.

With his financial future assured he decided to enter politics, running for mayor of Antananarivo in 2001. Starting as a relative unknown against a field of seasoned politicians, Marc organized a campaign staff drawn mostly from TIKO associates and presented himself as a humble, religious farmer who had become wealthy through his determination and intelligence. He also spent a small fortune from his company's coffers – over $110,000, unheard of in a mayoral race on the island – to put posters up and hold rallies all across the city. Although he was not a member of any existing political party and had never run for public office, he won the race handily, and became one of the most popular mayors in the capital's history over the next two years. He quickly expanded his base of power and formed his own party (I Love Madagascar, known by its Malagasy acronym TIM). By 2001, Ravalomanana was still just 51, and with a presidential election taking place the next year he was already thinking of using his new found popularity to challenge "the Big Man," Ratsiraka.

The presidential election of 2001 produced another descent into chaos in Madagascar when, once again, both major candidates, Ratsiraka and Ravalomanana, claimed victory. After the first round of voting, the Ministry of Interior declared Ratisraka the winner, while Ravalomanana contested the results and claimed victory for himself. The country's High Constitutional Court (HCC), which is supposed to intervene only in rare cases when the outcome is in dispute but is now routinely pulled into the political arena, ruled that the mayor had won over 51% of the vote and proclaimed him president. Ratsiraka objected to the independence of the court, pointing to the fact that four members of the HCC had attended Marc's staged inauguration in February shortly before handing down their decision. Ratsiraka supporters, mostly those from his Betsimisaraka tribe, began to cut off routes from the port city of Tamatave to the capital, a Ravalomanana and Merina stronghold. Ethnic rivalries thus came surging back to the fore during the dispute and the country seemed on the verge of civil war. Sporadic violence and considerable economic disruption ensued for several months until Ratsiraka conceded the race and went into exile in France with several of his most prominent supporters in July 2002. In just five years Ravalomanana had gone from CEO of a dairy company to president of over 20 million people.

Thus began Ravalomanana's career on the national stage, one that would showcase almost a decade of promise before ending in a stunning fall from grace from which he has never recovered. As president, Ravalomanana began several reform projects, advocating "rapid and sustainable development" and launching a crusade against corruption, a perpetual scourge on the island. The December 2002 legislative elections gave his party a large majority in the National Assembly, allowing him to press his agenda more aggressively. The central government's rule over the provinces has always been a flash point in Malagasy politics and, like others before and after him, Ravalomanana implemented his own form of centralization by passing a constitutional amendment that established 22 regions in the country. Each of these regions would be headed by regional chiefs who reported directly to him, thereby sidelining the provincial governors who had previously held power outside of the capital. Backed by strong economic growth and widely popular, Ravalomanana was re-elected president in 2006, again with a majority in the first round. Whispers of corruption surrounded his re-election, but with the island finally peaceful and progressing economically, most people – especially those in Antananarivo – welcomed the new political climate rather than challenging it.

An era of brief stability thus descended on Madagascar during Ravalomanana's eight years in power. His government made significant advances toward development targets and experienced an average of almost 7% economic growth per year. Thousands of new schools and health clinics were constructed, while thousands of miles of new roads improved rural farmers' access to markets. The establishment of the independent anti-corruption agency BIANCO (*Bureau Independent Anti-Corruption*) and the adoption of supporting policies resulted in a decline in government corruption. Conservation of land and forests expanded in fulfillment of Ravalomanana's "Madagascar Naturally" environmental program. In 2007 he released a comprehensive development strategy, the "Madagascar Action Plan," which set realistic goals for his second term across a wide range of areas, including governance, infrastructure, agriculture, health, economy, environment and national solidarity.

As time went on, however, opposition members criticized Ravalomanana for his increasingly authoritarian style and accused him of using his presidency for personal gain through a variety of questionable schemes. As we'll see, these voices in opposition began to coalesce around Andry Rajoelina, the new mayor of Antananarivo. The main reasons for Raoelina's revolt were at first personal, focused on Ravalomanana's blatant efforts to stifle his businesses. But there were plenty of other people willing to join Rajoelina for their own reasons, mostly having to do with Marc's turn away from democracy during his second term. By 2008, the ruling power's monopolization of politics and economics was breeding distrust: according to one survey, more than one-third of people with a secondary education felt freedom of expression was not respected in the country and more than 65% were not satisfied with the way democracy was working.[14] Some analysts have even claimed that Ravalomanana did more to push the country back toward Ratsiraka's dictatorship than to consolidate democracy.[15] This goes too far, but after winning reelection it became clear that Ravalomanana was at least as interested in promoting his family's business as in developing and democratizing the country. Tariff protections and tax breaks for his products gave his companies a virtual monopoly and allowed TIKO to move from agribusiness into other industries like construction, oil and – in a direct challenge to Rajoelina – even the media.[16] Moreover, while Ravalomanana became the first president to raise per capita incomes across the island for an extended period, thus reversing the downward economic trend across the island since independence, the percentage of people living on less than $1.90 a day actually increased from 69% in 2001 to 74% in 2005. With inequality and inflation rising along with incomes, Rajoelina was plowing fertile ground with his calls for an uprising.[17]

In 2008, a controversial land deal with the Korean agricultural firm Daewoo, the purchase of a costly presidential jet and the closure of media channels owned by his budding rival Rajoelina combined to strengthen popular disapproval of his policies. But as a two-term president Ravalomanana seemed more than capable of riding out the storm. And then suddenly in 2009, just when it seemed as if the country's volatile past had receded forever, political conflict quickly exploded again and the country's brief embrace of democracy ended in a matter of days.

* * *

Andry Rajoelina would become famous across Africa – or infamous, depending on your point of view – for overthrowing a popular president and improbably wresting control of Madagascar's entire political system. But who was Andry Rajoelina? His meteoric rise culminating in his seizure of power in 2009 had few parallels in modern African history, but he had hardly emerged from nowhere. Born to a middle-class family in Antsirabe in 1974, his father was a colonel in the Malagasy army, and Andry inherited dual French-Malagasy citizenship from him. Rajoelina moved to the capital at an early age and became a disc jockey for several years before trying other jobs in the music industry and eventually forming his own media company. By the time he reached his early thirties, he had become a media mogul, amassing a small fortune through his television and radio stations that came to dominate the island. No longer considered "just a disc jockey," he was already wealthy, well known and a highly regarded businessman by the time he ran for mayor in 2009.[18] He quickly rebranded himself as a politician, running for mayor of Antananarivo at age 35 and winning easily, just as his future rival Ravalomanana had done. But the two men sparred almost immediately, not so much over policy but over the President's attempts to regulate Rajoelina's businesses, leading to their epic confrontation in 2009 and Ravalomanana's calamitous overthrow.

By 2019, it was easy to forget how drastically things had changed over the last ten years. When Rajeolina became president in 2009 he did so under a cloud of suspicion and endless controversy. His heavy-handed leadership of the country through something he called the High Transitional Authority (HAT) was largely unsuccessful and his bid to hold onto power in 2013 was rejected by the HCC, but Rajoelina decided to accept the court's decision and bide his time until he could run again. His long-awaited rematch with Ravalomanana in 2018 ended in his resounding victory, albeit with some lingering claims of fraud, and for the first time Rajoelina obtained the legitimacy, both at home and abroad, that had eluded him as leader of the HAT.

In time his power would only grow larger. After the legislative elections of 2019, which saw his IRD party win an outright majority of seats in the new Parliament, Rajoelina was the undisputed leader of Madagascar. He now had full rein to implement his program, but he had effectively turned the country into a one-party state, rigging the system to give himself and his allies a permanent lock on power. He did this partly as populists across the globe have done, by carefully silencing dissent and making symbolic gestures to appeal to the masses, but partly also through methods that are uniquely Malagasy. By 2019 his rise was complete, and marked a dangerous turn away from the slow march toward democracy that had energized the island since independence.

But we are getting ahead of ourselves. The story of Rajoelina's rise and Ravalomanana's fall needs to be understood in greater detail, not only to better understand the most powerful man in Madagascar but to appreciate why the country remains so divided today. While many factors have contributed to the island's current plight, it was the coup in 2009 that left many Malagasy feeling disenfranchised and contributed to the heightened distrust of the political system that still characterizes so much of public life here over a decade later.

* * *

As we saw earlier, there were rumblings of discontent over Ravalomanana's presidency as early as 2006, but most Malagasy were willing to ignore allegations of his corruption so long as the country's impressive rates of economic growth remained high. Rajoelina, the upstart mayor of the capital city, set out to challenge this tacit agreement by fair means or foul, and by the time of the president's re-election the rivalry between them was already in full swing.

The coup that took place in 2009 had its antecedents years earlier. Some Malagasy will tell you it started in 2008, when the feud between Ravalomanana and Rajoelina devolved into open confrontation, but others who follow the nation's politics closely say it began as far back as 2003 or 2004. It was during those years when the mayor of Antananarivo, an ally of Ravalomanana, blocked Rajoelina from installing billboards across the city to promote his marketing companies INJET and Domapub. Rajoelina concluded that perhaps he needed political power to advance his business interests, and many people believe he ran for mayor in 2004 for exactly that reason. But becoming mayor only set him more firmly in Ravalomanana's sights. The president wasted no time in downgrading the status of the city to make it more financially dependent on the state, while forcing it to pay on short notice debts incurred by previous mayors and moving the upcoming African Union summit out of the capital city to the neighboring suburb of Ivato.[19]

By 2008, the relationship between the two men had become poisonous. On December 13, Ravalomanana took the extraordinary step of shutting down Rajoelina's VIVA television station, claiming it had aired an inflammatory interview with former president Ratsiraka that unfairly criticized the president. At this point Rajoelina had a choice to make: continue to accept the harassment from the presidential palace or fight back. Instead of backing down, the mayor issued an ultimatum to Ravalomanana that would reverberate for the next several months: allow my television station to begin broadcasting again within 25 days or I will lead people into the streets to protest against your regime. When no response came from Ravalomanana, the mayor followed through on his threat and began what became known as the Orange Revolution on January 17, 2009. Thousands of people joined him on that initial march through the streets of Antananarivo.[20]

At first, Ravalomanana did nothing, allowing the protests to continue and slowly grow in size. Meanwhile, Rajoelina used this breathing space to heighten his demands, quickly shifting from an emphasis on economic freedom to calls for a genuine revolution. By January 30, he was openly calling for the president's resignation, going so far as to declare himself the new president at one of his rallies that began to fill a central plaza in the capital that was soon renamed Democracy Square. The protesters filling the square only grew louder as days and weeks passed, becoming a venue not only for music and speeches but also for a sort of national catharsis, with multiple speakers rising daily to denounce the corruption and rigidity of the Ravalomanana regime. While some continued to rail against the shutdown of VIVA and Ravalomanana's monopolization of various industries, others highlighted two new grievances that would in some ways resonate more broadly than calls for greater media freedom.[21]

The first involved Ravalomanana's sale of 1.3 million hectares of arable land on the island to Daewoo Logistics, a South Korean company. Negotiations for the land began in May 2008 when Daewoo approached the Malagasy government to express its interest in a huge tract of land to produce corn and palm oil; talks continued for several months in total secrecy until Ravalomanana announced the deal to a nation where sales of land to foreigners, while certainly legal, are highly unpopular. The size of the concession was one cause for alarm: four percent of all arable land and fifty percent of land actually under cultivation in Madagascar would now be under foreign control. Nor did the terms of the lease do anything to quell suspicion over Ravalomanana's motives: the land was leased to Daewoo for 99 years *for free* in exchange for the company's agreement to give significant employment opportunities to Malagasy people living in the area. Rajoelina, of course, claimed Ravalomanana and his associates had sold parts of this land and pocketed the proceeds.[22]

The second controversial act by the president was Ravalomanana's purchase of a second presidential jet, named Air Force II, with a mix of public and private funds. Madagascar was a relatively small and certainly poor country, and many observers wondered why one presidential plane wasn't enough. The second jet cost $60 million, with half of that money coming from the national treasury. Rajoelina seized on the purchase as another blatant act of corruption, claiming that Ravalomanana had in fact purchased the plane for himself, not the nation, by embezzling $30 million from state coffers. The World Bank and IMF seemed to agree, suspending aid in December 2008 over the matter.[23]

These were objections to the president's public acts, and Rajoelina restricted his objections to the realm of politics at first. Only when the president resumed his harassment of Rajoelina's businesses did the mayor move to overthrow him. When Ravalomanana's government refused to reopen Rajoelina's *Viva TV* station in January 2009, stating that *Viva's* plans to air an interview with exiled former head of state Didier Ratsiraka were "likely to disturb peace and security," Rajoelina decided to act. He boldly took his protest to the streets, leading marches against the government and essentially declaring war on the regime. He led a series of political rallies in downtown Antananarivo and issued an ultimatum to Ravalomanana to restore *Viva TV* broadcasts. After a week passed with no resolution, the mayor met with twenty of Madagascar's most prominent opposition leaders, referred to in the press as the "Club of 20", to develop a joint statement demanding that the Ravalomanana administration improve its adherence to democratic principles. He also gathered 30,000 supporters one day at a public park that he renamed Democracy Square, a site he would subsequently use as a staging ground for his attacks on Ravalomanana.

Then, at a rally on January 31, 2009, Rajoelina brazenly announced that he was now in charge of the country's affairs, declaring: "Since the president and the government have not assumed their responsibilities, I therefore proclaim that I will run all national affairs as of today." He added that a request for President Ravalomanana to formally resign would shortly be filed with Parliament. Madagascar had seen battles for power before but nothing quite like this, played out both in the streets and on the airwaves, with tens of thousands of Malagasy lining up to support either side. Rajoelina's self-declaration of power temporarily discredited his democratic aims, however, and the number of attendees at subsequent rallies declined, averaging only around 3,000 to 5,000 participants. Ravalomanana retaliated swiftly to such naked defiance. A few days after Rajoelina's declaration, the Ministry of Domestic Affairs dismissed Rajoelina as mayor of Antananarivo and appointed a special delegation to manage the affairs of the capital. But Rajoelina would not give up, continuing to apply pressure until the dam suddenly broke. For all their noise and disruption, the first protests at Democracy Square represented the views of a decided minority of the country, and the overthrow of the twice-elected president was anything but inevitable. It took an act of violence, sparking outrage across Madagascar, before Rajoelina's movement ever had a chance of succeeding. On February 7, 2009, Rajoelina organized a new rally at the Square with 100,000 supporters, calling his uprising the Orange Movement and declaring himself president of the High Transitional Authority, the name he later gave to his upstart regime. After speaking for over an hour about the failings of the current administration and listing his goals for his own presidency, he concluded by introducing Monja Roindefo as his next Prime Minister. Roindefo, the son of a legendary anticolonial leader from the southern province of Tulear during the French colonial period, gave a fiery speech that called for Ravalomanana's ouster. He then provocatively asked the crowd "What should we do next?" Someone in the crowd responded with "Let's go to Ambohitsorohitra!" essentially calling for a march on the presidential palace less than half a mile away. Others picked up the chant, and within a few minutes thousands of protesters were on their way to Madagascar's version of the White House.

It's still not entirely clear what happened once they arrived there. The march on the palace by Rajoelina and his supporters appeared to Ravalomanana as an attempt to overthrow him by force, and became the moment when events spun out of control. A small group of leaders from the mass of protesters approached the presidential guards blocking the entrance to the palace. Some sort of negotiation seemed to be taking place between the two groups when an unidentified man fired what appeared to be a warning shot into the air above the heads of the crowd.[24] That sparked an overwhelming response from the guards, who allegedly opened fire on the mass of people in front of them. As screams were heard and bullets rained down, the crowd ran for their lives, ending the threat of any takeover of the palace, at least for that day. But over 30 people lay dead on the streets in front of the palace, and hundreds more were wounded. The country would never be the same.

Denunciations of the shooting of unarmed protesters came in swiftly from all corners of the island. This massacre dramatically diminished Ravalomanana's popularity during the crisis and led to his loss of support from the Army, which subsequently blamed the President for ordering the shootings.[25] No one could believe that the guards had resorted to lethal force so quickly, and rumors of the president's involvement in the decision to open fire began almost immediately. Fissures between Ravalomanana supporters soon opened up, with the Minister of Defense, Manorohanta Cecil, resigning over the incident. Certain units of the army began to defect from the president's camp, with one leader saying, "We have been trained to protect the people and their property, not kill them."[26]

Tension mounted over the next few weeks. Although the protests continued, a sense of shock pervaded much of the capital in the wake of such unprecedented violence. On February 11 Ravalomanana agreed to enter talks with Rajoelina to try to calm the situation, but quickly abandoned them a couple of weeks later. The truth was that neither side was very interested in negotiations now: Ravalomanana still felt firmly in control, while Rajoelina believed that, with questions and criticism now being leveled at the president not just on the island but from foreign capitals as well, momentum was finally on his side.[27]

Ravalomanana timed his abandonment of peace talks to coincide with his decision in late February to take a more confrontational approach with the protesters still occupying parts of the capital. It was time to deal with them decisively and get the country back on a normal footing, he announced. To augment the police force and gendarmes in the capital he hired groups of foreign mercenaries and local militias, which won him no friends among Malagasy citizens, who resented the appearance of foreign troops on their streets. Nevertheless, the new attitude was captured perfectly when the new Minister of Defense, Vice Admiral Mamy Ranaivoniarivo, announced that "the use of sticks is now abandoned. We are now at the time of the assault rifle," while somewhat lamely adding "This will be done legally."[28] He also put Rajoelina under house arrest, but on March 6 the mayor managed to slip out of his residence late at night undetected and take refuge at the French Embassy, later coming under the official protection of the United Nations.[29]

By the second week of March, enough defections had occurred within the army that an armed standoff darkened the gloom already hanging over the capital city. The chances for civil war seemed to be growing daily in Madagascar. Ravalomanana hunkered down behind the protection of the presidential guards and those forces still loyal to him while Rajoelina welcomed various units joining his side. Both sides refused to compromise their demands. Just as in 2002, when Ravalomanana's narrow electoral victory over Ratsiraka split the country in two, the military was again divided into separate camps. The vast majority of officers and soldiers remained loyal to Ravalomanana, although some were already meeting with Rajoelina. The young mayor received a tremendous boost on March 8 when an elite and powerful military unit known as CAPSAT (Army Corps of Personnel and Services Administration), from central Antananarivo, mutinied against central command and switched sides to back him. More mutinies followed and by March 13, according to some observers, the vast majority of all armed forces (including the gendarmerie and national police), especially in Tana, had shifted their loyalty to Rajoelina.[30]

CAPSAT's defection proved to be decisive for several reasons. First, while many observers were skeptical that a relatively small unit of just 500-600 soldiers could swing the outcome of the crisis so decisively, CAPSAT was the most powerful unit of its size on the island, with elite troops strategically placed in the capital who possessed some of the most powerful weaponry in the country.[31] Second, it gave political cover to other units who wanted to move away from Ravalomanana after the massacre at the palace but were fearful of the repercussions of doing so alone. Finally, CAPSAT did more than simply announce they were switching sides; they acted quickly and decisively to install Rajoelina in power.

There has been endless speculation over whether Rajoelina paid members of the military, especially CAPSAT, to mutiny and join his camp. To be sure, CAPSAT had its own reasons for turning on the president. When Ravalomanana hired foreign mercenaries and local militia to help quell the protests, CAPSAT scoffed at the order to serve alongside the militias and take orders from foreigners.[32] Marc also created resentment in the army with his preference for the gendarmerie, his decision to name a civilian defense minister (the country's first), and his promotion of colonels over generals to positions of command in the army.[33] Nevertheless, rumors have persisted of a military sellout to Rajoelina for cash, and even pointed to France, long concerned over Ravalomanana's close ties to the United States, as one of the sources of the funds. The fact that Rajoelina rewarded CAPSAT officers with prestigious posts in the army after he seized power is neither a confirmation nor a refutation of the idea that they were in his employ at the time of the coup. More damning are on-the-record statements by a former government official, a military officer and a diplomat claiming the entire operation was planned in advance by Rajoelina and his close associates in the weeks leading up to the coup. Multiple reports described a cadre of uniformed soldiers protecting Rajoelina and other key opposition leaders in the days just before and after the coup.[34]

The charges of French involvement in the coup cannot be discounted. France clearly saw Ravalomanana as a Francophobe and was one of the last countries to recognize him in 2002 during his battle with Ratsiraka. Once he became president, Ravalomanana returned the favor by designating English as the third official language on the island in 2005 and declaring the French Ambassador *persona non grata* after a spat in 2008. During the crisis of 2009, France came to Rajoelina's rescue when Ravalomanana turned the full force of the state against him, hiding Rajoelina when the government sought his arrest. By contrast, Ravalomanana established very close relations with the United States and Madagascar became the first country to receive funds from President Bush's Millennium Challenge Account and one of the first to benefit from the African Growth and Opportunity Act, a major trade deal between Washington and the continent. A contest for influence over Madagascar was clearly brewing at the time of the coup, and France sought to hasten Ravalomanana's downfall with its covert support of his rival.[35]

After building every week for the past three months, the crisis reached its climax in mid-March in a sudden military coup by Rajoelina. On March 15, Ravalomanana appeared on television to issue a statement to the nation and called for a referendum to resolve the struggle. This was immediately rejected by Rajoelina. By now much of the public had swung firmly behind

Rajoelina, and Ravalomanana was under increasing pressure to resign. In a move clearly orchestrated with the army, Rajoelina called for the president's arrest; then CAPSAT, just over a week after mutinying and stationing its troops across the city in support of the protesters, attacked and easily captured the presidential palace at Ambohitsorohitra on March 16. The president could see the writing on the wall, and on the afternoon of March 17, Ravalomanana met with representatives from the United Nations, African Union and the American ambassador at a second presidential palace in Iavoloha, handing them a document known as Ordinance No. 2009/01 that transferred full powers to a group of military officers known as the Military Directorate. Ravalomanana took some solace from the fact that these men had pledged their neutrality during the standoff between the two leaders, and perhaps he thought they might reinstate him as president after a cooling off period and outside intervention to restore democracy on the island.[36]

This was wishful thinking on the president's part. Reports from the meeting on March 17 at which Ravalomanana handed power to the Military Directorate show a recalcitrant Rajoelina storming out of the room as the ordinance transferring power to the Military Directorate was read aloud. He was either upset with the naming of someone other than himself as the new head of state or was already in a hurry to organize the replacement of the Directorate. Whatever the reasons for his sudden departure, a small group of CAPSAT soldiers then entered and kidnapped the three members of the Military Directorate, taking them to their camp in Soanierana. Rumors surfaced immediately that Rajoelina had ordered the kidnappings as a way of forcing the members of the Military Directorate to hand over power to him. People across Antananarivo feared the Directorate's members had been murdered and wondered what that would mean for peace in their city, but by 11pm the men had resurfaced, calmly announcing on the radio that they had decided to "transfer their full powers to Andry Rajoelina to lead the country." This became known as Ordinance 2009/002. By midnight, Rajoelina had announced that he was at the helm of a transitional government that would organize presidential elections within 24 months, and he was sworn in as President a few days later at Mahamasina Stadium before a crowd of 40,000 supporters. Ravalomanana fled the country, taking exile in South Africa.[37]

The crisis thus ended without more bloodshed. This is not to say that the coup was entirely peaceful, however. In fact, the 2009 crisis would come to be seen as a departure from previous political crises in terms of violence. Aside from the massacre on February 7th, over 68 people were killed just from the civil unrest that accompanied the daily protests leading up to that day.[38] Still, the crisis ended peacefully and even the attempted coups that followed were relatively small in scale with little attendant violence. This has led some analysts to advance other reasons for the low number of deaths in early 2009, stressing Madagascar's cultural values rather than the military's sudden intervention as the best explanation for the peaceful conclusion to the coup. While it may be true that an idealized kinship among all Malagasy people known as *fihavanana* exists and has helped in the nonviolent resolution of previous conflicts, it would be idealism in its most undiluted form to ascribe the end of the military standoff in 2009 to an entire country's supposed aversion to conflict.[39] Instead, it was the overwhelming power of CAPSAT that led to a peaceful conclusion to the crisis. Ravalomanana quickly realized that he had been outmaneuvered and was now outgunned. By forcing the army's chief of staff to resign, capturing the two presidential palaces, and threatening to use tanks and powerful weapons, CAPSAT had forced Ravalomanana's resignation and the double transfer of power. This is what prevented the conflict from reaching the stage of armed conflict or all-out civil war.[40]

The nation was aghast at the sudden transfer of power

and the unfathomable rise of an unproven mayor to the presidency. Rajoelina took the oath of office on March 21 while Ravalomanana's supporters vowed revenge. The High Constitutional Court, hoping to lower the temperature and put the crisis to rest, quickly ruled both transfers of power (from Ravalomanana to the military and from the military to Rajoelina) to be legal. Street protests soon broke out in Antananarivo in favor of Ravalomanana, who continued from exile to decry the injustice of his removal. Rajoelina's first major act as president was to dissolve both the Senate and the National Assembly, both of whom might challenge his takeover. Tensions abated over the next few months, but not completely: an attempted military coup against Rajoelina was suppressed in 2010, just a year after he took power.

International condemnation of Rajoelina and the coup was swift and cacophonous. Foreign governments and international non-governmental organizations, who had not closely followed the crisis in Madagascar until its sudden climax, focused solely on the upending of democracy on the great island. Nearly all of them called for a reinstatement of Ravalomanana to his rightful place as president, but as Rajoelina consolidated power and any return to the *status quo ante* became increasingly unlikely, they called for a process that would quickly lead to elections. International mediation of the conflict under the auspices of the Southern African Development Community (SADC) began in June 2009, by which time international sanctions against Rajoelina's government were already taking full effect. The suspension of aid by the EU, the exclusion in December 2009 of Madagascar from the landmark African Growth and Opportunity Act and the sanctions levied by the African Union against 109 members of the regime in March 2010, were all starting to bite. These sanctions, along with Madagascar's near-total dependence on foreign aid, forced Rajoelina to participate in this process, though with only halfhearted interest in restoring democracy.[41]

* * *

The struggle over the narrative of what had just happened began almost as soon as the transfer of power was complete. Almost every independent analysis agreed that the threat of force implied by massive protests backed by the army had led to a democratically elected president's overthrow, and it was immediately labeled a coup by the international community. But one man's coup is another man's revolution. Some in Antananarivo and beyond scripted a narrative of popular revolt against a president drifting toward authoritarianism. Others called it a brazen military intervention. Scholars have now begun to describe the line between coups and revolts as blurry, or even nonexistent, with the overthrow of Evo Morales in Bolivia just the latest example. Often they are one and the same: mass public uprisings alongside military defections that cause the resignation or removal of a country's leader. The events give way to linguistic warfare, in which a leader's removal can be seen as legitimate by labeling it a revolt, or illegitimate if labeled a coup. This affects what comes next, as the new government scrambles to attain a veneer of legitimacy. So while coups are seen as taboo in today's world, citizens have become bolder in challenging elected leaders who, in this age of rising populism and authoritarianism, also feel emboldened to test the boundaries of their power. Meanwhile, militaries now see themselves as arbiters of last resort, not potential rulers themselves. And a structural problem exists for many democracies in which strong presidents, strong militaries, polarized societies and weak institutions almost seem to invite extra-constitutional outcomes.[42]

All of this was on full display in Madagascar. Something of a cottage industry has now grown up over the events of the

2009 coup in Antananarivo, principally among Ravalomanana's supporters. One of his advisors sent me documents and a video purporting to "prove" that Rajoelina and his camp had planned the events of February/March all along. The video showed Charles Andrianasoavina, a repentant colonel from Madagascar's armed forces, apologizing for his role and naming the architects of the coup, all from Rajoelina's camp. He went so far as to claim that Rajoelina had himself orchestrated and financed the coup with the help of several members of the military. But Rajoelina's own supporters, including General X, later produced their own video of that fateful day that purports to show Ravalomanana's presidential guard firing on unarmed protesters. Together they are Madagascar's version of the Zapruder film, with each side seeing what it wants and using it to stoke their sense of grievance. History in this case remains elusive, but that doesn't stop either side from invoking "the coup" or "the uprising" to justify its ongoing vilification of the other.

Delving deeper into the crisis and instability of 2009 leads to an uncomfortable question about whether Madagascar's democracy is too young and fragile to survive the sort of cataclysmic showdown between two powerful leaders determined to seize or hold onto power at any cost. As we've seen, these sorts of crises are if anything becoming more common on the island, not less, and some scholars believe the events of 2009 never would have happened if Madagascar had been a mature liberal democracy. Political conflicts tend to escalate in countries that are not fully democratic, the theory goes, because peaceful mechanisms of conflict resolution are lacking, and leaders often prefer violence over other, more rational methods of resolution. Under this reading of the island's history, the failure of Malagasy leaders to consolidate democracy by 2008 created the conditions for an uprising. Even the noticeable improvements in people's economic condition from 2002-06 was not enough to overcome the sense of disappointment they felt toward the regime by 2007-08. If anything, Ravalomanana's initial success as president created rising expectations that were only partially met by his semi-democratic regime.[43] Rajoelina was able to find easy converts for rebellion by brilliantly cloaking his personal ambitions for power through denunciation of Ravalomanana's excesses and the failures of the justice system under the president. Opposition groups joined him not to rescue Rajoelina's business interests but as a way to stop the president's power.[44]

With Rajoelina firmly entrenched as president, it came as no surprise when most of Madagascar's political leaders came to his defense for his role during the coup, in most cases refusing to even label it as such. Only Ravalomanana's most loyal supporters would go on the record with me and condemn the current president for his overthrow of Marc. Everyone else embraced the narrative of Rajoelina as a servant of the people who had acted boldly to depose a corrupt leader. And yet the evidence is clear of Rajoelina's use of extra-constitutional means to depose a democratically-elected leader, including his collaboration with the military. While the international community's decision to label the event of 2009 a coup is entirely justified, many people on the island refuse to do the same.

Sylvain Rabetsaroana, for example, witnessed all of Madagascar's recent turmoil firsthand. He served as a Senator from 2001-09, then as a member of Parliament under the HAT from 2009-13 before launching an unsuccessful run for President in 2013. Now in his early sixties, he spends most of his time managing his businesses and spending time with his family and their two dogs. Rabetsaroana supported Ravalomanana during the first few years of his presidency but eventually grew disenchanted with him. "Ravalomanana deviated from his original path as a good leader and everyone in the country could see it. He became corrupt, and tried to make Madagascar another part of his companies. By the time he left he was the most corrupt of all of our presidents." The former Senator supported Rajoelina's takeover in 2009 but refused to call it a *coup d'etat*. "It was a people's movement," he told me. "At first there were just three thousand people in the street protesting, then the rallies grew and you had 10,000, 50,000, or 100,000 people calling for the president to resign. When Ravalomanana ordered the shooting of all those protesters, that was the beginning of the end for him."

He continued listing the former president's deficiencies and compared him to predecessors and the man who unseated him. "Ravalomanana was not a good listener – when you had a meeting with him he would say 'I only have two minutes for you.' Andry is a good listener," he said of Rajoelina. He now speaks to him regularly and offers advice when the President asks for it.

Monja Roindefo was an even more direct beneficiary of the coup. He served as Rajoelina's Prime Minister for about seven months in the immediate aftermath of the uprising. The son of Monja Jaona, the legendary leader from the south of the country who challenged France's imperial rule in the 1940s and 1950s, he now leads a small political party in Antananarivo called MONIMA, a party originally created by his father during the colonial era.

Recall that it was Moindefo who led the protesters to the presidential palace on the fateful day of February 7th. "2009 was a popular movement, not really a coup," he told me when I met him at his home. This was exactly the language used by former Senator Rabetsaroana. But as we discussed the events at length and I pressed him on how history should remember the uprising, he conceded that perhaps it was a coup. "In practice maybe it was," he said, "but not really in theory because the overthrow was not originated by the military. It came from good intentions but maybe we used the wrong vehicle."

People were inspired by Ravalomanana's sudden rise to the presidency in 2001, he told me, but as Rabetsaroana had told me, Ravalomanana "personalized the office." By this he meant that the former president used his position as a platform from which to destroy his business competitors. The international community, which was charmed by Ravalomanana's leadership style and impressive results, "became blind to his corruption and overreacted to his removal."

Roindefo then listed a series of moves made by Ravalomanana that upset him and many Malagasy at the time. "He banned the commemoration of the 1971 uprising and repression in the South. This angered a lot of us from that region. He dismissed Chirac's expression of regret over French misdeeds during the colonial period. He monopolized many industries in the capital and used foreign aid for his companies. GDP increased during his tenure but it wasn't evenly distributed and most people didn't benefit. He imprisoned opposition politicians, including many coastal politicians."

The former Prime Minister expounded on why he and others like him supported the overthrow. "Different people supported his removal for different reasons. For me, it was about the economic structure and the political culture he had created. The contracting process for our largest industries became corrupt and it was clear he didn't understand the ultimate goal of politics, which is the inclusion of all members of society. His models abroad were business leaders and not the famous figures from American history – Jefferson, Lincoln, Martin Luther King. I know you can't just overthrow the government, but for me it had become a matter of conscience – our president no longer respected the basic rights of the people. Rajoelina had different reasons, more personal: his businesses were under attack and his TV station had been shut down. Others had their own reasons. But the bottom line is that Marc became more aggressive against his political opponents in his second term, and it became a toxic situation here."

I couldn't resist asking him about a rumor I had heard several times regarding the coup, which held that France backed Rajoelina's uprising as a response to Ravalomanana's increasingly cozy relations with the United States. He didn't seem surprised at all by the charge. "There is a theory here that the French supported Rajoelina in his revolt against Marc, who was then supported by the U.S., but that has been exaggerated. Events were decided here in Tana, not abroad. But I do wonder why I'm still not able to get a visa to visit the United States!"

* * *

Rabetsaroana and Moindefo were political leaders of a certain generation, men who had grown up with the coups and countercoups of Malagasy politics over the last forty years. Their wisdom and insights were extraordinary as they recounted the tortuous path the island has followed in its quest to become a stable democracy. But the events of 2009 would surely look different to someone younger, perhaps more idealistic, and as the weeks went by I sought out members of the next generation of leaders in Madagascar who had experienced the coup firsthand and were willing to go on record about what had happened. Many came forward to share their experiences with me, but none were as eloquent or as thoughtful as a young woman named Lovatiana Gontare Ramaroson. Her story, parts of which were vehemently contested by others I met, was nevertheless a poignant and at times moving description of the coup and its legacy.

Ramaroson currently serves as the Chief of Staff at the Ministry of Agriculture, a position she secured through the direct intervention of President Rajoelina. Now in her mid-thirties, she exudes an air of calm and sincerity that belies her youthful appearance. When I met her at a restaurant above a popular supermarket in 2019, she had just spent the night partying at a popular downtown club with some colleagues from the president's administration in celebration of some recent political triumph. She apologized for her tired appearance, but in truth I had never seen anyone looking so refreshed after an all-nighter.

Lova, as her friends call her, graduated from college in 2006 and, like all of her classmates, started looking for a job. She responded to an ad in the paper for a job as a personal assistant with a company called Injet, a media and marketing company. When she arrived at the designated office she was surprised to see Andry Rajoelina himself there to conduct the interview, along with his wife. Rajoelina was a year away from running from mayor of Antananarivo at the time, but was already well known across the capital. "The President likes to give opportunities to young people in both business and government," she told me. "He knows that most jobs require five years of experience and very few people in their twenties have that, so he does what he can to help them." Lova got the job despite having no professional experience and says she will be thankful to him forever, "because it changed my life."

In late 2007, Rajoelina became mayor of Antananarivo. In his first year he had already taken steps to change the city and begun his feud with Ravalomanana. Lova said it was clear to everyone in the capital that the President "wanted to monopolize the marketing industry in Tana so that his daughter could take it over. That's when he started to persecute Rajoelina." Lova moved with him to the mayor's office, telling me it was a good opportunity because she had studied law and political science and dreamed of becoming a diplomat someday. She knew this would be her chance to learn the political system.

By 2009, the tension between the two men was palpable, and those close to the situation knew that conflict at some level was imminent. "We had more influence in the city by then than the

President did. We created TGV [Rajoelina's political party]. The movement soon expanded to the provinces, who saw this young man leading the capital and wanted to follow it. They felt a lot of sympathy for the mayor and his movement and decided to join it."

She was adamant that the protests were never intended to oust Ravalomanana – until they were. "Before that time, Rajoelina never explicitly said he was going to overthrow the government and take over the country. But he didn't have to because it was a general feeling that as the movement grew and people became more dissatisfied with the President, something dramatic might happen. But it's important to understand that it wasn't a conscious decision to take power and we didn't plan for it to happen at the beginning. But at some point in the days before February 7th of that year he decided he was going to become president. By that time we all knew it would happen."

As I asked her about her involvement in the coup itself, Ramoroson grew somber, as if the memory of those fateful days was difficult for her to share. "I've never really talked about this publicly before, and I realize now that I've wanted to," she said slowly. "I was there that day, because my mom's house is in Analakely [a neighborhood in central Antananarivo] and I could just walk over to the protest site. The leaders of the protest never planned to go to the Presidential palace, for all of us it was just another day of protests downtown. Then suddenly I heard people saying, "We're going to the Palace, We're going to the Palace!" And then everyone headed in that direction. Before I knew it we were there and things just spun out of control. I heard gunshots, saw people running in every direction. I still can't believe all of that happened. When I think about it now it's like a dream, you know?"

After the coup Lova took a leave of absence from Rajoelina's staff for six months. "I was shocked, I really couldn't believe what had just happened, and maybe I needed some time off to come to terms with it and decide what I wanted to do next." She agreed to become head of the Ministry of Youth and Sports for TGV. But when Rajoelina created a new parliament in 2010, he asked her to join it and she agreed almost immediately. "I felt it was my duty. I saw that the President wanted to do the right things for the country despite the international condemnation." She became the youngest woman in the Parliament at age 26 and is proud of her service during that time. "The HAT years [2009-14] were like a normal presidential term [5 years] and we made the most of it. We won something back during those years. We had removed a corrupt president and helped the country move on to something better."

But the consequences of those few weeks still weigh heavily on her. We talked about all of the ramifications of a coup on a country as inherently unstable as Madagascar. In the end she still believes in the ideals represented by the rebellion but said she would let history decide whether what they did was right. "I understand the views of Ravalomanana and his supporters. He was the elected president. You can judge it as a *coup d'etat* if you want, and many people here and abroad did, but for us it was a popular movement. Our goal and our feeling was that we were liberating the country."

A popular movement. A national liberation. A massacre by a corrupt leader. These were the things I heard repeatedly from the President's supporters. As I talked to more people, however, I quickly learned that there was another side of the story. Ravalomanana's supporters just laughed when I told them how Rajoelina's camp had justified the coup. "We can tell you what really happened, they said, but why don't you go talk to Marc? He was at the center of it all; he knows more about it than anyone." I soon realized that these people were right. An understanding of the uprising that led to the overthrow of Madagascar's best hope for democracy in a generation couldn't be fully told by those from the outside who watched it happen.

I needed to go straight to the culprit – or the victim – depending on who you believed. And so with equal doses of excitement and trepidation I set out to ask the man himself.

* * *

It's not easy getting an audience with a head of state, even one who's been out of office for ten years. I had a journalist friend, Bruno, who was close to the Ravalomanana camp and swore he could get me an interview with the former president within a week. A week went by and nothing happened. When I talked to Bruno he gave me two numbers to call, supposedly the numbers of two of Ravalomanana's top aides. I left messages with both of them and never heard back. I was leaving Antananarivo on a trip through the South in a week and time was running out. I began to make arrangements to interview someone else instead – a close advisor or a member of his cabinet.

"There's a woman we need to find," Bruno told me four days before my trip. "She controls Marc's schedule and helps run his political party. I think I know where she works but I'm not sure." By this point I had lost all faith in my friend's close connection to Ravalomanana, especially when our search for the mysterious woman began with a trek through labyrinthine alleys that seemed to lead nowhere. After two hours of urban sleuthing we emerged on a main road. "Ah, this looks familiar!" Bruno exclaimed. A few blocks down we turned into a large compound, where half of Tana's under-30 population seemed to be congregating: college students, campaign volunteers, candidates themselves, kids just hanging out with their friends. "Yeah, this is it," he said. We climbed two flights of stairs and walked down a hallway, then knocked on a door. A woman opened it and the first thing I saw was a classroom of students behind her.

"Madame Michelle!" Bruno bellowed and offered some mix

of Malagasy greetings and apologies for interrupting her class. He gestured to me a few times and seemed to be doing his best to persuade the woman to hear me out for a few minutes. She looked thoroughly displeased, but at last she waved me in to her classroom and asked me to sit down. Her class stared at us in total silence as she proceeded to interview me in a hushed tone that was nonetheless overheard by everyone.

"Why do you want to interview the president?" she began. She made some notes and asked to see my passport. She asked me how many books I had written before and which newspaper I worked for. When I just shrugged she sighed and closed her notebook. "How long will you be in Tana?" she asked. "Four more days?" I said, more like a question than an answer. She pursed her lips and said "Thank you for coming - I'll see what I can do."

When we walked outside Bruno slapped me on the back excitedly. "That went great, don't you think?" I gave up, and continued packing my bags for the trip south. Two days later Madame Michelle called and told me Ravalomanana would see me the next morning.

* * *

How many times had I climbed the grand staircase that led up out of Analakely into the calmer hills of Mandrasoa and Faravohitra? Most of the time I was running up them, sporting Nike running shoes and a bright orange t-shirt, enduring the stares of the peasant woman selling grilled fish and boiled frogs, the girl offering fluorescent hula hoops, the man peddling knockoff sneakers. This time I walked past in a suit and bright orange tie, and the same merchants looked at me more closely, nodding and laughing at my transformation. I took another set of narrow stairs into Faravohitra, from which you could see most of Tana down below, then a sharp fishhook onto

Ravalomanana's street. I arrived at his compound ten minutes early and Madame Michelle was there waiting for me. "Good luck," was all she said as she walked me through the foyer and showed me into his living room.

The former president was informally dressed when we met, his jeans and running shoes a testament to his carefully crafted image as a man of the people. A servant arrived and offered me a selection of juices from which to choose. I think I selected mango. "Twenty years ago all I could have offered you was yogurt," he joked.

After Ravalomanana's decade in the political wilderness I was expecting to find a tired, defeated man, but Ravalomanana looked relaxed and in good spirits. We started talking about Malagasy history, and he immediately confirmed his anti-French bias. "Look at the difference in the colonies controlled by the French and the British. The British colonies were well run. Madagascar has the worst roads of any former colony, and that's because the French invested so little in them."

We talked about his record as president and whether he was proud of his leadership for seven years before the coup. "When I was in power we did a lot. I erased up to $7 billion in debt after the World Bank told me I had to do it to make the country economically competitive. But we did it, and after that we received $2 billion from the World Bank for development. We were on the right track here."

He was defiant when I brought up the coup itself, accusing Rajoelina of cynically exploiting a minor land deal by Ravalomanana as a pretext for launching daily protests against him. "I bought some land with my own money from local people and filled it in. He said I took it from poor people for myself. That was the excuse he used to start the coup." There was no question in his mind about the military's involvement. "[Rajoelina] was the leader, but he had some or most of the Army with him. He did it for two reasons. First, to advance his personal interests. Second, because the French were supporting him and encouraging him to do it. Why? Because they want a puppet in Madagascar. They had already tried to stage a coup twice before." In a way, the former President agreed with Ramoroson that Rajoelina did not begin his quest to oust Ravalomanana as a means of becoming president – at least not initially. "[Rajoelina] got greedy as he got more support. First, he just wanted to overthrow me, but then he decided to take power himself," he said.

We came around to the events of February 2009, and the day the protesters stormed the palace. He immediately dismissed any personal responsibility for the deaths of that day and pinned the blame squarely on Rajoelina, going so far as to say the march was a pretext that was always designed to lead to violence that could be laid at his – Ravalomanana's - doorstep. "He brought people from Analakely to the palace. His supporters tried to break into the palace. He tried to start a civil war. The whole thing was a setup; his men shot the protesters as a reason to do the coup, to discredit me. I asked the Hague to investigate the coup and they never did."

This was not the first time I had heard a high-level official say the march on the palace and the ensuing bloodshed were orchestrated from Rajoelina well in advance. Indeed, Colonel Andrianasoavina said as much during his controversial interview years later. At first I thought it strained credulity to believe that a man and his movement would be so cynical as to murder scores of innocent people just to start a revolution that would install him in power. But world history is replete with such Machiavellian schemes to take power that frequently devolve into bloodshed. And besides, if Ravalomanana didn't order his guards to open fire, who did? Either they did so on their own, without authorization, or the shots came from elsewhere. The video footage isn't clear. The truth may never be known. But most of the evidence and testimony unearthed later exonerated Ravalomanana from the massacre, without being able to prove Rajoelina's direct involvement either. The uncertainty haunts the country to this day.

As the former president pivoted to the current day, he kept his anger toward his usurper in check and focused on the dire conditions in the country rather than the man who, in his opinion, created them. In fact he never even said Rajoelina's name during the entire interview, choosing instead to refer to him as "the President," "They" or simply as "He" when speaking about his rival. "Now in Madagascar we have a social crisis, a political crisis and an economic crisis at the same time. He tries to copy me, my style of bonding with the people. And the French hate me, because I am a nationalist and I put the interests of Madagascar first. The Malagasy people are hopeful but disappointed in their leaders now. Madagascar is not a democracy today. The president, he wants to create a dictatorship. Democracy means you have to listen. But free speech is disappearing, it will soon be finished here. They are sending people to prison who speak out, even journalists. The way they govern now is just an extension of the coup. And they still block any attempt I make to create new businesses."

He seemed to be suggesting that foreign powers and crucial donors were already starting to back away from Rajoelina. "We need the international community to continue to lend and invest in Madagascar. But they say, 'We have to trust you first, you have to show us good governance. You have to show the country is well managed.' That's why they are being so careful now."

I knew Ravalomanana would allege fraud in the last election, but he went much further than that, proclaiming, "I won the election last year. The HCC is corrupt, they took money from the President's people not to investigate it. They said, 'We received your complaint but we can't do anything about it.' What was that?"

The accusations of fraud coming from Ravalomanana's camp never really died, and were resurrected a year later when the Vice President of the National Independent Electoral Commission (CENI), said his team had discovered over 1.1 million duplicate national ID cards in their system. This seemed to corroborate Ravalomanana's claims of massive fraud, but Rajoelina's Minister of Interior and Decentralization stepped in to claim that irregularities on such a massive scale were not only impossible but irrelevant, because other checks had already been put in place to ensure people couldn't vote twice.[45]

I moved on to other topics, but eventually Ravalomanana returned to his denunciation of Rajoelina. "During the campaign he said he wouldn't touch the Constitution. That he will respect it. But they appointed governors [in the provinces] instead of electing the regional chiefs, and they ignored the law respecting the opposition by refusing to recognize me as the leader of the opposition in Parliament. The President wants to control everything as a dictator would. The new city he's building, Tanamasoandro, is badly planned; it will result in flooding, just watch."

He ended our interview with a commonly heard lament on the vivid contradiction between Madagascar's natural wealth and its unbreakable cycle of poverty. "We have lots of resources here, lots of water. We should not be so poor. But three things hold us back." He said, ticking them off on his fingers. "One, civil war; two, natural disasters; three, a bad government that doesn't respect the rule of law." I asked whether he was optimistic about his country's future. He looked at me as if I had asked him whether he would like to live on the Moon. "With this president? No, I am pessimistic."

* * *

By any measure Rajoelina's ascent was stunning. He was just

35 years of age when sworn in, making him the youngest president in the country's history and the youngest head of government in the world at that time. Just three years before he had been unknown to almost everyone in his own country, not to mention the rest of the world. Now he assumed power over 20 million people that desperately needed leadership and policies to reverse their nation's staggering poverty and insidious corruption. He failed on both counts during his first term, and his failure was one of exquisite irony, because the very act of usurping power had made him a pariah - at least temporarily – to so many potential global partners who could have helped Madagascar.

Indeed, the international community was swift to react to what most people were now calling a *coup d'etat*. In March 2009, the SADC announced that it would not recognize Rajoelina's new government. The African Union suspended Madagascar and threatened sanctions if the previously elected government was not restored within six months. The United States, Madagascar's largest bilateral donor and provider of humanitarian aid, also refused to recognize the Rajoelina administration, and ordered all non-essential embassy employees to leave the island. Madagascar was removed from the list of beneficiaries of the African Growth and Opportunity Act, the vital trade pact it had signed with the U.S. in the early 2000s. In May, the UN responded to the coup by freezing 600 million Euros in aid while the IMF went even further, freezing all support to the country. All of these organizations stipulated that Rajoelina's legitimacy would be conditioned upon the county's holding free and fair elections as soon as possible. And yet his time in office was only getting started.

In August 2009, the two rivals along with former Presidents Ratsiraka and Zafy signed the Maputo Accords, which provided guidelines for a period of political transition. Rajoelina promised to hold elections soon, but a year went by without any timetable for a vote. Then, in November 2010, he strengthened his own power further by passing a referendum to adopt the nation's fourth constitution, with 73% of voters supporting it, although voter turnout was under 53%. One critical change made by the new constitution was to lower the minimum age for presidential candidates from 40 to 35, making Rajoelina now eligible to stand in presidential elections, whenever they occurred. It also mandated that the leader of the High Transitional Authority – Rajoelina – be kept as interim president until an election could take place, and required presidential candidates to reside in Madagascar for at least six months prior to any election. Since Ravalomanana and other opposition leaders had been living in exile in South Africa since the coup and dared not return while Rajoelina was in power, this last stipulation effectively barred the former president and his party's leading members from running in the next contest. The coup was now complete.

Rajoelina used other tricks to turn the government back into a dictatorship soon after taking office. He dissolved the Senate and the National Assembly and transferred their powers to the HAT. Legislative authority now rested in practice with Rajoelina and his cabinet, composed of his closest advisers. A military committee established in April 2009 increased HAT control over security and defense policy. The following month the HAT strengthened its influence over local government by replacing the country's 22 regional governors that had been installed by Ravalomanana. The National Inquiry Commission (CNME) was established shortly thereafter to solidify the HAT's control over judicial and legal matters.

Rajoelina then turned his wrath on his rival, seeking revenge for the latter's attempts to thwart his business ventures before the coup. First, he canceled Ravalomanana's unpopular land deal with Daewoo Logistics. Then in June 2009, he fined Ravalomanana $70 million and sentenced him to four years in prison for alleged abuse of office which, according to Rajoelina's government, included the December 2008 purchase, with public funds, of the second presidential jet. Ravalomanana was by this time living in exile in South Africa, and these steps were meant to ensure that he would not return anytime soon. Rajoelina also pursued legal action against Ravalomanana's company TIKO to reclaim $35 million allegedly due in back taxes. In 2010 the HAT sentenced Ravalomanana in absentia to hard labor for life and issued an arrest warrant for his role in the deaths of the protesters who were shot in front of the presidential palace during the coup. Rajoelina then took aim at several key policies initiated by his predecessor, terminating Ravalomanana's development strategy, known as the Madagascar Action Plan, and abandoning education reforms that had adopted Malagasy and English as languages of instruction, instead returning to the traditional use of French.

By this time it had become clear what a disaster the coup had become for the country. The HAT dispensed with all notions of democratic fairness by increasing the number of members of parliament from 160 before the crisis to 356 in November 2010 and 526 in December 2011, packing the chamber with its supporters who proceeded to stifle freedom of speech and imprison journalists who criticized the regime. The disappearance of foreign aid forced them to seek new sources of revenue, like rosewood exports. Rajoelina quickly lost control over trafficking of various natural resources while corruption and embezzlement shot up. Roads, healthcare and education deteriorated while poverty grew even worse. Crime rose to new heights and the *dahalo* flourished.[46]

The condemnation of Rajoelina's seizure of power went beyond rhetoric, and various sanctions put in place by donor governments and organizations had a deep impact on the country's ability to govern. In June 2010 the EU announced the suspension of its 600 million Euro financial aid package to Madagascar for another year. Sanctions and suspension of donor aid amounted to 40% of the island's national budget and 70% of public investments, and much of these penalties hit the poorest sectors of society hardest. Rajoelina occasionally organized events to distribute basic items to the people, including medicine, clothing, cleaning materials and school supplies, and his administration spent millions of dollars to subsidize basic needs like electricity, fuel and food staples. In 2010, two years after Rajoelina launched the project as mayor of Antananarivo, the HAT completed the reconstruction of the *Hotel de Ville* (town hall) of Antananarivo, which had been destroyed by arson during the political protests of 1972.

Meanwhile, international pressure to hold elections continued to hound the new president. Finally, in September 2011 – more than two years after the coup – the SADC's mediation resulted in an outcome acceptable to all parties. Known as the Roadmap for Ending the Crisis in Madagascar, the settlement called for national elections to be held in 2013, giving Rajoelina another two years in office. The SADC won high marks for bringing all of the major parties to the table and restoring the constitutional order after other attempts at mediation had failed, but it gave Rajoelina virtually everything he wanted. The Roadmap named Rajoelina the only president of the country until new elections could be held, said he did not have to share power with anyone, and that he would not be prohibited from running in future elections. He faced no penalty for leading a military coup in 2009, an event that was largely ignored by the settlement. The only stipulation that may have displeased him was the requirement that he stop the persecution of the opposition and let all political actors in exile, namely Ravalomanana, return. Rajoelina would blatantly ignore this last point by threatening to arrest Ravalomanana and denying his plane permission to land when the exiled president tried to return in January 2012, but by that point the world had moved on. The Roadmap was quickly accepted by the international community, legitimizing

Rajoelina and his transitional government while setting the stage for elections of a new president in 2013 and a new National Assembly in 2014.[47] In very short order the deep freeze in relations with the rest of the world after the coup began to thaw. Rajoelina was rewarded by the international community for signing the Roadmap just months later with an invitation to address the 66th Session of the United Nations General Assembly, marking the first major form of international recognition of the HAT regime. In December 2011 he was officially received by French President Nicolas Sarkozy.

Rajoelina was in no rush to carry out his obligations under the Roadmap, but eventually several factors coincided to force Rajoelina to hold the elections he had gone to such lengths to delay. First, after significant pressure from the SADC on both men to resolve a new standoff, Rajoelina and Ravalomanana met in the Seychelles in May 2012 and agreed to an election in May of 2013. Second, the World Bank issued a report in October 2012 that detailed the economic impact of the coup. The report estimated that Madagascar's economy had grown just 2.7% in 2012 and was projected to grow by only 2.6% in 2013, even as inflation slowed and work began at Ambatovy, one of the largest nickel mining projects in the world. The country had lost $6.3 billion since 2009, the World Bank said, based on the assumption that the economy would have grown 5% per year had there been greater political stability. In addition, its economy had been crippled since the coup by a significant drop in tourism, the suspension of foreign aid and wariness among foreign investors in its gold, oil, and mineral reserves.

Four years after seizing power and agreeing to hold elections, Rajoelina finally gave in. After months of haggling, an election was scheduled for 2013 in which both Rajoelina and Ravalomanana agreed not to run, bowing to international pressure to give the nation a fresh start. But however well intentioned, the plans for a new election soon degenerated into farce, Malagasy style. For example, while the agreement barred the two rivals from running it said nothing about spouses, and in May 2013 Ravalomanana's wife, Lalao Ravalomanana Rakotonirainy, announced her candidacy for president, despite having no political experience. Rajoelina immediately proclaimed her announcement a breach of contract and announced that her entry now permitted him to re-renter the race. A new furor erupted over this announcement, both at home and abroad, and led to the postponement of the election several more times until Rajoelina's candidacy could be resolved. Things got even more confusing when former strongman Didier Ratsiraka surprised everyone by announcing he was running as well, after an 11-year exile in France. A special electoral court stepped in and ruled in August 2013 that the candidacies of all four of them – Rajoelina, Ravalomanana, Ravalomanana's wife and former president Ratsiraka – were invalid and that none of them would be permitted to run in the election. Rajoelina declined to press the issue further and announced his endorsement of former finance minister Hery Rajaonarimampianina, who won the race with 53.5% of the vote. Most observers credit his victory to little more than being the last man standing. After winning just 15.8% in the first round, Rajaonarimampianina won the second-round runoff in large part because of a sharp dropoff in turnout – from 61.6% of registered voters to 50.7%. Some quick math shows that garnering 53% of the votes cast means he was elected by just 27% of registered voters.

Rajoelina officially stepped down in January 2014, nearly five years after seizing power. Rajaonarimampianina assumed the presidency later that month but, in an ominous sign for a country trying to heal its collective wounds, his inauguration was marred by an explosion from a grenade that killed a 12-year old child and wounded dozens after the ceremony. The World Bank announced that the resumption of normal lending would hinge on the appointment of a prime minister, and projected modest 3.7% growth in 2014, followed by 4% in 2015. Meanwhile, Rajoelina's party won almost 50 seats in Parliament, becoming the largest bloc and giving rise to rumors that he might become prime minister. Jean Louis Robinson, the losing candidate, pledged to unite the country's fractured opposition. The AU signaled its acceptance of the result by lifting its suspension of Madagascar's membership in the regional body and urging the international community to provide support to the country's troubled economy. Foreign aid would resume soon thereafter.

A classic technocrat, Rajaonarimampianina set about organizing the selection of his cabinet, a process that extended over several months. During this time, Rajoelina had the temerity to seek the nomination for the position of Prime Minister, which would only have caused more outrage, but Rajaonarimampianina wisely nominated someone else. In April, a cabinet was announced that comprised 31 members from varied political affiliations. Rajoelina returned to private life until the next election, scheduled for 2018.

Madagascar then went about a year without any major political strife. In 2015, however, lawmakers voted 121-4 to impeach Rajaonarimampianina, a devout Catholic, for violating the constitution's separation of church and state, and for "general incompetence." Critics claimed he had achieved as little success curbing rampant corruption as his predecessor. The constitutional court threw out the impeachment vote and allowed him to remain as President, but confidence in his leadership had reached a new low and would remain there for the rest of his term.

The economy continued to struggle. The World Bank issued a devastating report near the end of Rajaonarimampianina's term in office that showed in stark relief how damaging the recent instability had been for ordinary Malagasy. Madagascar's per capita income of $420 made it one of the poorest countries in Africa, according to the report, while half its children still suffered from chronic malnutrition. The suspension of aid by the IMF and other donors had resulted in severe damage to its poorest citizens. The report also highlighted political risk as one of the biggest factors in the island's recovery. Coralie Gevers, the World Bank's country manager in Madagascar, drew a clear link between political stability and a reduction in suffering: "Madagascar needs to prove first, not just to the international community but to itself, that it can have elections – stable elections, peaceful elections – in late 2018, that will enable them to continue implementing reforms – economic reforms – and investing for the long term benefit of the country not only in infrastructure but also in human development. If we see that, we have every hope and every belief that Madagascar will be able to reduce its poverty."[48] In addition, a 2017 outbreak of bubonic plague severely impacted the tourist industry and killed 124 Malagasy.

The election of one of Rajoelina's former acolytes and the defeat of his handpicked candidate must have been a bitter pill for ex-president Ravalomanana to swallow. From 2009 to 2012 he had lived in exile in South Africa, where he engaged in active negotiations with Rajoelina and former Presidents Zafy and Ratsiraka to organize national elections. He had acquiesced to the demands of the international community that he would not run in the 2013 election, leading to Rajaonarimampianina's victory. As we saw, after being sentenced in absentia by Rajoelina to a lifetime of hard labor, he was arrested in October 2014 when he tried to return to Madagascar. It must have been immensely gratifying when, after his sentence was lifted and he was freed from house arrest in May 2015, Ravalomanana was re-elected as the president of a new opposition party and was allowed to reopen TIKO, his primary business before Rajoelina began his fervid acts of persecution. With his return to civilian life now assured, he began to focus his sights on a much bigger comeback. But gaining power a second time would prove infinitely harder for Ravalomanana than it had been fifteen years earlier.

Chapter 3

The Return of Rajoelina

Here you have to buy an election, and to do that you have to have money, and to get money you have to plunder the country. And that's what our politicians do.
Monja Roindefo, Former Prime Minister

As the calendar flipped to 2018, Madagascar braced itself for another period of instability. Ravalomanana had finally been absolved from any crime and was allowed to return to the island to resume his political life and business career. Another presidential election loomed just several months away and there was no question that Rajoelina and Ravalomanana, each of whom had been barred from running in 2013, were headed for another showdown.

Rajoelina became the first to register his candidacy for the upcoming race. Among his early campaign promises were vows to close the Senate (to save money), build more universities, increase access to electricity, work towards agricultural self-sufficiency and increase security. The campaign started in earnest in October 2018, with Rajoelina facing his archenemy Ravalomanana and his former underling, Rajaonarimampianina, who no longer felt compelled to support Rajoelina after serving his own term as President. The three men quickly became the favorites in a campaign of 46 candidates, a campaign *The Economist* dubbed "Night of The Long Names."

Violence came early in the campaign. After Rajaonarimampianina passed a new law in April that sought to pave the way for his re-election by somewhat blatantly restricting Rajoelina's and Ravalomanana's ability to run, supporters of both leading candidates took to the streets. In a troubling reprise of the events of 2009, police shot and killed two protesters at an April opposition rally in the capital. Since many of the protesters were calling for him to resign, Rajaonarimampianina called it an attempted coup. The High Constitutional Court (HCC) was forced to intervene in May and declared the president's new law unconstitutional, and order was temporarily restored. The HCC's decision also required the President to form a transitional government in sixty days that included the leading parties in Parliament. Rajaonarimampianina did so, but new protests then broke out alleging the new government was not as inclusive as required by the HCC's ruling. More calls were made for the President to resign, which he finally did in September 2018 to prepare to run in the coming election. Once free of the office, Rajaonarimampianina ran on his record as Finance Minister and President for the last five years, gaining Russian support for his candidacy but otherwise considered too weak to challenge Rajoelina and Ravalomanana. In true Malagasy fashion, he sought to have the election canceled at the last minute because of what he described as an uneven playing field, a request that was promptly denied by the HCC.[1]

The constitutional court had thus temporarily cooled temperatures around the campaign on several occasions, and it's worth pausing for a minute to consider the growing impact of the court. The HCC has shown itself to be a significant force – one of the few – in resolving disputes and maintaining political stability in Madagascar. This has become commonplace, and if the constant need for a neutral arbiter to settle political disputes can on one level be seen as a troubling sign for a young democracy like Madagascar, perhaps we should be thankful that at least one institution exists whose decrees are respected by everyone. Somewhat surprisingly, all political candidates and parties seem to accept the HCC's decisions as final and binding, even if they disagree with those decisions. This is obviously a positive step toward creating a system of checks and balances and something the country can build upon. Moreover, Malagasy civil society is still not strong enough to keep ruling elites in check without the court, as only a small percentage of civic organizations on the island are involved in government oversight and monitoring.[2]

I was curious as to how the HCC sees its role and whether it even wants to be involved in these high-profile political cases. I met with Jean-Eric Rakotoarisoa, the President of the court, in his office in November 2019 and asked him exactly that.[3] Rakotoarisoa is an intelligent, businesslike, bespectacled man of about sixty who was elected by the other members of the court to serve as president. He told me straightforwardly that the court's involvement in declaring winners and losers is embedded in the court's mandate. "The HCC has two roles," he said. "First, to rule on the constitutionality of the laws passed by the Parliament and the government, as well as treaties. Second, to serve as the final electoral judge and give an official proclamation of results for the presidential, legislative and Senate elections."

He scoffed at any idea that the court was biased or had succumbed to any outside pressure. "The court is independent. The constitution reinforces its independence, as does the composition of the court. Three members are selected by the President, two by the National Assembly, two by the Senate, and two by the *Conseil Superieure*. Each member serves just one term of seven years. But our independence comes as much from the will of the seven justices as it does from the independence inherent in the structure of the court."

Rakotoarisoa welcomed a discussion about the charges of electoral fraud during the 2018 election leveled by Ravalomanana's camp and the court's unwillingness to validate those claims. "I have heard those things," he said. "But with respect to Marc, we received over 600 complaints from his campaign and we took them seriously. But there were no procedures followed and, in the end, no proof of any fraud.

For example, his party didn't have any delegates in the voting offices around the country, making his claims far less credible and harder to document."

Several aides to Rajoelina had confirmed to me that the court has kept them at a distance, but the court had shown little inclination to intervene on Ravalomanana's behalf at any point either. There was definitely a perception, at least among Ravalomanana supporters, that the HCC was intent on doing the current president's bidding. I asked the chief justice for an example of when the court had opposed Rajoelina. "Well, we rejected his proposal to modify the constitution earlier this year. That was a significant one." He said they will rule soon on the constitutionality of the president's appointment of governors to the regions outside of Antananarivo, and they may have to rule next year on the president's proposal to reduce the number of senators as well. If either decision goes against Rajoelina it would go a long way toward validating the court's independence.

Before we parted Rakotoarisoa shared his views on the structure of government in Madagascar and the possibility of a strongman president running roughshod over the other two branches. Predictably, he saw no chance of the court acquiescing in that, but gave only tepid support to Parliament's willingness to check a dictator. "A separation of powers exists here, and each branch has real power. Certainly with respect to the court, and also with the president. However, the legislature hasn't used all of its power to the extent it could. For example, 90% of bills passed in Parliament originate with the President and his ministers, not the legislature. They don't make many new initiatives and that is one of the weaknesses of the system." But he assured me the court would stay vigilant in its efforts to safeguard the constitution and the thin reeds of democracy that have begun to sprout again in Madagascar.

* * *

Election day finally arrived in November 2018. Thirty-six candidates formally appeared on the first-round ballot for president. Defense Minister Beni Xavier Rasolofonirina said 10,000 security personnel had been deployed across the country to bolster security. Nearly 10 million people registered to vote in a population of 25 million, but turnout in both rounds of this contest would be disappointing. The endemic poverty on the island must have been a reason for voters' indifference. Investors and donor governments had started to reengage after a four-year freeze and the peaceful election of 2013, and a modicum of stability had returned since then. And yet 80% of Malagasy citizens still lived on less than $2 per day, despite some slight rebound in the economy in recent years. With civil society groups accusing all three wealthy frontrunners of enriching themselves while in office (something each denied), is it any wonder that a majority of the island's people stayed home?[4]

In the first round, Rajoelina received 39.2% of the vote while Ravalomanana took in 35.4%, setting up a second-round showdown between the two longtime rivals. Rajaonarimampianina finished a distant third with 8.8% and immediately protested, alleging various irregularities and claiming that Rajoelina's votes should be invalidated. Despite being viewed as Rajoelina's puppet for much of his rule he would not endorse any candidate during the second round, scheduled for December. Only 54% of registered voters voted in the first round.[5]

The emergence of Rajoelina and Ravalomanana at the top of the polls surprised no one. Supporters of both candidates hoped that this contest would settle the rivalry between them once and for all. Their decade-long quest to seize control of the country had resulted in a coup in 2009 and an electoral battle by proxy in 2013, but the presidential race of 2018 would be the first time the two men would put their rivalry to a direct vote. Rajoelina ran a campaign touting both his youth and the experience he had gained during his four-year presidency from 2009-13. In recognition of his rapid-fire rhetoric and charisma, many in the media began calling him "TGV," after the fast French train. This time his campaign promoted infrastructure development – everything from hospitals to schools to sports stadiums – and pledged to improve the island's beaches "to make them like Miami and Cote d'Azur" in order to draw more tourists and create more jobs. Ravalomanana, for his part, made much of the fact that during his rival's years in power, poverty and corruption grew as aid and investment dried up. He took on the nickname "The Milkman" for his dairy conglomerate, or "Papa" in a nod to his seniority. He claimed the county had gone backwards since he was overthrown and promised to pick up where he was forced to leave off. "We will rebuild everything they have destroyed, repair the roads that we built when I was president and that have not been maintained."

The second round of voting took place on a warm summer day in December, amid predictions by each candidate that he would win. Indeed, with only 5% of polling stations reporting their results both men took to the airwaves to claim victory. When more polling centers reported Rajoelina with a slight lead, Ravalomanana launched a public protest even before the final votes were in. "Fraud and violence have prevailed and this has an impact on the results. The results of this election are not credible and the election is not transparent," he said in a statement. "It is true that I said that I will respect the results if the rules are respected. Unfortunately, that is not the case." In a dangerous broadcast given the country's history, he then called on his supporters, "whose rights have been violated, to stand up and defend their choices." The electoral commission, CENI, said it would help candidates verify the results for themselves. The EU observer mission reported that the runoff was as "calm" as the first round and that they "did not see any fraud."[6]

The final results showed Rajoelina as the clear winner with 55.7% of the vote compared to 44.3% for Ravalomanana. Rajoelina won overwhelming support along the coasts while Ravalomanana prevailed in the Merina heartland around the capital. Once again, only about half of all registered voters bothered to show up. Ravalomanana, still claiming he had been cheated, filed a formal complaint with the HCC in late December and asked for a cancellation of the results. Ravalomanana's campaign manager vowed to fight on: "Do not believe that we are giving up. There was fraud. There was a premeditated act [in favor of Rajoelina]," he said, alleging that the electoral commission "facilitated fraud" in favor of Rajoelina. Rajoelina, for his part, urged everyone to remain calm and respect the results: "The country no longer needs trouble. We do not cheat. We do not how to cheat."[7] With tensions running high the HCC ratified Rajoelina's victory in early January, handing him a five-year term and rejecting Ravalomanana's accusations of fraud and irregularities, which had cited over 200 occurrences. Three days of protests in Antananarivo by Ravalomanana's supporters ensued, with police using tear gas to disperse the protesters after they breached a security cordon and blocked roads with burning tires.

Rajoelina was inaugurated on January 19, 2019. His victory represented a remarkable comeback for a man who had been vilified by the international community and large segments of his own country for launching a coup less than a decade earlier. Some analysts found it paradoxical that the Malagasy people voted for someone who had already governed with such catastrophic results and whose previous term, according to surveys conducted across the island, was viewed as the worst since independence. Moreover, they claimed, the sketchy sources of Rajoelina's campaign funds and his penchant for promising all things to all people should have served as red flags to voters.[8] Whether one believes his election was tainted by fraud or not, he had clearly sidelined all potential rivals and become the undisputed leader of Madagascar. The landslide victory of his party in legislative elections a few months later confirmed Rajoelina as the dominant force in Madagascar for the next decade. In the ideological void that existed in Malagasy politics, what he would do with his newfound power was anyone's guess.

* * *

And yet allegations of corruptions continued to dog Rajoelina even after his election, including one bombshell report detailing Russian interference on his behalf. A year after the election, *The New York Times* devoted a front page story to clumsy attempts by Vladimir Putin to swing the election Rajoelina's way, or at least to deny Ravalomanana, still seen as uncontrollably pro-American, another term.[9]

The story called it one of Russia's most overt attempts at election interference to date. Moscow spent millions trying to reelect Rajaonarimampianina, the eventual third-place candidate, by publishing its own newspaper on his behalf, bribing opposition candidates to drop out and paying for television and billboard advertising. The operation was approved by President Putin and coordinated by some of the same figures who coordinated the 2016 disinformation campaign in the United States. But the motive in Madagascar was much simpler: seizing control of the massive profits to be made from the island's natural resources. Well before the election a Russian company controlled by Yevgeny Prigozhin acquired a major stake in a company run by the Malagasy government that mines chromium, a mineral valued for its use in stainless steel; with profits starting to roll in by 2018 Russia decided to do whatever it took to try to protect, and even enhance, its investment.

Russian meddling began just a few weeks after

Rajaonarimampianina sat down with Putin in Moscow in March 2018, at a meeting attended by Prigozhin, who had just been indicted in the U.S. for his role in Russia's effort to manipulate the 2016 election there. Rajaonarimampianina said the upcoming presidential election was not discussed, but Harison Randriarimanana, a former agriculture minister, told *The Times* that Rajaonarimampianina announced to his team after the meeting that Putin had agreed to assist with his re-election campaign. This came at a time when Russia was aggressively trying to revive relations with a number of Africa countries that had grown distant since the end of the Cold War. Rajaonarimampianina insisted he did not receive a penny from Russia, but couldn't verify whether the Kremlin worked to assist him without his knowledge. A letter obtained by *The Times* clearly requested Russia's help to "resist attempts by international institutions to interfere" in Madagascar's elections.

The operation mimicked Russia's effort in the U.S., using a disinformation campaign on social media and attempting to bolster so-called spoiler candidates. It included a "troll factory" that focused on social media, and ultimately enlisted more than 30 Russian operatives to swing the election. Few appeared to have any expertise on Madagascar or even Africa. Some lesser presidential candidates told *The Times* accounts of Russians turning up out of the blue, some with bags of cash and offers of up to $2 million in financing. One candidate, a pop megastar known as Dama, said the Russians tried to get him to support a delay in the election so Rajaonarimampianina would have more time to campaign. They also tried to get lesser candidates to support Rajoelina in the final weeks of the campaign. But word of their meddling began to spread, and an op-ed appeared in Antananarivo claiming that after interfering in the American election the Russians had now appeared in Madagascar to do the same thing. Even worse, their political acumen proved to be embarrassingly poor. Moscow initially chose the wrong candidate (Rajaonarimampianina, who they called 'The Piano' for unknown reasons), one that ended up with less than 9% of the vote in the first round. So in September 2018 they quickly dumped him in favor of Rajoelina, the man they had just tried to defeat. After paying local writers to write disparaging articles about Rajoelina during the first round, they asked the same writers to endorse him during the second. As in the American election, it is not clear whether the Russians directly colluded with the eventual winner (Rajoelina), or simply operated a parallel campaign to support him. And in the last analysis they appear to have succeeded: Prigozhin's company was able to negotiate with the new government to keep control of the chromium mining operation. His company now maintains a staff of 30 in Madagascar and owns a 70% stake in the venture.[10]

With or without Russian help, Rajoelina began his first real term as president with a decision intended to demonstrate his willingness to keep his budget-cutting promises. When naming his cabinet a few weeks after his inauguration he announced that the number of ministers would be reduced from 29 to 22, along with other symbolic gestures of cost cutting. "All of this is in the interest of austerity and not to spend public money," he said afterwards.

A much more controversial move would soon follow. In April 2019, Rajoelina introduced an amendment to the 2010 constitution that would have abolished the Senate, increased regional autonomy, and established new governors in each region of the country to ease development in those regions. The referendum was scheduled for May 27 to coincide with legislative elections planned for that date, but the HCC struck down the proposed amendment on April 26 on procedural grounds, ruling that the measure must be passed by Parliament rather than submitted directly to the people for a vote.[11] When I caught up with former Senator Rabetsaroana, he actually supported the move against the chamber in which he once served. "I have no problem with it," he said. "The Senate does absolutely nothing." Blocked by the court, Rajoelina simply reduced the number of senators from 63 to 18 – setting off another legal battle in which he eventually prevailed. His appointment of new governors to the six regions of the island despite the constitution's requirement that they be elected also survived, despite a vigorous protest by Ravalomanana's fading opposition party.

As Rajoelina consolidated his power and jousted with the HCC to enhance it, he received more good news that would effectively put a stamp of legitimacy on his recent victory over Ravalomanana. Five months after the 2018 election, the European Union's Electoral Observer Mission issued its report on the fairness of that contest. They again declined to cite any widespread fraud or even major irregularities in the voting process. They called for a cooling off period among the major parties and for everyone to respect the outcome of the election. The Mission also went out of its way to praise Ravalomanana for eventually accepting the results and the HCC for its careful weighing of the evidence before declaring Rajoelina the winner. But in a rare nod to Ravalomanana's claims that democracy was under threat, they also called for new laws to regulate campaign finance and to create a formal position for the opposition leader in the National Assembly.

The mood in Antananarivo had been cautiously optimistic since Rajoelina's election, hoping his decisive victory would usher in a period of political calm and allow the country to resume its halting steps out of poverty. But the new president's bold moves to restructure the island's government were not met with universal applause. Patrice Rabe, in a July 2019 editorial entitled "Back To A Strong Presidential Regime," which appeared in the daily newspaper *Midi Madagasikara* in July 2019, expressed a growing wariness over Rajoelina's early tendency to strengthen his own power at the expense of other branches of government:

The TGV [Rajoelina's party] is on the way to creating a strong presidential regime.

The relationship between the Executive and Legislative branches recalls the image of a glass half empty or half full. In its landmark decision of 25 May 2018 over a request for the disqualification of President Hery Rajaonarimampianina, the HCC specified that "the Executive and the Legislative must respect the principles of separation and collaboration of powers, the foundations of the semi-presidential regime of the Fourth Republic."...The semi-presidential system is a mixed regime borrowing characteristics from the parliamentary system and the presidential system. It's like a hybrid car that uses two types of energy - electric and thermal - to drive. But the TGV of the Fourth Republic gives the impression of operating with only one type of engine: the presidential one...The semi-presidential regime advocated by the HCC, which is actually only a variant of the parliamentary system according to many constitutional experts, appears to be on the way out. Without warning, the TGV is heading towards a return to a strong presidential regime.[12]

* * *

Andry Rajoelina is often called a populist and compared to more high-profile leaders around the world who wear that label, most of them proudly. But the comparisons with Erdogan, Modi, Orban, Duterte and others are for the most part overblown. True, Rajoelina is a highly charismatic politician who has rejected any particular ideology in favor of building any kind of coalition that will keep him in power. He has tried to subvert the rule of law and convert Madagascar from a multiparty democracy on paper to a one-party regime in practice. But he stops short of turning to crude autocracy and has so far avoided the xenophobic, anti-elitist rhetoric now being employed by populists in various parts of the world. Having overthrown an elected president once, he now craves the legitimacy that comes through elections even as he transforms his country into a paragon of illiberal democracy.

Rajoelina's style of governance is emblematic of a larger trend. By any measure it has been a terrible decade for democracy. As of 2019, according to Freedom House, the world was in its 13th consecutive year of a global democratic recession. Liberal democracies have weakened or given way to illiberal regimes in every region of the world, from Africa to Eastern Europe, Southeast Asia to South America. And not even the most affluent and long-established democracies in the world are immune, as recent elections have shown that populists can win elections there too. Skeptics dismissed the first few years of democracy's retreat as transitory, but the crisis in representative government is real.[13]

This represents a stunning reversal in the steady progress and consolidation of the franchise. For three decades beginning in the mid-1970s, a third wave of democratization swept the globe and, by 2000, made democracy the most popular form of governance by far. By 1993, a majority of states with populations over one million had become democracies. But sometime around the mid-2000s, the relentless expansion of democracy ended and soon began its current decline. Political scientists disagree about the causes of that reversal, but a consensus has emerged that democracy as we once knew it is in trouble.

Still, when democratic countries change into something else the result is not always dictatorship. Some take that path, of course, with no more prominent example than Venezuela. More often, however, they morph into competitive authoritarian regimes in which elections retain real significance even though the opposition is forced to fight on a highly uneven playing field. Illiberal democracies, or "populist dictatorships" as the political scientist Yasha Mounk prefers, share two important features: first, their rulers came to power by winning free and fair elections with an anti-elitist and anti-pluralist message. Second, these leaders subsequently use those victories to concentrate power in their own hands by weakening the independence of key institutions, sidelining the opposition and undermining the media.[14]

This is exactly what's happening in parts of sub-Saharan Africa. According to Larry Diamond, Africa has witnessed one of the world's swiftest declines in democracy and the rule of law over the past decade or so. The continent is now home to a disturbing trend that sees disguised autocrats, such as Kenyatta of Kenya, Museveni of Uganda and Magufuli of Tanzania, use rigged elections to gain legitimacy and keep their hold on power. But in addition to manipulating elections, these populist leaders use their power to weaken key institutions like the judiciary and the press, while attacking political opponents to ensure that no viable challengers emerge. Diamond sees reasons for optimism in places such as Ethiopia, Nigeria and Tunisia, but overall the decline in democracy has become alarming, in large part because it shows no signs of slowing down.[15]

Indeed, Rajoelina is riding the crest of a political wave, not just in Madagascar but around the world, where his brand of illiberalism is gaining ground. Populist leaders in every region are taking advantage of the growing support for radical outsiders and candidates proclaiming their own strength and decisiveness. Once in power, these leaders typically engage in a hostile takeover of governing institutions and move to consolidate power in their own hands. They exploit the rules and procedures of democracy by suspending parliament or packing the court with their own judges. What have some have called "constitutional hardball" is on the rise everywhere, pushing the limits of presidential power in a dangerous game that forces opposition parties to either fight back in an equally undemocratic way or acquiesce and potentially fade into obscurity. Either way, democracy is the loser.

Let's look at one well-known example of developing-world populism to see how Madagascar compares. Rodrigo Duterte, the wily strongman president of the Philippines, came to power in 2016 promising to end corruption, deal harshly with drug dealers and other criminals, and return real power to the people. He vowed to build roads and clinics, provide jobs across the island and end the lack of public services. His promise to break through the red tape of Filipino society and end the political infighting proved immensely popular. But some analysts see Duterte's presidency as representing more continuity than change. He has dispensed money and influence to his financial and political supporters, some of whom have been indicted on serious corruption charges. Like many populists who rise to power campaigning against corruption, he has used his position to perpetuate it. According to Sheila Coronel, Rodrigo's brand of populism has largely been a failure compared to others. "Modi has built a grass roots political party and a political movement on the back of Hindu nationalism. Orban has articulated an intellectual justification for his rejection of liberal democracy and the liberal international order. Duterte suffers in comparison. His illiberalism may be less enduring, as he is bereft of a movement, party or ideology that will carry on his legacy. For the time being, it is only Duterte's dark charisma that holds the country in thrall."[16]

Rajoelina's charisma is decidedly sunnier, and he has built a dominant political party (albeit centered solely around him), but like Duterte, the lack of any broader vision for the country makes his position inherently more precarious than his current popularity suggests. Most Malagasy were impressed by Rajoelina's stand on corruption during the campaign, and view him as a president who cares about them. But they also see a president who has undermined institutional checks on presidential power by attempting to dissolve the Senate, install his cronies as regional governors and prohibit Ravalomanana from taking his rightful place at the head of the opposition. Unlike more notorious populists, he has not done things like crack down on the independent press or jail members of Ravalomanana's party, and yet newspaper editors and other intellectuals I talked to were fearful of his democratic orientation, not to mention his proven track record as a usurper.

Rajoelina came to power with financial backing from a host of shady characters, and he has been loath to jettison them so far. In fact, he has assembled around himself an army of devotees, one that extends far beyond the administration, to the police, the Parliament and the military. Madagascar's political campaigns after Ratsiraka's disastrous tryst with socialism have been devoid of any deep ideological struggle; as several people told me, the candidate who distributes the best t-shirt and delivers the most bags of rice to voters usually wins. Once in power the winners forego the pursuit of any policy platform other than "development" and focus on doing whatever it takes to keep power. But if Rajoelina has been short on ideology, he has nonetheless played his hand brilliantly since taking office, outmaneuvering Ravalomanana and tightening his control of the state. Liberal voices among the opposition, wracked by infighting until very recently, are on the verge of being drowned out entirely. The most obvious result of Rajoelina's rise and the consolidation of one-party rule is a remarkable lack of dissenting voices throughout the island.

But all is not lost for democracy, either on the great island or elsewhere in the world. The good news is that the champions of illiberal democracy like Rajoelina, who have spent years constructing a seemingly impregnable political fortress, may soon reap the whirlwind. The legitimacy of populist dictators depends upon a carefully nurtured belief among the masses that their leader is representing *them*. But this belief inevitably begins to erode as these leaders try to seize more power for themselves. As Mounck has written, the new populist playbook raises the specter of a vicious cycle: whenever a national crisis threatens a populist regime's popularity, its leaders feel tempted to resort to greater levels of repression to stay in power. But the more it cracks down, the more the regime loses whatever legitimacy it had as a champion of the people. When enough of the population sees through the façade and recognizes that their leaders no longer work for them, they will begin to resist.[17]

Rajoelina should heed this warning. Like other populists, he will soon be forced to deliver on his promises to maintain popular support. He himself invited the Malagasy people to wait a year to judge his performance, and most have been willing to do so. That year is up, and many are questioning whether they are any better off and whether Madagascar is any closer to escaping its deep poverty trap. The island seems to suffer through a national crisis of one sort or another every couple of years, and when the next cataclysm arrives – whether it be the Coronavirus, or a catastrophic cyclone or drought – his sedulous efforts to accrue more and more power will put him at the eye of a political storm. And that could produce a crisis of its own.

* * *

I went back to several Rajoelina supporters to gain greater insight into the man that had just been elected to lead Madagascar for the next five years. Former Senator Rabetsaroana, who switched his allegiance from Ravalomanana to Rajoelina at a critical time in the nation's recent history, gives Rajoelina credit for learning on the job quickly. "Remember that he had four years – from 2009-13 – to prepare for this presidency. During that time he watched, he learned, and he became a better leader. I fully support him now and think he is making things better. He is ready now to lead the nation."

I asked the ex-Senator whether Madagascar is a democracy today. Once again, he didn't hold back when assessing the leadership present on the island today. "It's getting there," he said. "For too long though the politicians forgot that there are 25 million people living in misery here. They thought only of themselves. Once the political class starts acting for everyone we will have a real democracy. The problem is that the country is led by people who aren't ready to lead. They came to their position by chance and they are not responsible enough to carry out their duties as they should." This is especially tragic, he believes, because the island has so much potential. "We have everything here – food, water, minerals, mountains, beaches. It's a beautiful country and there is no reason why we should be so poor."

The exodus of bright, young Malagasy who leave the country in search of better opportunities in richer, more stable countries – the island's "brain drain" – has made the process of democracy building that much harder. "One of the most important things we can do in Madagascar is to build a middle class," Rabetsaroana told me. "That will create more jobs for people – better jobs – and make our democracy stronger. But the problem is that we have so many educated people leaving the country to live a better life elsewhere – in France, the United States, Canada. I went to France to study and I enjoyed my time there, but I always knew I would come back here because I love my country. There was so much poverty here and I knew I had to come back. We need more people to stay and help us build it for the future. Three thousand doctors have left the country, and that has a huge effect on development."

Monja Roindefo, the former Prime Minister under Rajoelina during the HAT and current leader of a small political party based in Antananarivo, had a markedly different view of the president. He is dismissive of Rajoelina's accomplishments and his promises of the future. Perhaps this is to be expected.

After the coup in 2009, Roindefo became the sacrificial lamb for the regime as a response to the international outcry over Ravalomanana's overthrow. He was replaced as Prime Minister after a long, drawn out process, and the years have not alleviated his disappointment, if not bitterness, over his treatment by Rajoelina and his camp. When he was fired he initially refused to leave because of what he claimed were constitutional concerns. As he told me, "I was supposed to be replaced by a consensus candidate acceptable to all the parties. But Rajoelina just tried to appoint his own man." The HCC then blocked Rajoelina's attempt to oust him until a more suitable candidate could be found. Roindefo told me he left with no regrets: "I'm proud of the work we did in nine months: violent crime went down, the private sector was energized, and we greatly reduced corruption in the government."

The former Prime Minister refused to state whether he supported the president or one of the major opposition parties. "I can't say I'm in opposition; you can't really define me. I am an *alternative* to the current regime." He preferred to answer my questions about the president by focusing on his policies rather than the man himself, other than to say "We don't talk anymore." But he could not find much to recommend even regarding the president's policies. "I am deeply skeptical of the development projects being undertaken now. They leave no lasting impact on Madagascar. We're not undertaking the right projects, as evidenced by the fact that poverty is not declining. The president's development plan has many weaknesses and it doesn't really advance the Sustainable Development Goals established by the UN."

There had been several recent newspaper articles in the country detailing a range of issues troubling the country, and Roindefo proceeded to lay most of them at the president's doorstep.

"Why can't he master all the problems now popping up? Cattle theft – even by the gendarmes; the negotiations he's undertaking with the oil companies to ensure gas and energy. I'm skeptical of the outcome of his policies and I can't endorse them. The country is going badly in all areas. Rajoelina sends bad signals to our international partners with some of the things he tries to do. The government is trying to outsmart the international community by changing the legal entities [it creates to oversee foreign aid], but they are much too sophisticated for that. The president appointed governors of the regions but the constitution says they should be governed by the regional chiefs and elected. The international community won't accept that. Sooner or later there will be bad consequences from all of this."

He was particularly critical of Rajoelina's plan to build new cities like Tanamasoandro to alleviate some of the pressures building on Antananarivo and other major metropolitan areas. "The idea of new cities is great, but there's no investment in the existing cities, so what will happen to them? As for the new city outside of Tana, it has been badly planned, and that's why there are protests. And he calls the protesters 'enemies of development'? This is like the rhetoric of a dictator. He ignores what they say. It's their historic land, but he wants to send them to Tulear so he can proceed with his project. This reminds me of the Indian removal in your country two centuries ago." He sat back and waved his hand. "But they won't listen to anything I say. They'll just say I'm against them personally."

As we've seen, Madagascar is not a country with deeply held ideological beliefs about the role of government in society. Roindefo picked up this theme and identified it as a challenge for democracy. "Part of the problem here is that the parties don't have different visions or ideologies, just different interests. We are at a crossroads and we need leaders who have a real vision. Otherwise we are on the verge of a serious crisis in

5-10 years. More African and Chinese will come here to manage our projects because they have the expertise. It may result in the type of xenophobia we saw in South Africa recently. Why can't Malagasy be trained to run these things? We are at the bottom tier of African development, and you have to ask why." With regard to the South, his native land and the region where his father became a powerful national leader in an earlier era, Roindefo was equally pessimistic. "In the South, I haven't seen any long-term impact from the aid projects going there. There is massive aid there but I'm skeptical that much will change. The EU and World Food Program teams monitor the droughts that hit the area but I'm not sure we're all ready for the next severe drought and famine there."

He saved his greatest impatience for the ongoing corruption that plagues the island's democratic struggles. His candor about the need to participate in such graft was astounding to me, even after hearing dozens of other politicians deplore it as well. "Here you have to buy an election, and to do that you have to have money, and to get money you have to plunder the country. And that's what our politicians do. The international community knows that happens but they don't care so long as we have an election. But there's no real choice for voters. Poor people – the vast majority of the population – will vote for a new t-shirt, because if you're living on $2 a day that t-shirt means a lot. In the end it shows how powerful poverty can be during an election. So nothing will change until the high level of poverty changes."

Roindefo's comments were tinged with resentment toward the man that had dismissed him so unceremoniously, but his insights into the weaknesses of the current president were enlightening nonetheless. Many Malagasy, however, are much more willing to give Rajoelina the benefit of the doubt, at least for a couple of more years, and some verge on idolatry. Several young staff members I met believed he would undoubtedly turn the country around. One of them is Patrick Rasamoela, a bright, well-spoken young man in his thirties who frequently appears on Malagasy television as a spokesperson for the government. Rasamoela met Rajoelina at the end of 2017 and instantly agreed to join his campaign for president. After Rajoelina's victory he served as the President's representative to the Ministry of Foreign Affairs. Rasamoela is also an entrepreneur in the software business, winning the Tony Elumelu Entrepreneurship Award in 2018 given to young African entrepreneurs. He told me he joined politics to set an example for the rest of his fellow citizen and to devote his time to improving their quality of life. He tempered his ambition with disarming bursts of humility, as when he told me "I want to change the country but I can't do it by myself; that's everyone's job."

Over the years Rasamoela has come to see Rajoelina as a man of the people who also values his privacy. "There are only three people truly close to the President personally," he related. "The first is his wife. The second is Mamy Ravatomanga, the richest man in Madagascar and the principal financier of his campaign. The third is Niaina Andriantsitohaina, the [now former] Minister of Foreign Affairs and the fourth richest man in Madagascar. Everyone else is kept at a professional distance." Rasamoela told me the President takes no salary for his position as a way to show people how serious he is about serving them and not himself. As he and other aides told me similar stories about the President's selflessness, it became apparent to me that Rajoelina, still a young man himself, liked to surround himself with young, smart acolytes whose unstinting loyalty he could depend upon. Rasamoela played this role perfectly, and went on to hold a series of increasingly important roles in the administration.

Lovatiana Gontare Ramaroson, his former aide who now serves as Chief of Staff at the Department of Agriculture, is another loyal defender of the president. While other supporters seem to have made a tactical decision to sign up with Rajoelina, the rising star who had come dominate politics in their country, she is a true believer in his vision. Whenever I started to feel cynical about the island's leadership or its future, one conversation with Lova made me reconsider all of my conclusions about the president. She felt a political loyalty to the man that I didn't often find in Madagascar, and I actually found it refreshing to be reminded that not everyone here had become resigned to the corruption and empty promises of the establishment.

She told me that in 2013, when Rajoelina was effectively barred from running for president by the constitutional court, he took the decision in stride. "He wasn't disappointed at all. He accepted the decision gracefully," she said. "I knew then that he was a humble man." As for Lova, she went back to school, getting a Master's degree in Diplomacy from the National School of Administration. "We kept in touch during those years out of power," she said. "A couple of times he told me he wanted to return to politics because he felt he still had a role to play in the future of the country. But he didn't need to run again in 2018 to prove anything. He had already been president and been the most powerful man in the country. He had achieved all his goals and risen to the very top of the system. He could have stayed home with his family rather than subject himself again to the attacks, the endless stress, the long hours of work. But he wanted to help the country again."

Ramaroson talked about Rajoelina's leadership style and who he listens to in government. "Actually, his closest adviser is his wife," she told me, echoing Rasamoela. She said his wife's desire to stay out of politics actually helps them, because he knows her advice is coming not from personal ambition but from a genuine desire to help him and their country. Then she talked about why she – Ramaroson – had stayed loyal to him for so long. "He is an inspiration as a man. He has a very clear vision of his life and of life in general. He's really smart. He had a normal life when he was young but I think he always knew he had a huge destiny. As a boss, he's someone you want to work with. He's a real leader and he will succeed in the end." She said they talked at length after his election victory in 2018 and what it meant for the future. "Now he really wants to put his stamp on his country and do the best he can for the next generation. He told me: 'We are going to do something for this country, Lova. We are going to change this country."

"I'm very proud to work for him. He inspired me to dream of becoming president myself someday. He told me that as a woman, I would have to work twice as hard as a man to succeed – and I saw this when I was in Parliament - but that I should believe in my dreams and follow them despite any hardships. He's like a big brother to his staff, but one who listens, one who trusts. We all share a mutual respect with him, and I think that is the basis for all the important relationships that he has."

One of the president's goals is to give the capital city a facelift. He rebuilt the Hotel de Ville on Independence Avenue and Lova was the first person to get married in it once it reopened. He is building a new city project, Tanamasoandro, outside of Tana. He also declared a goal of making Tamatave like Miami. "People laughed when he said that but he's serious about it," Ramaroson said. She told me he wants to expand access to education for young people and end the island's apprehension about giving any responsibility to young people, whether in business or politics. "He really cares about their future. He once asked me, how can they have a good life if they don't get an opportunity while they're still young?"

Ramaroson is convinced the President will govern not for the financial interests that put him in power but for the great majority of Malagasy locked in a cycle of poverty. "Poverty is his biggest concern. I toured the poor districts of Tana with him after the election. He saw the poorest slums in the city, people living outside with no house, no running water. The president has a big heart. In the car afterwards he asked me, 'How do they do it? How can they survive like that? And how do they keep smiling? No, we cannot accept this. We are going to do something for them; we have to make sure their children have access to education and create enough jobs for them. I can't leave them like that.' There were tears in his eyes when he said that."

Lova said Rajoelina was over his feud with Ravalomanana. She understood why people wanted to rehash their rivalry but was hopeful they and the country could one day move past it. She did her best to place those dark days in a broader historical perspective. And she ended with a heartfelt appeal to focus on what's changing in Madagascar and how important that change can be:

The negative image after 2009 is the story of our country. We have always had a negative image since I've been alive. But you know, all countries have good and bad stories, not just Madagascar. Europe went through its world wars, Rwanda went through a genocide. Now we are starting a good story. I really believe that. Yes, the things that happened, they happened. The important thing now is to focus on what comes next. We in the government have to write the next story, and the president is already creating it. He has made mistakes like everyone but he has learned from them. Now he just wants to give back to his country. I share his impulse to do good things for Madagascar. I want to write a good story and educate my son in this story.

Historically, Madagascar has not had a patriotic spirit. You don't really hear people here saying how much they love their country, like they do in America. Now, you see that people are starting to believe in their country, to feel patriotism in their hearts. I am raising my son to always ask, what can I do for my country? The president is creating that sentiment. And he pushes others to change the things that they can change, because he can't do everything by himself and he knows that. Each person has to do his part to help the country advance, each of us must make an effort and make sacrifices toward a greater objective of building Madagascar.

* * *

After Rajoelina's victory the country turned its attention to the legislative elections scheduled for May 2019. The country's electoral commission, CENI, tried to impose some order on the process by issuing a list of campaign rules and regulations, then following up with occasional harangues regarding the latest egregious violation, but with no threat of any penalty the candidates simply ignored them. Several candidates alleged fraud in their districts, and one well known candidate was inexplicably left off the ballot in Tamatave province. Ravalomanana's party, TIM, pledged to fight the results, claiming they stayed silent after the presidential election but would not do so this time. In the end, 100 candidates appeared before the HCC to allege fraud or abuse during their respective elections. Once again, nothing came of it.

The campaign came to be viewed as the third round of the Ravalomanana-Rajoelina feud. And once again, Rajoelina dealt a decisive blow to Ravalomanana and his party, with the new president's IRD party winning 84 seats to just 16 for Ravalomanana's TIM. Independent parties also made a strong showing, winning 46 seats. But the biggest loser ended up being Malagasy democracy itself. After almost half of all registered voters participated in the presidential election, less than 25% voted in the parliamentary elections, prompting Ravalomanana to say afterwards that people in the country were "fed up with politics" after back-to-back elections and the constant stench of corruption coming from the government. Turnout in both contests was so low that one has to agree with the ex-president, and conclude that Madagascar's people are simply not heavily invested in democracy yet.[18]

An editorial in the daily newspaper *Midi Madagaskar* in the midst of the campaign captured voters' apathy perfectly:

It is an election campaign without passion that takes place under the eyes of a population that's rather uninterested. There is no debate of ideas proposed by the candidates, who are content to simply make vague promises to voters in their constituency. Only a few stalwarts still resort to the old propaganda methods that have proven themselves in the past. Popular rallies with fiery speeches are still recipes for votes, but they do not guarantee a real connection with the people today. The chaos and disrespect of electoral rules are the defining characteristics of this campaign, which is mostly taking place in a joyous mess.[19]

And yet, this being Madagascar, some people still cared enough to try to take matters into their own hands. As results from the election started to leak out, the electoral commission's office in Tulear province was set on fire the night before the final tabulation of votes was announced. Almost all of the voting records in the office were lost forever. The commission said the results in Tulear were not affected, but it was one more sign of the instability inherent in the nation's elections.

* * *

A trend is developing across Africa, one that combines authoritarianism with competitive multiparty elections. Indeed, since the return of multiparty politics in the early 1990s, the most typical kind of regime in Africa seems to be an electoral autocracy, a system that mixes tried and true authoritarian practices with regular elections. In good times such regimes use the natural advantages of incumbency and whatever legitimacy they may have earned, only to switch to fraud, repression and even violence when necessary to stay in power. This schizophrenic approach to governing, according to some experts, explains how regimes like those in Mozambique and Tanzania have managed to stay in power. Others worry about a domino effect across the continent, as new leaders who are elected without any predisposition towards autocracy see the electoral success of leaders like those in Uganda and Rwanda employing a harder-edged authoritarianism to fend off any challengers. Such success may also influence international donors who prize economic efficiency above truly free societies. As we'll see below, quasi-authoritarian regimes often benefit from the willingness of foreign governments and international organizations to overlook failures in democratic governance so long as elections continue to be held.[20]

Madagascar has slowly drifted into all of these traps. Rajoelina has consolidated power to such an extent, and in such a short amount of time, that it's hard to see anyone challenging him anytime soon. The world already knows to distrust his professed commitment to democracy thanks to his unconstitutional seizure of power in 2009. But Rajoelina's control over the presidential and legislative branches gives him such built-in advantages over any would-be opponent that he may never need to resort to fraud or vote rigging to remain president for another term. And yet with a Parliament in thrall to him and an independent judiciary reluctant to challenge him over anything but the most egregious violations, one can legitimately ask how democratic Madagascar really is.

One widely used yardstick for anointing a country a democracy examines whether power has rotated twice in two successive free elections, a test Madagascar has passed thanks to its two elections in 1993 and 1996. Two leading surveys of democracy around the world, however, judge it only partly democratic. Freedom House ranks every country in the world using its Global Freedom Score, an index based on each country's political rights and civil liberties observed during a given year. Their 2019 report made a bigger splash than usual by reporting that 2018 was the 13th consecutive year of decline in global freedom and concluding that democracy is in retreat, though the overall losses are still shallow compared to the gains of the late 20th century. Freedom House ranks Madagascar as an Electoral Democracy (barely) but says that the country is only "Partly Free" overall. It gave Madagascar an aggregate political freedom score of 56 out of 100 in both 2018 and 2019, with a modest improvement to 61 out of 100 in 2020, after Rajoelina's election. As points of reference, South Africa received a score of 79/100, the United States came in at 86/100, France earned a 90/100 and Canada received an almost perfect score of 99/100.[21]

The Economist Intelligence Unit largely concurs, calling Madagascar a "hybrid regime" in its 2019 report on democracy around the world. A hybrid regime is the EIU's third tier out of four, meaning Madagascar has a long way to go to become a full democracy. In hybrids, elections have substantial irregularities that often prevent them from being both free and fair. Government pressure on opposition candidates and parties is occasionally present, corruption is widespread, and civil society is weak. There are also serious weaknesses in the functioning of government and in political participation by the electorate. Madagascar's overall score in 2019 was 5.64, up from 5.22 the year before, while the world average was 5.44. Sub-Saharan Africa had a score of just 4.26, and Madagascar, despite all of its problems, now ranks in the top ten democracies in the region. The country has made incremental improvement every year since 2012, according to the EIU's rankings, but is still not back to its 2006 level of 5.82 (when the world average was 5.52).[22]

The island thus qualifies as an electoral democracy and sits slightly above the world average for democratic practices, but is nowhere close to the leading democracies outside its region. More importantly, while these statistics tell us that Madagascar's overall level of democracy is low, they don't really explain why. To understand the reasons behind the country's lack of political freedom we need to explore four major weaknesses in its political system and its electoral process. The first is corruption, a problem so widespread in Malagasy culture and history that it has persisted for generations even while millions plead for its disappearance. The second is the ethnic divide between the Merina and coastal tribes that undermines national unity and breeds distrust. The third weakness is the lack of a unified opposition, which allows Rajoelina the opportunity to govern mostly as he sees fit. And the final flaw has nothing to do with Madagascar and everything to do with the international community, which continually opts to look the other way when elections are less than free and fair.

Nothing is more corrosive to Malagasy democracy than the rampant corruption that now plagues all levels of its society. Madagascar ranked 158th out of 180 countries in Transparency International's Corruption Perceptions Index in 2019, but this actually sells the problem short. There are so many examples of corruption I could cite from my time there, but one high-profile example that garnered national attention when it happened will suffice. In 2018 three Malagasy delegates to the United Nations were tasked with selling their country's UN residence in Manhattan as part of their mission's relocation to a larger building. Not content with moving to a nicer house, the men hatched a plan to underreport the sales price of the residence to their government, who presumably would never check the details of the transaction. The mansion sold for $10 million, but the three officials reported the price to their bosses in Antananarivo as $7 million, pocketing $3 million for themselves. They got away with the scheme for several months before the national anti-corruption agency (BIANCO) caught up with them, landing them on the front page of Madagascar's newspapers and in Antananarivo's largest prison. This type of brazen corruption at the highest levels of government is not as common as the more garden variety requests for bribes and other favors that most Malagasy undergo on a daily basis, but it happens nonetheless and does untold damage to the country's economy and reputation.

BIANCO has had a mixed record of fighting graft since its inception over ten years ago. Most presidents tolerate the agency as a necessary evil, one required by the international community and business investors as the cost of joining the global economy. Their hope, clear but unspoken, is that it nets enough high-level actors without probing too close to home. Similarly, BIANCO's effectiveness is also limited by the mandates of the nation's leaders. In May 2019, for example, the agency processed its annual report and regretfully reported that it was not able to achieve its goal to reduce public perception of corruption in the country, "due to a lack of political will." The Director General cited as examples fraudulent public works projects and occasional embezzlement, and estimated the total loss to the state from these scams at over $300,000. He deplored that the agency "was not able to work in all serenity" to achieve its goal. He was clearly referring to the amount of political pressure put on BIANCO from the highest levels of the government.

Laza Eric Donat Andrianirina is the new Director General of BIANCO, taking over in August of 2019. Before that he was in charge of investigations at Bianco from 2007-15. I met him on November 26 at his office, which was on the outskirts of Tana, demonstrating either its independence or its irrelevance, depending on your point of view. Clearly concerned about the angle I would take with him, he was the only person I interviewed on the island who insisted that I submit all my questions to him in advance and in writing; he then proceeded to ignore most of them during our interview, which was cut short after only 20 minutes because he had suddenly run out of time.

Nevertheless, Andrianirina was adamant that BIANCO is fully independent from any political pressure. The 2007 law that created the agency mandates independence, he said. Also, the appointment process for the Director General is careful to avoid any single institution's influence. First, a commission conducts an exhaustive search for the position and selects three final candidates; then the president chooses one from the short list presented by the commission. That process, while not a total prophylactic against meddling, meets a minimum threshold for independence. Once in power, the Director General operates with a modicum of freedom. He can name his own investigators and is not beholden even to the Attorney General, who is powerless to stop any investigation even if it's against a government minister.

Andrianirina went out of his way to assure me of his own personal integrity. "I don't receive any orders from any political or judicial officials," he told me. "I haven't received any pressure yet. If it does come, they won't do it directly, that's for sure. But it could happen indirectly and I'm ready for that. I will stay professional even if they try to influence me. I won't sell my soul. I have a reputation to uphold."

Others I spoke to indicated that BIANCO had a monumental task ahead of it, regardless of the good intentions of its leader. One prominent journalist in Antananarivo who has been covering the issue for over a decade (and who agreed to speak to me only on the condition of anonymity) told me the problem is getting worse, not better. "We've had corruption here before but never this bad. The last Parliament was the most corrupt we've ever had, unfortunately. They vote for laws in exchange for bribes." She laid part of the blame with the High Constitutional Court, which she said allowed the corruption to continue. "The President paid many deputies in Parliament to switch parties, which is not constitutional, but the court allowed it." She echoed others I had spoken to in her skepticism of BIANCO's willingness or ability to clean things up. "BIANCO is doing what they can, but they're obliged to stop investigating after a certain point because of pressure from the top. They're also compromised because they need funding from the government and so can't always investigate them freely."

Sylvain Rabetsaroana, the former Senator, identified corruption as Madagascar's biggest problem immediately when I met him in his office in May of 2019. "Of course it's corruption," he said. "How else do you explain the fact that the state had a monopoly on various enterprises – the national airline, the telecom company – and they all went bankrupt? It's obvious to me that people in the government were stealing. What you have to understand is that the political class in Madagascar are thieves. They live off the state. That's what they do. And they know they probably won't be in office very long, so they have an incentive to take as much as they can while they're there. And the World Bank knows about it too."

Rabetsaroana then listed the most corrupt presidents he had seen in his lifetime and those that were more honest. One of his takes surprised me. "Ratsiraka wasn't corrupt – he just loved the power of being president. I don't think anyone accused him of stealing from the state." The former Senator went on to blame a certain ethnic community for taking corruption to new heights in recent years. "Later, the problem became the Karana – the Indo-Pakistani community. They started paying the president and other politicians, and the corruption became too much." He went on to defend Rajoelina's early record on corruption. "The President takes the issue very seriously. He has already thrown some high-level people in prison and made it clear he won't tolerate stealing."

Rajoelina seems to be entirely serious about ending corruption in his country, announcing zero tolerance for it soon after taking office. Several people I talked to, both among his supporters and his political opponents, gave him credit for taking on the issue so directly. He continues to make it at least a rhetorical point of emphasis. In August 2019, for example, he convened a conference of senior judges to denounce corruption and ordered the Justice Minister to deal harshly with any judges found to be accepting bribes. Yet the problem is bigger than just one man, and corruption will certainly outlast his presidency, even if he serves for several terms. I personally witnessed buses on the national road to and from Tulear being stopped at multiple checkpoints along the road by policeman demanding a few dollars from drivers. Meanwhile, surveys within the country reported most Malagasy still had to deal with corruption on a regular basis.[23]

Patrick Rasamoela told me an interesting story about the new president's stance on corruption. When Rajoelina got elected in 2019 he told his senior campaign staff that most of them would soon have important government positions, but that he expected them all to be clean; he would have no sympathy for them if they got caught practicing corruption. "You will be on your own then; I won't help you," he said. Rasamoela added that one reason corruption has proven so hard to slow down in Madagascar is that elections have now become very expensive. He told me it takes $20 million to run a legitimate presidential campaign in Madagascar. That's a lot of money in Madagascar, and the donors presumably want something for their investment. Echoing Rabetsaroana, he told me the Karana finance most of these campaigns. Another reason is that government officials need to dress well and drive a nice car to get respect in Madagascar's political system. This forces them to look for other sources of income, though he himself has managed to live on his salary alone.

Monja Roindefo also identified corruption as a major obstacle to the island's political development, and for him it goes back much further. "We have always had a culture of generosity here. People expect rewards for doing something for someone. First it was a cow or a goat, now it's money. Second, poverty and inequality cause some people to take advantage of their position, such that now they expect payment as their right. The situation is not getting better. But it can change if the right example is set by our leaders. Otherwise, why stop if the next guy is doing it?"

To see just how rampant corruption was in Madagascar, I spoke to a policeman in Antananarivo named "Rindra." He joined the force in 2017 after acing the entrance exam and finishing near the very top of his class during basic training, thus guaranteeing himself a job offer. He told me that others were not so lucky. "For every 1,000 police officers accepted each year, 900 of them have to pay to get in or use family connections. The typical payment is four million Ariary. Then, once they are accepted, most offer bribes of up to another six million Ariary to choose their post (traffic, crime prevention, etc.). Their salary is only 600,000 Ariary a month." As a result, he said, twenty percent of their income comes from corruption.

Corruption at the police department flows from top to bottom, or perhaps the other way around. "People at the Ministry who have office jobs make more than those working the streets," Rindra related, since they can demand bribes before giving their signatures on important documents people need. "The Directors at the Ministry of Public Security make their money that way. Plus the regular officers have to make annual payments to the Directors just to keep their jobs at the same post." Those who don't pay risk being sent to remote regions of the country to battle the *dahalo* or other armed groups.

Rindra hasn't seen any real change in the system of corruption within the national police since Rajoelina's election. "But now we have to offer up someone to BIANCO every so often so the President can show his supporters and the donors that he is waging war against corruption. It's mostly symbolic." He understands that corruption hinders the country's development but he sees it as a necessary evil. In fact, he believes it actually helps people here get along with their daily lives. "If there wasn't a system of corruption no one could get anything done." This, of course, was his view of Malagasy society as presently constituted, which was all he had ever known; ridding the culture completely free of bribes seemed almost unfathomable to him. What he didn't seem to consider was that if by some miracle the whole system ended everyone would be living on a level playing field and there would be no reason to bribe someone, making everyone better off.

Rindra finished on a note of contrition but also seemed resigned to taking bribes if it continued to be the only way to ensure a basic quality of life. "I do feel bad when I participate in corruption," he told me. "I went to university and so I'm better educated than most people on the force. This wasn't my plan, to become a police offer and start taking bribes from people. But I had no choice, I couldn't find any other work, and now I have to pay my superiors to keep my job, otherwise I'll be sent to the 'hot zones' around the country. So I have to keep earning and paying." To fix the problem, Rindra would start by paying higher salaries to public officials, so they don't have to resort to corruption to maintain some semblance of a decent life. He also thought prosecuting people at higher levels, a job BIANCO is supposed to be doing, would set a better example. "We shouldn't just focus on the police. Putting some members of Parliament in prison for *their* corruption would send a strong message that the President is serious about the problem."

* * *

The ethnic divide between the Merina of the high plateaus and the coastal tribes is a real and enduring problem in the country, and the second weakness of the island's democracy. The Merina are immensely proud of their heritage as the descendants of the first kings and queens of Madagascar, and rightfully so, but they are also guilty of a certain arrogance toward the other tribes that can quickly morph into resentment when those tribes assert their numerical superiority (as a collective group) and challenge Merina power. One Merina friend I had in Antananarivo believes the old caste system still predominates among her fellow Merina, in a tacit agreement of exclusion that they are smart enough to keep to themselves. She traces her family line back to the noble caste of the monarchical period, and insists her caste still retains some racial purity. "The noble caste here is divided into seven groups," she told me. "All nobles adhere to those groups but don't talk about it in public. Only Merina are accepted as nobility. Nobles may only marry nobles, but it's not safe to talk about that since we might be killed for it."

The Merina, the traditional ruling class of the island, have come to feel besieged by the steady rise of other ethnic groups. And while their fear might seem paranoid at first, this phenomenon is not unique to Madagascar. Around the world, dominant ethnic majorities increasingly see themselves as imperiled minorities, in what many are calling a "majority with a minority complex." Demographic change and, surprisingly, the rise of democracy itself come to be viewed as a threat to the traditionally dominant group, who fear a permanent loss of status as other ethnicities grow in number or in stature. Under this theory, when both sides in an ethnic conflict begin to perceive themselves as the aggrieved group, vulnerable to being outnumbered or displaced, violence can erupt. A violent turn can occur even in democracies, and especially in ones with weak institutions.[24] The Merina, while not a majority overall in Madagascar, are still the largest single tribe – a "majority minority" – and have by far the most power through their control of the capital city and many of the key positions in government. They guard their status jealously, well aware of the higher birth rates along the coasts and the simmering resentments against their privileged position.

On the other side of the divide, the coastal peoples will never forget their enslavement at the hands of the Merina and others to whom the Merina once sold them as slaves. This is somewhat ironic, for during the centuries when commercial slavery was developing in size and intensity, it was the interior of Madagascar that served as the main reservoir for the slave trading kings of the coasts. Only later did the Merina monarchy become a slave power and seek to expand its kingdom in order to capture slaves from other tribes. When France finally abolished slavery in 1896, colonial officials estimated that 400,000 people categorized as slaves existed at that time, half of whom lived in the central highlands, thus accounting for a substantial proportion of the island's population. In any event, the subjugation of the coastal tribes over centuries of Merina rule was brutal and enduring, and the resentment of this fact, together with the stigma of slave ancestry, which still exists, remains a challenge to democracy for the foreseeable future.[25]

One night I joined a group of French doctors in the northern city of Diego Suarez for drinks and dinner at a local family's house. The young man mixing mojitos for us spent half the night railing at the central government's unwillingness to give him a passport. "It's because I'm not Merina," he told us. "In Antananarivo they make it harder for us to do anything – get a job, get a passport, anything that requires an official signature from the capital." His father chimed in with what sounded like nostalgia for the colonial era. "There used to be a French consulate here in Diego that made things so much easier for us. But the Merina in Tana closed it so they could have more control over the coastal people." His daughter, a slim young woman sporting an impressive Afro, seemed much more resigned to it. "Yeah, they like to treat us like we're nothing to them," she said. "But don't worry," she said with a wink, "we give it right back to them when we have to."

It isn't as if the ethnic divide on the island is entirely taboo. Everyone I met was willing to talk about it, but the Merina in particular rarely brought it up themselves. When I asked former Senator Rabetsaroana about the claims of discrimination, he addressed it in his usual straightforward fashion.

It's terrible, but it exists. And the worst thing is that we as a nation don't really talk about it. We're sly in the way we discuss it, and most people will only talk about it indirectly. But it's blocking our development as a nation. In a way we're hypocrites because we say we have no problem, but believe me, tribalism is a big problem here. When President Rajoelina said 'I am Merina but my heart is coastal' that was a big moment for us all. He wants to be the uniter of Madagascar. The last two presidents were tribalists. And before them, Albert Zafy was even worse. The problem goes both ways, you know. We Merina have a certain arrogance sometimes and the *cotiers* like to call us 'bourgeois.' The coastal people are 30 years behind the highlanders in education and culture and they resent that. But try talking to other politicians about this problem – they are too timid to even address it, and we need to change that in our society.

Former Prime Minister Roindefo, a proud member of one of the southern tribes, sees the ethnic divide as real but perhaps too complex to be categorized as outright discrimination. Part of the divide is the result of Merina oppression, he acknowledges, but some of it is simply the result of each tribe's efforts to hold on to its distinctive culture. He traces the problem back to the monarchy, and faults all of the island's leaders for its endurance.

170

"We haven't tackled it seriously since the end of colonization, which of course perpetuated it. There has been no serious integration since. The separate customs and characteristics of the tribes still exist. But we need a policy of integration. One way would be to have the government start sending representatives of different tribes to their non-native regions. But people are right to complain that the national government is still 90% Merina. We haven't achieved social, ethnic homogeneity yet, and part of the reason is that our leaders still only know their own culture."

Thankfully, ethnic violence occurs infrequently and only when national political crises erupt. One reason may be the prevalence of a single Malagasy language across all tribes, which is said to be an antidote to ethnic tensions. Claims of a common language on the island are something of a myth, however, and linguistic unity should not be considered a balm for the general wariness among the country's people. Yes, there is an official Malagasy language, but one with so many dialects and regional variations that the members of different tribes often can't understand each other, and several people laughed when I suggested that everyone in Madagascar speaks the same language. The regional differences in vocabulary and pronunciation are growing wider, not smaller, according to experts I spoke to, and French is only spoken by about half the population, and is thus in no way a *lingua franca*. A woman I met in Antananarivo who grew up in one of the Northern provinces told me she spent six months trying to adapt to the Merina dialect of the highlands. "I had to learn their language to communicate here," she told me. "Their language" was an interesting way of putting it, I thought.

A third weakness holding back Malagasy democracy is the ongoing lack of a strong opposition to the party in power. Much of this phenomenon is the direct result of populism's deleterious effect on democracy the world over. In robust democracies, the largest political party feels harassed by opposition parties but are tolerated to a high degree. In democracy's latest iteration, opposition parties are threats to be crushed, outlawed, and dismembered. Populism's impact in Madagascar became apparent almost immediately after the election of the new legislature in 2019, which wasted no time in passing a law stripping the opposition of much of its traditional power, effectively sidelining it in the coming debate over many of the nation's most pressing problems.[26] This set off alarm bells in Antananarivo and led to small-scale protests over what some called a second coup by Rajoelina and his allies.

Marc Ravalomanana, who has led the opposition in Madagascar since his overthrow in 2009, has valiantly tried to battle back, but the crushing defeats he and his party suffered in 2019 only reinforced their weakness. The new law targeting the opposition was clearly an attempt to remove his voice from the political scene. This kind of silencing of the opposition has a long history in Madagascar and only seems to be getting worse. When large swathes of the populace hear from only one source of authority, propaganda becomes truth in their minds, and alternative visions of society are dismissed. Questionable claims of economic progress and miracle cures for the Coronavirus are taken seriously, to the detriment of the country's future.

Ravalomanana's response to Parliament's gutting of his party is nevertheless instructive. He reacted by creating a new alliance, the RMDM, after reaching an agreement with 21 party leaders from across the island. The RMDM strives to be a robust opposition to Rajoelina's regime but holds very few seats in Parliament. Ravalomanana said it would hold the country's leaders accountable for the promises they make and shine a spotlight on any excesses committed by them, though he made sure to mention that it would not be a platform for overthrowing the government. He claimed that his movement represented the will of most Malagasy. "The idea is to preserve the interest of the majority and not just a part of the population and their relatives," he said.[27]

RMDM immediately denounced the new law passed by Rajoelina's IRD party, calling it contrary to the Constitution and an obvious effort to gag the opposition in Madagascar. "This law will only serve to nullify the power of the opposition and is already being used to prevent it from performing the tasks entrusted to it by the Constitution," Ravalomanana said. "But this is also an obstacle to democracy ... This bill is really an absurd interpretation of Section 14 of the Constitution that specifies the appointment powers of the leader of the opposition. That is to say, it is a law intended to reduce my power and the other opponents of the government ... who have the right to constitute an opposition, according to the Constitution."

Ravalomanana then looked for international support for his foundering party. He alerted the Southern Africa Development Community, then meeting in Tanzania, on the political situation in Madagascar. In an open letter addressed to the Secretary General of the SADC, the former Malagasy President stated his belief that the regime in place had violated democracy and was attempting to circumvent the country's Constitution. He went on to deplore the current regime and its impact on democracy in Madagascar:

With the current political manipulations, I wonder if this country will be governed in the same way as during the transition [after the coup], with the return of police forces to repress the opposition parties that hinder the current power. Was the bill drafted in the National Assembly written to target a few opposition leaders, including me? As leader of the opposition leading the RMDM, I have the legitimacy and the authority [to serve as opposition leader] in accordance with the Constitution and with the Malagasy people because I got the most votes cast after the current president and I was elected by the opposition parties...Madagascar will not develop without democracy, without good governance, and without respect for the rule of law. The RMDM that I lead with my colleagues will not stop criticizing the government when the conduct of national affairs brings no benefit to Madagascar and its people.[28]

Ravalomanana's passionate defense of the opposition party's right to be heard was impressive, but with less than 15% of the delegates in Parliament his power is increasingly on the wane. Rajoelina and his party have now successfully sidelined their opponents and have ample opportunity to run roughshod over them for the foreseeable future. One can only hope they will use their newfound power to rule in the interests of everyone, but early indications of their intentions don't hold much promise.

* * *

The final weakness in Madagascar's democracy has little to do with the island itself and everything to do with the anemic response of the international community. If developing countries like Madagascar aspire to reach a point of development where it can credibly claim to be a democracy – leave aside Denmark and just think Botswana – it will need outside actors to advocate for fair elections on its behalf and hold those who undermine the democratic process to account. Unfortunately, those few outside governments and organizations who care at all about the island have been only too happy to give its dubious elections a passing grade out of some curious combination of fear (of causing a crisis through its condemnation) and optimism (that questionable elections now will gradually turn into more efficient ones).

As we've seen earlier, a troubling pattern is emerging in Malagasy politics. Either a coup is launched or the loser of an election creates chaos by claiming the election was stolen from him – sometimes with great justification but often with none. Then the HCC steps in – the one institution to have earned widespread respect – and issues a verdict that forces everyone to fall back into line and allows the country to move forward again – until the next election. But the process is unforgivably destructive. This kind of selfishness on the part of its politicians is one reason why Madagascar is so unstable. The cynicism of the international community is another, more subtle cause of its turbulence.

In *The Despot's Accomplice,* his excellent book on the precarious state of democracy around the world, Brian Klaas argues that the West has become an unlikely enabler in the decline of democracy, in two ways: by deliberately embracing an undemocratic regime for geostrategic expediency (what he calls the "Saudi Arabia Effect"), and by setting incredibly low standards for counterfeit democracies (the "Madagascar Effect"). In Madagascar, according to Klaas, the West set such low expectations for the 2013 elections following Rajoelina's coup that almost any election would have earned its stamp of approval. Western institutions were quick to pronounce the 2013 contest free and fair despite its obvious flaws because it was more politically convenient than calling it what it actually was. Madagascar, he writes, has never been more than an "empty shell for democracy" and became less, not more democratic after that election.[29]

And the tepid Western approach to judging elections in Madagascar is now becoming common practice, Klaas believes. Something has changed in our evaluations of democracy around the world. Unless there is widespread violence, Western institutions now face great pressure to label an election free and fair because to do otherwise turns off foreign aid and dooms a country like Madagascar to an economic recession. As he points out, in the 2013 election in Madagascar, two major candidates were excluded, illicit funding was the main source of campaign financing (with no oversight), and millions of voters were left off the rolls because the last census was taken in 1993; and yet most Western governments called it free, transparent and credible.[30] This does a disservice to democracy around the world, he argues, and Western interests are far better served by genuine democratic partners than by counterfeit democracies like Madagascar.

Klaas reprised his argument after the 2018 election in an article for *Foreign Policy* magazine. Bribery and corruption, he wrote, take place each election cycle and yet no one is ever called to account. Rajoelina may have won against Ravalomanana in 2018 because he amassed so much money through corruption after the coup that he could simply buy more votes than anyone else. And the runoff system used in Madagascar allows candidates who garner just a couple of percentage points in the first round to sell their votes to the highest bidder left in the second round. The result is a sham election that calls into question Madagascar's claim to be a democracy:

"These days, it seems that any election that is nonviolent is deemed "good enough" for Africa. The United Nations highlighted the "peaceful and orderly" process in Madagascar. And the European Union, despite witnessing cash bribes in exchange for votes, still gave a firm thumbs-up to the election, peppering its initial report with praise for the "calm" process — a phrase commonly used in places where there's a threat of electoral bloodletting. But an overemphasis on an absence of violence can lead to an absence of democracy...Low-quality elections are being approved as high quality by the international community because the bar is too low. The message that gets sent to figures like Rajoelina is unmistakable: Buying votes with bags of cash is not an obstacle to securing a much-coveted badge of international legitimacy."[31]

Klaas's clear-eyed reflections on this subject are a welcome corrective to the mantra of democratic progress on the island.

Each of Madagascar's last two presidential elections has seen widespread corruption and abuses of power, but the international community has not even hesitated to proclaim them acceptable. This has the effect of propping up exactly the types of leaders the West says it wants to condemn. Rajoelina knew full well in 2018 that as long as no violence took place he could basically get away with anything to ensure his election, and as Klaas and the EU both pointed out, the man who actually deserves credit after the debacle was Ravalomanana, for his graceful acceptance of such a dubious outcome. The West's complicity in Rajoelina's rise is only half the story, of course. Malagasy leaders themselves are responsible for ultimately restoring the country's democratic future in a sustainable way. But foreign organizations like the UN and the EU are perpetuating Madagascar's intolerably weak democracy with a wink and a nod. The failure of the international community to insist on real elections only encourages candidates in Madagascar to disrespect the outcomes of its elections, a phenomenon that dates back to Ratsiraka's refusal to concede defeat and leave the presidential palace in both 1993 and 2001. A culture of rejecting electoral results and threatening violence is never a positive step in building a democracy, but when foreign actors refuse to make any attempt to hold developing countries to a higher standard, is it any wonder that losing candidates and their supporters feel tempted to protest against a rigged system by taking matters into their own hands?

What happens next in Madagascar is anyone's guess. With his cool, self-assured, unflappable demeanor, Rajoelina is an expert at giving the impression of being a man of the people while keeping almost everyone at a distance. Discerning his true intentions and any sort of political ideology is an exercise in reading tea leaves. One clue to his hopes for Madagascar might be found by considering the small list of other African leaders he holds in high regard. In 2019 Rajoelina invited

Rwandan President Paul Kagame to Antananarivo to celebrate the country's independence day. It was a telling choice. Kagame has earned iconic status both in Africa and abroad for the miraculous transformation of his country following its descent into genocide in 1994. Rwanda has boasted impressive rates of economic growth and societal transformation, but has also suffered intense criticism for the stifling of its political opposition and its weak record on human rights. Rajoelina apparently holds only admiration for Kagame. "The President told me he wants to imitate Paul Kagame with everything he has done for Rwanda," Rasamoela related in the days leading up to Kagame's visit. "One day we were talking about it and he said 'I took power about the same age that Kagame did, and in the next 20 years I hope to achieve what he did in Rwanda over the last 20 years.'"

Others have speculated on the link between the two as well. A long editorial in the days prior to independence day appeared in *Le Tribune*, one of Madagascar's leading newspapers, wondering how conscious the mimicry by Rajoelina actually was. It is worth quoting at length, not only to understand Rajoelina's hopes for Madagascar but to hear a leading Malagasy editorialist's views on the importance of democracy to the island.[32]

The Rwandan Miracle, 25 years after the genocide of the Tutsis, has made Paul Kagame a hero of African development. Internationally, everyone recognizes that he has brought stability and economic growth to a country ravaged by a tragedy two decades ago. All the statistical improvements that followed in various socioeconomic categories, not to mention all the technological innovations taking place in that country, attest to the leadership qualities of the former warlord. One example, considered quixotic at the time but which now appears more important in light of the serious problem developing all over the world: Rwanda banned plastic bags 15 years ago. Because of the progress that Rwandans themselves acknowledge, Kagame faces little visible opposition in his country. It's true that his control of press freedoms and democratic liberties (from a Western viewpoint) play a role. In 2019, Rwanda is classified as non-free by Freedom House. Indeed, all the positive rankings on Rwanda exclude those relative to democracy and human rights.

Paul Kagame has therefore earned his undisputed title as the godfather of African heads of state, partly through his longevity in office (in power for 19 years) and partly through his success in making Rwanda a landmark country on the African continent. He has reached a status his peers can only dream about, and they are now quick to court him for his imprimatur. Andry Rajoelina and his staff are among that group: taking official visits, opening direct air links between the two countries, cutting and pasting their counterparts' monthly work schedules, etc....

The eternal debate is therefore before us now: should we privilege democracy or development in poor countries? Because let's remember that, despite all of its undeniable progress and the press surrounding it, Rwanda is still classified among the countries eligible for [development] funds from the World Bank group dedicated to poor countries.

To what lengths will Kagame inspire Andry Rajoelina? The Malagasy chief of state, presiding over a country that has known only a very relative sense of democracy since his coup in 2009, has made it his mission to develop Madagascar through his program known as the Initiative for the Emergence of Madagascar (IEM). A lot of people suspect him of wanting to modify the constitution to erase the constitutional limit of two terms, in order to stay in power as long as possible. If his IEM program shows palpable results over the course of his first term, his autocratic leanings will undoubtedly garner a certain level of support, which will allow him to build on his base of 25% of the electorate from his 2018 election (he received 55% of the vote with a 52% abstention rate in the second round).

Andry Rajoelina also knows that the international community has learned to put water in its wine since the pitiful failure of certain previous democratization experiments, and realizes that stability is ultimately more important than electoral transparency. To stay in its good graces, it will suffice for the country just to have official elections, ones that the international community will hasten to validate even while they make some mild protests. We've known how to play that game for a long time in Madagascar.

The notion of enlightened dictatorship also seduces more and more Malagasy. However, in the context of Madagascar's political culture, this path is a slippery slope. As a blogger said, in "enlightened dictatorship" the second word is just as important as the first. Kagame wants both.

Let's remember for example that Kagame has made the fight against corruption his battle cry. Rwanda is currently ranked 48th out of 180 countries by Transparency International with a grade of 56/100. It's one of four countries of sub-Saharan Africa among the top 50. His efforts to clean up corruption therefore make it easier for Rwandans and the international community to swallow the dictatorial pill he has offered. It's not perfect if one compares Rwanda to Denmark (first in the 2018 rankings), but remember that Madagascar is 152nd out of 180 countries, with a grade of 25 out of 100. The experience of the High Transitional Authority here from 2009-13, and the continued presence of some rather shady people in the close entourage of the Malagasy president since his return to power through the ballot box, ensure that doubts will still exist about the real will, and above all the capacity, of

Rajoelina's administration to tackle this phenomenon that is ruining the life of the country. People also know that electoral campaigns have cost a lot of money and that the financial backers expect a return on their investment. This is undoubtedly one of the advantages of a dictatorship: you don't need to invest a lot to get elected, which reduces the accountability to your "sponsors."

Madagascar's version of democracy has proven to be nothing if not unpredictable. The state's ability to contain violence and avoid a total collapse of its institutions seems paradoxical next to the recent fragility of its presidential regimes.[33] One theory holds that its leaders become more autocratic over time because they have no real structural bases of power – political parties on the island are notoriously weak – forcing them to rely almost exclusively on support from the masses, which can crumble quickly in a crisis.[34] And yet despite the coups and countercoups, the idea if not the practice of democracy has taken a tenuous hold on the island in recent years. Almost 90% of the country support democracy in the country, with even higher levels of support in Tana.[35] Rumblings of discontent with their government are nevertheless growing: Fifty-eight percent of people in Tana said they were satisfied with democracy in 2006, but just 20% said so in 2015, even after a new election in 2013. Trust in the administration shrank from 64% to 35% over the same period.[36]

Looking ahead, only the Malagasy people can decide whether Rajoelina's brand of populist politics is best for them. Having finally vanquished his chief rival, orchestrated his party's landslide victory in the legislative elections that followed and overseen the weakening of the opposition, the President now has free rein to govern as he pleases for the next four years. Thus far the Malagasy people, weary of chronic instability in their country and thankful for some semblance of stability, have shown themselves to be more than willing to go along with Rajoelina's plans for development. Even the spread of the Coronavirus wasn't enough to dampen the enthusiasm of the country as of 2020, especially when the President announced the discovery of an herbal remedy for the virus that would soon be exported to other African countries. Most Malagasy remained willing to indulge Rajoelina's request to give him a year in office before judging him. His sudden return to power was striking not only for its emphatic end to his decade-long confrontation with Ravalomanana, but also for the sense of democratic optimism it inspired among large swathes of the population. Faith in elections, if not as a means of expressing the national will then simply as a vehicle toward achieving stability, had been temporarily restored by someone who first came to power openly dismissive of them. It was a curious and unexpected turn of events for an island that had learned to distrust its political leaders. Perhaps only in Madagascar can a former coup leader be seen as the last, best hope for a nation's democracy.

Chapter 4

Trapped In Poverty

There is a concentration of wealth in a certain number of people in Madagascar. The poor are becoming poorer and the rich are becoming richer, with a smaller middle class each year.
- Professor Aime Jaony

Gladonia Razaiarizafy is a maid at the hotel where I stayed in the northern city of Diego Suarez. Shy at first but radiating energy as she warms up to people, she wears her expressions openly in a way that confirms her simple origins. A few days after I arrived we began to exchange greetings every day at the hotel and became somewhat friendly after a couple of weeks, and in time I considered her one of my favorite acquaintances in Madagascar. Her wide-eyed reactions to some of the prosaic things I occasionally said to her were both hilarious and revealing of her and the culture she embodied. I learned a lot from Gladonia.

One day we were chatting while she cleaned my room and she asked me what I did for a living. When I told her I was a lawyer in the United States she dropped her mop and turned to face me, a look of terror on her face. "Are you here to put me in prison for something I've done?" she asked. I started to laugh, but when I saw she was serious I tried to reassure her, explaining that I had no authority to do something like that in Madagascar even if I wanted to, and now that we were friends, why would I want to? She relaxed, but for me it was a profound lesson on the degree to which the powerless respect and fear the actions of those above them.

And Gladonia is nothing if not poor and powerless. She grew up in Andapa, in the Sava region, where she lived until she was 12. When one of her older brothers ran out of money while studying at the university in Diego, she and her mother, two sisters and four other brothers packed up their things and took a bus to help support him. That is what families do for their eldest sons in Madagascar. When they arrived her mother worked as a tailor, making about $200 per year. "Life was very difficult for us," Gladonia told me. "We had never been here before so everything was new. Before we lived in a small town and we had a garden so we could cook our own food. Here we had to pay for everything. Also my mother was alone and she was often very sad at first."[1]

She quit school at age 16 after becoming pregnant. Her boyfriend, a taxi driver back in Andapa who visited her frequently after her family moved, left her when he found out she was pregnant. "I was very sad for a long time. Plus my family hated me for getting pregnant by someone who wouldn't support me, so I left Diego. I went back to Andapa to live with my father for eight months. I had the baby, a boy, but I suffered a lot there too. I worked in the rice fields, and one day my mother called me on my friend's phone and told me to come back. I was happy because I missed my family and I thought I could continue my studies."

So Gladonia returned to Diego in 2015 with her son, training for six months at a local cooking school. With no job prospects as a cook she sold used clothing in one of the stalls along the street for a year, making about $200 per year. "It was hard work, 12 hours a day and six days a week," she said. "I lived alone with my baby as I've done ever since I returned. I've learned that when I live with my family it always starts a war. We get along better this way, living separately."

In 2016, she left the clothing stall to try to make more money on her own. Putting her cooking skills to work, she sold cakes and other snacks on the street in front of her small house in Diego. "I was cooking again and I liked that, and I was my own boss so I liked that too, but I was only making about $260 per year, so I had to try something else." So the next year she found work as a server for a wedding caterer for several months, but that turned out to be only part time work and she could barely feed her son. Unsure what to do next, Gladonia went to her mother and asked her if she could help with her tailoring business. Her mother agreed and they worked together for about nine months, sharing all the money that came in. But by the next year her mother said she was getting too tired to work full time, and the work dropped off. Gladonia knew she would have to find something else, and after several opportunities fell through she found a job washing clothes in a hotel, making about $200 per year; but after a while the hotel could only offer her part time work and she went back to selling food on the street in front of her house.

In late 2018 she started her current job as a maid at the hotel. "I wanted a steady income and they offered me more [about $430/year] than I had ever made before," she said. I think I'll stay until I find a way to sell clothes again in my own shop, this time without another owner so I don't have to share the money that comes in. Right now I have nothing saved, but if I save a little from this job and try to do some other odd jobs in the afternoons after my work at the hotel finishes, I think I can do it someday."

On a typical day, Gladonia wakes up at 1 am to go fetch water, a task she carries out three times every week. Usually there are four or five people ahead of her when she arrives at the tap, so she has to wait. Sometimes she takes her son with her, and sometimes she leaves him at home alone. She usually arrives back home around 3 am, when she cooks breakfast and lunch and cleans the house. At 5 am she takes a bath before leaving for work at 6 am to arrive in time for her 7 am shift. She goes home at noon, by which time her son has returned from school and has already eaten the lunch she prepared earlier.

He goes back to school at 2 pm, which leaves most afternoons free to rest and clean the house. She typically cooks dinner at 5 pm and eats with her son around 7 pm. "Then we spend time together. I teach him things like colors, songs," she said. They go to sleep together around 9 pm, and the routine starts all over again the next day.

Gladonia lives near the university in a small house that's divided into two apartments. Her apartment has two small rooms, a bedroom and a small living space with a pantry. It has no electricity and no running water or toilet. She pays about $11 per month to live there, and about $1.60 a month to access water from the public fountain, the one that forces her to wake up at 1 am three times a week because that's the only time it's sure to have water flowing. If she goes at any other time there's rarely any water coming from the tap, and sometimes there's no water running at 1 am either, so she has to go home and come back at 3 am to try to again. And once every few months the water stops running for a week at a time, meaning she has to walk to a natural source over an hour away.

She pays $8.50 per month for rice, $5.50 per month for charcoal and $1.75 per month for her son's preschool. Sometimes when she's too exhausted to fetch water in the middle of the night she'll pay someone 75 cents to get it for her. Her diet consists exclusively of rice and water, except for birthdays and other special occasions, when they might eat pasta. Drinking water is only available from the public tap. She eats twice a day, at noon and at night, and has found that breakfast is not necessary when you're so poor. As a treat for her son, once a week she'll buy a small fish from the market for 75 cents on her way home from work. When she gets home she cuts it into small pieces to make it last for three meals. "Sometimes we're hungry," she said, "and I think it's not just because we lack the right quantity of food but because we also lack the right quality. We have no vegetables, no juice, hardly any meat." I was struck by this;

she was one of the few people I met in Madagascar who were cognizant of the devastating effects of their meager diet beyond the need for more calories.

And she is painfully aware of the precariousness of her plight. "On $37 per month I can't save anything. If one of us gets sick or there is some other emergency, I have to take an advance on my salary, which means less money at the end of the month." She's calculated that if she could in fact save enough to open and operate her own used clothing stall, she would triple her salary to over $1,200 per year. "I know it's possible but I have no idea when it will happen or how I will ever save up that much money," she said.

"Now I'm poor. My life is very difficult. I know I'm poor because I buy nothing and still my expenses are always more than my earnings. But most people I know live like me. The problem I think is that those in power don't care about us, they don't even see us. They just do whatever they want. So it's a political issue to me, because people who have power control everything. For example, my family had grown some vanilla and I was taking it to the market to sell when two policemen stopped me and said I couldn't sell that here because I needed a permit. So they took the vanilla and later I saw them sell it in the market for themselves. I wanted to do something, to tell someone, but what could I do? I am no one to them."

Gladonia has already become a cynic about the island's political leaders. People who are rich in Madagascar have gained their money illicitly, she believes, or "in secret." They must have connections to powerful people in the government and abroad, maybe even to the President himself. This allows them to sell their products abroad for a high price. Regular people here without those connections have no chance of competing with them, she believes. And corruption will always exist in Madagascar, it will never go away. "Money rules the island, not laws, so corruption will always be here." She acknowledged that BIANCO has reduced it somewhat but only in the smaller institutions of government – in the "big offices" like the police it's the same as ever. "BIANCO itself is even corrupt – you can pay them to look the other way, which is what the rich do." She implored President Rajoelina to build a system where even those without diplomas can find work. "Everyone must have work for the country to succeed, and they must earn at least a little to save a little and keep it in the bank. It's very hard to find work here, and I'm lucky to have the one I have."

With inequality rising across the island, I was interested to learn whether she felt any resentment toward those who had used their connections to get rich. But Gladonia harbored no animosity toward them. "I don't get mad or jealous at rich people. Instead I just dream of being one of them, of living their lives, of seeing my son play with their sons at school one day. I want my future to be better and I believe it will be better. I know I have the courage to continue working and to fight my way out of poverty. I will always dream of success, even if it never comes."

Like countless people I met, Gladonia holds no illusions that life for people like her will get better. "When you live in poverty it's difficult to leave it. I think the easiest way might be to leave Madagascar," she said. She knows several girls who have gone to work as domestic servants in various Arab countries. "That's probably the best choice now. My cousin did that and now she sends money home every month." When I asked her if anything was getting better for her, her face brightened and she mentioned the improving security situation in Diego, which once saw armed thieves and bandits, known as *foroche*, roaming the city at will. "The new president is really working hard to improve security here and the *foroche* are gone," she told me. "So I'm happy about that."

We talked at length about the chances of her escaping her situation one day, either through her own hard work, better job prospects through economic development on the island, through marriage to a stable partner, or simply from pure luck, but every time Gladonia expressed some small measure of hope for the future she quickly dismissed it as probably unreachable. There were simply too many obstacles in front of her, she concluded. "Once you're in poverty it's hard to leave," she said one day. "If you have courage and don't lose heart it's possible, but still your situation will only change a little bit. I actually don't know anyone who was poor and is no longer poor – they've all stayed poor. Part of the problem is that our political leaders don't care about us." She summarized her life this way:

> My life is not happy but I'm still proud of myself for working at the job that I have. And I'm hopeful that one day I can improve my situation. I have a lot of hope actually. Five years from now, maybe my life won't be that different but I believe little by little things will get better. But my life now is sad and I cry every once in a while. I'm used to crying, actually. I wonder why I am so poor, why my life is so difficult and why I have to raise my son like this. Sometimes I get really angry, really pissed off. But after several hours of crying or being angry, I hear certain words in my head that calm me down: Keep your head high, don't give up, keep working hard for your son, the voice says.

There are obvious temptations for young women to earn more money in Madagascar by selling their bodies at bars and night clubs found in every city, Diego included. Gladonia has never considered it but understands why some of her friends have. Those who sleep with men for money have simply run out of options, she believes. "When I see girls my age who have become prostitutes I think it's because they have lost hope about the future. I could never do that, even though I would make more money. I'm a blunt person, an honest person, and I can't fake things with people, especially about the way I feel, or about love. I don't want to share my body with someone if it's not for love. I only want a serious relationship."

Gladonia dreams of finding a man who will love her, but after several experiences with heartbreak already, she mostly tries to put it out of her mind. She told me she would actually be afraid to marry if the chance ever came, even if it were with someone she knew well. "Men are all the same, and they always hurt me. It used to be my dream to marry, but now I don't like the idea of getting married. But destiny will decide, and maybe it will happen. I don't want any more kids right now, but maybe in the future, if I meet someone who loves me."

And so the daily grind for Gladonia and millions like her goes on, with each day that brings two meals a day and no major catastrophes considered a minor miracle. The will to persevere amidst unspeakable hardship is breathtaking to watch, and unfathomable to those of us who never have to experience it. Perhaps it's made easier by the example she feels she must set for her son, and the daily inspiration he provides for her. "I will do everything in my power to make sure my son doesn't end up in the same situation as me. I want him to go to a better school than other kids – one where he can learn French and English. I want him to be a tourist guide so he'll have to speak a lot of languages, maybe Spanish and Italian too. But mostly I just don't want him to live like me."

* * *

Gladonia's story, and her plight as one of the island's millions of poor people, is unfortunately all too common in twenty-first century Madagascar. The tragedy is that the island's staggering poverty has deepened even while that of the rest of the world has begun to recede. Madagascar is thus in much the same position economically as it was a generation ago while almost every other developing country has forged ahead. The country now stands at a crossroads: it will either begin to catch up to its former peers or fall permanently behind.

No one can deny the incredible transformation that has overtaken the global economy, and particularly in the developing world, over the last thirty years. As Steven Radelet points out in *The Great Surge*, beginning in the 19th Century, the percentage of people living in extreme poverty began to decline, but their number in absolute terms continued to grow rapidly until the mid-20th century. Then in the early 1990s the total number of people living in extreme poverty began to fall for the first time in world history, and the decline was swift and significant. After rising relentlessly from the beginning of human history, the number of people living on less than $1 a day dropped by more than half in less than 20 years. Moreover, the sudden drop in the number of extremely poor people around the world has come amid an era of rapid global population growth, which means that the percentage of people living in extreme poverty has been falling even faster (from 53% to 17% in 30 years). Radelet considers the decline in extreme poverty one of the most important achievements in the history of the world economy.[2]

Just as encouraging as the overall decline was how widely the impact was felt. Almost every developing nation on Earth, from all parts of the globe, took part in the historic reduction in extreme poverty over the last generation. Out of 109 developing countries, only 21 achieved per capita economic growth exceeding 2 percent per year from 1977-94, but 71 did so between 1995-2013, including 30 countries that achieved 4% growth rates during that period. Meanwhile, very few have failed, with only 10 countries witnessing negative per capita income growth since 1995.[3]

Madagascar's per capita GDP is still below its level in 1990, and even more astounding, its 2018 average of just

$432 per person remained 40% below its figure at the time of independence in 1960, using constant dollars. As we'll see, much of the country's stagnation has been the result of its two political crises in 2002 and 2009, but rampant population growth and other factors played an important part as well. Jeffrey Sachs, in *The Age of Sustainable Development*, cites seven root causes of extreme poverty, including things like poor governance, bad economic policies, insolvency, disadvantageous physical geography, cultural barriers (to women, for example), and geopolitics. But the seventh reason, known as poverty traps, has particular relevance to Madagascar, given its prolonged stagnation. Poverty traps, a term first termed by the economist Paul Collier, occur when a country is too poor to make the basic investments it needs to make to escape extreme poverty. Much of sub-Saharan Africa, with its high levels of extreme poverty decade after decade since independence, has been afflicted by this debilitating phenomenon until very recently, and Madagascar continues to suffer its effects.[4]

It's important to note that not everyone sees the end of extreme poverty as inevitable. Sachs, for example, speculates that the number of people living in extreme poverty may actually be undercounted. While acknowledging that the percentage of people living in extreme poverty in the developing world has declined from 52% in 1981 to 21% in 2010, he takes aim at the $1.25 income threshold used to define extreme poverty by the World Bank and others. It is surely too narrow, he says, and a better measure is whether people can meet their most basic material needs. When a more holistic measure is used, the actual number of extremely poor people as of 2010 was closer to 2 billion than the reported number of 1.2 billion.[5]

David Rieff is also skeptical of the so-called progress in combating extreme poverty around the world. Three-fourths of the global decline in extreme poverty since 1981 occurred in China, he says, and without that accomplishment, the MDG goal of halving extreme poverty by 2015 would not have been met. In Africa, extreme poverty fell only 8% between 1990-2010, and undernutrition and stunting remain stubbornly high.[6] Rieff rightfully questions whether the modest reduction in extreme poverty in Africa is sustainable, and though he doesn't cite Madagascar as an example, the island's recent economic demise is another reason to be cautious in proclaiming victory.

Perhaps the larger question is why Africa, after so many years of independence, economic reforms and foreign aid, is still poor. Even some prominent economists admit they don't have a good answer for what works and what doesn't. "Economists, ourselves included, have spent entire careers studying development and poverty, and the uncomfortable truth is that the field still doesn't have a good sense of why some economies expand and others don't. There is no clear formula for growth," proclaimed Abhijit Banerjee and Esther Duflo, who, it should be noted, won the Nobel prize in economics in 2019 for their work on fighting poverty.[7] Others, like Jeffrey Sachs, think their pessimism over finding solutions is nonsense, and that development experts do in fact know how to stimulate economic growth. As Sachs points out, extreme poverty has come down in Africa since 2000 but poverty traps continue to constrict the region's ability to generate growth on its own. "Governments there do not possess the domestic revenue bases needed to build infrastructure or provide vital public services such as health care and education. Financing their own escape from poverty would be too slow and accompanied by much avoidable suffering: tens of millions will be lost unnecessarily to disease and hundreds of millions of lives will be hindered by illiteracy and other extreme privations unless the developed world supplies these countries with increased assistance to ensure investment and vital public services." More foreign aid to Africa is therefore key to its rise, but poor countries can also do more to catch up by following fairly basic steps to promote growth. Focus on exporting labor- and resource-intensive products, he advises, and use the proceeds to build human capital and physical infrastructure.[8]

If only it were that easy. Madagascar's economy has been in shambles since Rajoelina's coup in 2009, and is only now just recovering. Always a poor country, the island has now become one of the poorest in the world. A 2014 World Bank report began with this stark declaration: "Madagascar has been entirely unsuccessful in reducing the number of its people that are poor, or extremely so, in the ten years since 2001, when poverty was already at a very high level."[9] By 2010, a year after the coup, the numbers were staggering. A large majority of the population was extremely poor, whether you define that term by income or one's ability to meet his or her basic needs. In terms of income, over 82% of people lived on less than $1.25 per day in 2010; in terms of ability to consume basic amounts of food, 60% of the population, or close to 13 million people, lived on resources whose value fell below the cost of basic sustenance - about 2100 calories a day.[10]

What makes the increase in the poverty rate so troubling is that it was occurring at a time when the population was growing rapidly, resulting in an even more significant increase in the number of people falling into both absolute and extreme poverty. An estimated 15.6 million Malagasy were below the absolute poverty line in 2010, while 17.1 million people in Madagascar lived below $1.25 US dollar a day.[11]

A lack of natural resources has doomed many poor countries to a dismal fate, but Madagascar can't use that excuse. Its wealth of land and relatively high levels of human capital mean the source of the island's lack of economic growth must lie elsewhere. Moreover, its natural resources, both mineral and agricultural, are evenly balanced, allowing it to avoid the resource curse that has plagued so many other developing nations. This balance explains the absence of protracted conflicts both internally and with external actors, but its relative peace compared to other sub-Saharan countries only makes its low growth rates more puzzling.[12]

Many factors led to the unacceptably high level of poverty in the country, but the effect of the coup on Madagascar's economic growth was paramount. The country's economy was growing at a 7.1% clip in 2008, Ravalomanana's sixth year in power, but then shrank by 4% in 2009, the year he was overthrown. By 2013 it had only recovered to 2%, and did not reach 5% again until 2019, ten years later. Similarly, the island's per capita GDP levels did not return to their 2008 high until 2018, when it was still around $500. (Per capita GDP has doubled since 1995 but is roughly the same today as in 1980 and 2008.) This lost decade, when the island's population grew by an astonishing six million people, is the single largest factor in the country's urgent plight today.

The 2014 World Bank report made a direct link between the country's recent political strife and the increase in poverty. Twice over the decade from 2001-10, the slow process of economic growth that had emerged already by the mid-1990s was stopped in its tracks by political crises, in 2002 and 2009. The report found that over ten years GDP would have grown by 65% if the island had managed to avoid both upheavals. In the event, however, cumulative growth over 2000-10 only reached 30%, less than half of what it could have been. And again, Madagascar's high rate of population growth caused per capita GDP and income to actually decline. With population growth at close to 3%, per capita GDP fell by 4% cumulatively for the decade as a whole, and continued to fall until 2014.[13]

The report tried to put a number on the missed opportunities for poverty reduction caused by the two crises. Growth of per capita GDP at about 2.8 percent a year – well within reach for Madagascar – would have translated into a reduction of poverty from 71 percent in 2001 to 55 percent in 2013. Instead, as noted above, the report found poverty levels approaching 76 percent in 2013, using the national poverty line. Thus, a full 21 percentage points more people – 4.5 million people – became poor than under a counterfactual of sustained growth. And if you just eliminate the second crisis in 2009 by itself, poverty would probably have declined to 63 percent in 2013 versus the actual figure of 76 percent.[14]

Looking back beyond the lost decade, the report also concluded that if Madagascar had been allowed to continue its normal, "off-crisis" growth rate (2%), it would have doubled its per capita GDP in 35 years; a long-time, to be sure, but at least it would have grown. This belief is supported by the fact that in the 6-year period between 2003 and 2008, when things were relatively stable, per capita GDP grew by a cumulative 14 percent. Not surprisingly, most of the loss in per capita GDP during the decade took place during the two crises sub-periods. And while economic growth isn't everything, these shocks to the system had undeniable consequences to regular Malagasy people, because without it fewer people can find jobs or grow their businesses, and the government is unable to generate the resources necessary to pay for the public goods and services the country needs to grow faster and improve the welfare of its people. In short, the poverty trap continues.[15]

The lost decade made the island a clear outlier even among sub-Saharan African countries. As noted above, the recent global trend has been for low-income countries to grow significantly, but not Madagascar. And while the first decade of this century had a devastating impact on the country, the economic decline of Madagascar began well before. Cumulatively, the real GDP per capita of Madagascar fell more than 30 percent between 1980 and 2010. Such a poor growth record long ago became the exception, not the rule, among developing countries. Madagascar is in fact one of a handful of countries in the world that have experienced a cumulative decline for 30 years, measured by GDP per capita in real terms. The report found that of 155 countries for which a measurement is available, only 19 experienced a cumulative economic regression between 1980 and 2013. Among these 19 countries with a declining economy, only 11 were very poor countries with per capita GDPs below$2,000 in 2010 in purchasing power parity, an unenviable list that includes Madagascar. In fact, the island's results were just behind those of Liberia and the Democratic Republic of Congo, two countries that, unlike Madagascar, had suffered through prolonged periods of violent conflict. Even these two countries were on the road to recovery in the years after 2010 (both posting double digit growth rates in the following five years), while for Madagascar, the next five years continued to be years of decline.[16]

Those are the macro numbers, and they are startling. But a deeper look at Madagascar's poverty sheds more light on its worsening plight. For example, children are the poorest segment of Madagascar's population. Over the lost decade, poverty in Madagascar was less a result of joblessness or inactivity than of low earning and limited opportunities. People were working, doing anything they could to make ends meet and support their families; but the political crises pushed more of the population toward agriculture, which has now become the main source of labor income. With lower incomes resulting from agricultural work, this shift has had a depressing effect on the economy as a whole, such that 80% of the island's population lived in rural areas by 2015. Since poverty in rural areas is higher than in urban zones, 86% of the country's poor now live in rural areas.[17]

Interestingly, Madagascar is not an outlier in non-income measures of well-being, especially human development indicators. For example, it is actually below the sub-Saharan average in adolescent fertility. But it is hard to read the World Bank report with any sense that things are improving, even leaving incomes aside. The UN's Human Development Index, which ranks countries on a variety of factors ranging from health, education and standard of living, placed the island 161st out of 189 countries in 2018. This is hardly surprising, given that food consumption shifted to lower quality food items over the decade, while access to tap water at home declined sharply over the decade. Less than 6% of the population in rural areas had any access to electricity. Illiteracy fell sharply between 2000-10 but still stood at 32%. School enrollment rates increased over the decade but, in the face of the two political crises, contributed little to poverty reduction. (Still, in 2010 one additional year of education led to a 5% in earnings.) Health care remained a serious source of concern: 32% of the poorest quintile, and 23% of the population overall, did not have access to a primary health care center. Taken together, these measures of non-income poverty reveal that about one-third of Malagasy people in 2010 were what the World Bank calls "have nothings" – people who are poor, have no education and no electricity.[18]

In addition to political crises and poverty traps, the country's geographic isolation may be another reason for its high level of poverty since independence. Even before the coup, the country had trouble finding its place in the world, oscillating between two potential sources of external support: the smaller islands of the Indian Ocean and the larger region of Southeast Africa. Neither has proved to be a natural partner for the Malagasy. As others have pointed out, if the great island has never become a Creole version of Francophonia like the other Mascarene islands, it has also failed to forge close bonds with either the Swahili coast of Africa or the Persian Gulf (unlike its neighbor Comoros). "Neither Asian nor African nor European in cultural affinity – despite centuries of influence from all three continents – Madagascar remains Malagasy," according to Phillip Allen. "Madagascar today belongs to several networks without being incorporated into any." The best possible partner may be Mauritius, an economic success story just over 700 miles away.[19]

Not surprisingly for a country facing such high levels of

chronic poverty, foreign aid continues to be a vital source of support for the nation's struggling economy. After years of receiving a cold shoulder from Western donors following Rajoelina's coup, lending resumed after the election in 2013, and large foreign aid institutions have now fully embraced Rajoelina since his reelection in 2018. The World Bank pledged $1.3 billion to Madagascar in 2016 to support its three-year National Development Plan, and has supplemented that amount in the years since with loans in the hundreds of millions of dollars almost every year since. The most recent installment was a $100 million loan announced in 2019 to improve the population's access to electricity, a category in which the island currently ranks 185th in the world. Foreign aid has risen from $324 million in 2000 to $779 million in 2018, though the second figure is slightly lower as a percentage of national GDP. Foreign aid still accounts for close to 40% of the government's annual budget.

And yet foreign aid, while vitally important to Madagascar, is still incredibly low compared to other countries. The total received by the island's people in 2013 averaged out to just $21 per capita; only Angola received less. And the volume of aid sent to Madagascar was only 5% of its GDP. This is surely due to its low visibility to the rest of the world: Madagascar has not been strategically important for decades, its political instability, while crushing to its own hopes for development, doesn't affect the developed world and its economic tragedy is a long term phenomenon, with no famines or spectacular crashes that might arouse public opinion.[20]

The country is now pinning its hopes on mining, tourism and the export of a few key commodities. Madagascar's substantial natural resources include oil, gas, nickel, titanium, cobalt, iron, coal, uranium and ilmenite (used as a pigment in paint, plastics and dyes around the world). The island is the largest producer of vanilla in the world and has major reserves of oil and minerals, most of them discovered fairly recently. Europe is its key economic partner, accounting for 80% of its tourist arrivals and receiving about 50% of its exports. The mining sector, like everything else, took a major hit in 2009. Until that point it had been the main source of foreign investment in the country, accounting for almost 80% of foreign direct investment (FDI) in 2009. FDI slumped to $455 million by 2013 after reaching a high of $1.36 billion in 2009. Only a handful of new mining permits were issued after the coup and the army-backed government did little to stimulate the sector, failing to pay tax refunds for exploration and threatening to hike royalty fees. The government says the freeze in new permits was the result of a deal in 2011 to end a crisis that left Rajoelina struggling to get international recognition, and that normal licensing has since resumed. Overall, the sector has the potential to generate substantial revenues for the island. Under current law, mining companies pay a 2% royalty on gross exports of raw commodities or 1% on minerals processed locally and exported with added value.

Two projects currently dominate the mining sector. First, a nickel plant in Amabatovy jointly owned by Japan's Sumitomo Corp., Korea Resources Corp. and Sherritt International Corp., was brought into production in 2014 and nickel quickly became Madagascar's largest export (averaging $30 million per month). However, Sumitomo has been suffering losses at the plant as the $8 billion project has struggled to ramp up and nickel prices have slumped. The other project is an ilmenite mine on the southern tip of the island that is 80% owned by Rio Tinto, but it too has faced sharp growing pains. Slower growth in China has meant lower prices, since China is the largest buyer of many African minerals.[21]

By contrast, development experts are encouraged by the island's stimulation of the oil and gas industry, which has seen some positive movement in recent years. Madagascar has yet to prove offshore oil reserves but shares a maritime border with

Mozambique, which definitely has them. Onshore, a company called Madagascar Oil planned the country's first commercial crude sales by 2020 but will need a decade to reach full capacity.

The United States is one of Madagascar's largest foreign aid suppliers and a huge potential market for its emerging textile industry. Madagascar gained duty free access to the United States in 2000 under the African Growth and Opportunity Act, causing a boom in exports of apparel, then lost it in January 2010 after Rajoelina's coup. The country regained its privileged status under the Act in 2015 and is now trying to make up for lost time. The potential to tap the American market once again holds great promise for the island's underclass, who have seen their wages stagnate in real terms since 2000. In recognition of this fact, in April 2019 Rajoelina asked employers nationwide to raise the minimum wage by 19%, to 200,000 Ariary per month. Though there was nothing compulsory about his request, most businesses complied with it, giving low wage workers a small raise that equates to about $675 per year.

But even with these modest signs of growth in key new sectors, the business climate in Madagascar remains far behind that of its peers in sub-Saharan Africa and most foreign multinational companies still see too many risks to invest significant sums. Forbes Magazine ranked Madagascar 22nd out of 47 African nations in business climate for investment, with neighboring Mauritius ranking first. The president has made some legal reforms to attract more FDI and there a number of infrastructure projects across the country that should make Madagascar more attractive to foreign investors, according to Forbes, but the high cost of energy and lack of basic infrastructure continue to hold the island back. For its part, the World Bank recently ranked Madagascar 161 out of 190 countries in its Doing Business 2020 report, citing its poor infrastructure and struggles to supply enough gas and water to its people and businesses as major impediments. But despite its low grade overall the bank ended its report on a note of optimism, pointing to several reforms in progress that could show results in the near future.[22]

Other reasons for the island's perpetual underperformance have been suggested by analysts both at home and abroad. Its low tax base and the inadequate government revenue and spending that results (both among the weakest in the world) mean there simply isn't enough cash available to rectify Madagascar's multiplying problems. Others have pointed to the island's cultural values acting as a brake on development, with the Malagasy's traditional respect for authority perhaps undermining its newfound support for democracy. And yet the most incisive analyses continually return to the political dimension, where the otherwise inexplicable timing of political crises following periods of economic growth leads to the inevitable conclusion that the island suffers from an inability to establish any lasting consensus on the process of distributing whatever meager gains its economy starts to produce.[23]

* * *

Madagascar has always been a rural country. Its capital, Antananarivo, remains the only city with more than one million residents, and only five cities have more than 100,000 people. Despite a slow rise in urbanization the vast majority of the population continues to reside in the countryside, making agriculture a key to its future growth prospects. Agriculture employs roughly 80% of Madagascar's population and accounts for over 25% of its GDP, so any plan to increase economic output in Madagascar will have to start with farming. And yet the island faces many of the same challenges that threaten Africa as a whole when it comes to agriculture.

A decade ago, experts were hopeful that Africa could shed its past as the largest recipient of food aid and begin feeding itself. The fact that Africa was largely left out of the green revolution that sparked incredible increases in crop yields in other part parts of the world was viewed not as a cause for despair but as an opportunity. Some began calling it "agriculture's final frontier," and predicted that by boosting agricultural yields Africa could one day feed not just itself but the rest of the world. If farmers there simply used existing seed, fertilizer and irrigation technology already used in other parts of the developing world, the thinking went, agricultural production would jump enormously. A study by the McKinsey Global Institute claimed that, if a green revolution ignited in Africa, the continent's agricultural output could increase from $280 billion per year to as much as $880 billion per year by 2030. Such growth is possible, the institute postulated, if Africa raises its yields on key crops to 80 percent of the world average and brings more of its potential farmland into cultivation. The moral imperative was there too, of course: without a revolution in agriculture, it was understood that the number of food insecure people in Sub-Saharan Africa (those living on less than 2100 calories per day) would soon reach 500 million, or half the region's population, but the hope was that Africa could finally move beyond its own survival and actually alleviate food insecurity globally. "The continent that has been fed by the world's food aid must now feed the world," as one writer put it.[24]

But by the end of the decade, analysts were returning to a more sober assessment of Africa's agricultural potential, and in some cases had begun to return to predictions of a darkening future. No longer viewed as a possible food supplier for the rest of the world, the continent would have its hands full simply feeding itself, because, as one New York Times article put it, "Africa has a land problem." With relatively few industry or service jobs, 70% of Africans make a living through agriculture, more than any other continent; yet the triple threats of population growth, climate change, and soil erosion are conspiring to cause a crisis for 40 million Africans trying to survive off of land whose agricultural potential is declining. And the problem will only get worse. High birth rates and lengthening life spans mean that by the end of this century there could be as many as four billion people in Africa, about ten times the population forty years ago. This could cause a furious contest for arable land, fueling conflict between ethnic groups, not to mention that with land scarcity comes overuse, leaving no time for soil to replenish. Climate change threatens to make things harder, with scientists now predicting more drought, desertification and hunger for the continent in the decades ahead. In fact, the future is already beginning to take shape before our eyes. A bad year used to see one country in Africa hit by famine, but 2017 saw millions of people in three countries – Somalia, Nigeria and South Sudan – on the brink of starvation. And rising living standards will only mean higher demands for meat, which requires even more land to produce. Experts are now starting to agree that a looming food security crisis exists in Africa, and that more and more countries on the continent may become reliant on food imports and foreign assistance in the near future.[25]

And yet the dream of an agricultural boom in Africa refuses to die. The number of agricultural startups in Africa has grown significantly in the last few years, as a new generation of agricultural entrepreneurs hopes to cash in on a recent boom in technology that aims to increase productivity and make agriculture more modern and lucrative.[26] Their goals, not dissimilar from those of earlier pioneers hoping to induce a green revolution out of tough African soils, are to make money and feed millions of Africans. They too point to the fact that the continent holds about 65% of the world's most arable uncultivated land but imports over $35 billion in food each year, according to the African Development Bank. And that African crop yields are only 20-30% of what could be produced if more modern farming practices became widespread and new technologies were introduced. There is no doubt that new blood and larger, more efficient processes are necessary, as the average age of farmers in Sub-Saharan Africa is 60 and most are smallholders, barely able to feed their families, but they are racing against time in a sense, trying to scale up production before the population crisis grows acute and the soils are thoroughly depleted.

* * *

No economic issue gets as much attention today as the rise of economic inequality in societies around the world. In the United States, the political left has made the fight against inequality one of its signature issues, with President Obama calling it the "defining issue of our time" in 2013, and every Democratic candidate in 2020 unveiling a plan to combat it. Thomas Piketty's book on the causes of inequality in the West, *Capital In the 21st Century,* became an instant classic among academics and political pundits alike. But the discussion over inequality both in political discourse and in Piketty's tome was focused on Western societies and had little to say about the problem in developing societies. Nevertheless, countries like Madagascar are forced to grapple with the issue just as much as Europeans and Americans, with more and more questions arising as to the source of inequality on the island and its long-term implications.

But there are some caveats to make before delving into Madagascar's case. First, it's important to note that, at a global level, inequality *between* countries is decreasing thanks to a historically significant process in which the big emerging economies of Eastern Europe, Asia, South America and Africa are catching up with the advanced economies. Inequality *within* most large economies, on the other hand, is on the rise, thanks to competitive pressures caused by globalization.[27] Historically, global inequality was insignificant for most of human history, exploding only in the 19th century (due to the

Industrial Revolution) and continuing to rise for most of the 20th century. But such inequality declined sharply starting in 1990 and continued to decline for the next 30 years. Overall, emerging economies are likely to continue catching up with the advanced economies, and inequality within countries will continue to replace inequality between countries as the primary locus of divergence.[28]

Second, an academic consensus is emerging that inequality is rising in Western nations and may well be inherent in capitalist systems, with only radical measures available to contain it. Piketty, for example, posited that if the rate of return on capital remains significantly above the rate of growth of the economy, then the risk of divergence in the distribution of wealth is very high. This is precisely what has happened in the US and Europe in the past few decades when growth rates have been relatively low. And as inequality rises in these advanced economies it is perpetuated by the role of inherited wealth, which over time comes to dominate wealth accumulated from a lifetime's labor by a wide margin, thus concentrating wealth in ways that may be incompatible with a modern democratic society.[29] According to Piketty, with returns on capital in the 21st century expected to be 4-5% and global economic growth expected to be no more than 1.5% per year, the consequences for wealth distribution over time are potentially terrifying. The only solution he sees is a global annual tax on capital.[30]

A global wealth tax appears to face enormous political obstacles, however. And according to Walter Scheidel, the alternative methods are even less appealing: historically, he writes, the only surefire ways to stop the onslaught of inequality in capitalist societies are through violence and death. "For thousands of years, civilization did not lend itself to peaceful equalization. Throughout history, the most powerful economic leveling resulted from only the most powerful shocks: mass mobilization warfare, transformative revolution, state failure and lethal pandemics."[31] Exhibit A and B to his thesis are the two world wars of the 20th century, which were among the greatest levelers in history. Inequality, he and others believe, is currently resurgent because the traditional catastrophic levelers lie dormant and are unlikely to return in the foreseeable future. (The Covid-19 pandemic, while killing at least one million people worldwide, was not catastrophic enough to reduce inequality in Western societies in any meaningful way.) With the four traditional levelers now gone and unlikely to return, one can only wonder how we will begin to combat the high levels of inequality now present in advanced economies.[32]

And yet while scholars like Piketty may have little to say about inequality in places like Madagascar, the issue is creeping higher into the nation's political discourse with each passing year. What began as a first-world issue has now become so central to developing economies that the UN included "the reduction of inequalities" as one of its Sustainable Development Goals for 2030, and economists agree that societies with highly unequal economic growth fare worse at reducing poverty. A quick look at the situation across the continent of Africa reveals why the level of concern for the developing world is growing. As a region, sub-Saharan Africa has one of the highest rates of inequality in the world, and Madagascar's Gini coefficient, the most common measuring stick of economic inequality, puts it in the middle of African countries. With the top 10% of all Malagasy owning one-third of all the wealth in the country, it's now almost in the top third of countries globally - more unequal than most European countries and almost as unequal as the United States. As might be expected, the lost decade of 2001-10 saw a drop in inequality on the island, caused partly by a sector shift toward agriculture and a premium placed on education, but it is starting to rise again.[33]

Public opinion surveys on the island reveal a population that largely accepts the high levels of inequality among the

Malagasy. One poll found roughly 25% support for each of four responses to the question of why there are extremely rich and extremely poor people on the island – that such inequality is normal because it's fate, it's normal because the rich have earned their wealth through their work, it's not normal but nothing can be done about it, or it's not normal and something should be done about it. With a total of 75% choosing one of the first three answers, the study showed that a healthy majority in Madagascar currently accept the high levels of inequality across the island either because it's the natural order of things or because they feel there is nothing that can be done about it.[34] Nevertheless, as we'll see below, those who study the issue closely view it as a more serious problem that could get worse.

* * *

The two regions of Diana and Sava that make up the province of Antsiranana are rich in basic natural resources, and are thus a far cry from the impoverished southern regions where drought has wrought havoc in recent years. So Diego seemed to be a better candidate for economic improvement than the other provinces. If this region, home to a lush countryside and visited by a relatively large number of tourists to Diego and Nosy Be, wasn't close to reversing its fortunes, then other regions would have an even harder time. I decided to seek out two local experts who could help me understand the rate of progress here – one working for the national government and one with a local development agency.

Professor Aime Jaony teaches Economic Development at the University of Antsiranana in the northern city of Diego Suarez. He sees inequality growing every year and threatening to undermine the social fabric of the country. "There is a concentration of wealth in a certain number of people in Madagascar," he told me. "The poor are becoming poorer and the rich are becoming richer, with a smaller middle class each year. There is an 80% poverty rate nationally and it's over 94% in the south." He cited the lack of education and the rise of crime as key factors in the persistence of the nation's poverty. "For example, the price of vanilla has risen, which is good for the people, but now more people are being killed over it in the northeast. That sense of fear hurts the entire region's development."[35]

Professor Jaony believes social mobility is nonexistent in Madagascar, primarily because the poor can't afford good schools. "The rich are always rich and the poor are always poor," he said. "The people of Tana have an advantage because there are better schools in the capital. Especially compared to the south of the country. Some people in the South don't have a birth certificate, so they can't even attend school. Also, you have 70 kids per class in the south compared to 40 per class nationally, so the quality of education there is terrible." The southern region, long the most destitute of Madagascar, also has trouble attracting enough teachers willing to go there to teach.

Like most experts I met, Professor Jaony cited corruption as a scourge that plagues Madagascar every day, and one that only increases during election season. "There's a lot of it," he said. "Gifts like soap, rice and kitchen utensils are given to people who would otherwise struggle to afford them. Five Thousand Ariary [about $1.25] per head is the going rate for buying votes." He told me there is more corruption in the provinces than in the capital because there is less authority there and fewer people report it. And while he believes the amount of corruption is unchanged now from ten or twenty years ago, there is more fear now in the ministries about getting caught than before, largely because of the rise of the anti-corruption agency BIANCO in 2006. Professor Jaony applauded BIANCO's efforts to crack down on corruption, but says it's mostly the opposition party members who are arrested. And voter fraud is highest in districts where there is less authority, like the South, where investigations have found fraudulent ID cards and people voting more than once.

Professor Jaony's harshest criticism was reserved for his nation's leaders. "Governmental action here is not really focused on poverty," he told me. "The country must create jobs at the local level, but that's not happening. The President wants to make Madagascar's big cities like Europe's cities. 'Make Tamatave like NY,' he said. It's not a bad idea to attract more people and investment, but it doesn't provide any immediate assistance for people who are poor and need help now." A common refrain heard in all the provinces is the government's continual neglect of districts outside Antananarivo, and Professor Jaony, as a native northerner, agreed. "The government needs to do a better job partitioning resources around the country. It should send more development projects to the provinces. And part of the problem is political – mayors from the president's party receive assistance for their cities, but others don't." Politics, he believes, is at the heart of so many of Madagascar's problems.

McGordon Ranaivo Arivezo is the regional coordinator for GFA, a local development group in Antsiranana. Tall and angular, with an inquisitive face and glasses that give him a professorial air, Arivezo is beloved by his staff at GFA and has inspired dozens of them to travel to nearby rural areas to assist with their development needs. I came to admire the man as well, for his generous nature, his easy sense of humor, and his ceaseless efforts to lift up his countrymen. I would often see him walking home at night along the main road in Diego after a long day at the office, head bent and lost in his thoughts, and I would wonder how much better off Madagascar would be if only hundreds more like him existed.

GFA has two years left to implement their development strategies for the villages they serve in the region. "We've actually found the best strategy is to ask the villagers themselves what they need, Arivezo told me. "And we've found they are more interested in getting help with basic social infrastructure than with small business development – at least at first. So in the communes our first task is often to find partners to supply clean water sources, clinics and schools. And since we are prohibited from giving cash directly to them, these are the best options to help them now."[36]

Like Professor Jaony, Arivezo believes that no economic progress is possible on the island without reasonable security measures in place to keep people safe. In the distant villages he and his staff visit around Diego, security is often the first issue local governments have to tackle. And in this region where vanilla is one of the few lucrative cash crops, he has seen crime recede in some areas simply through the establishment of a formal market that registers reputable sellers of vanilla and banishes thieves from the village for ten years if they're caught stealing. This was a vast improvement over the previous system, which allowed anyone with a little money to avoid jail time through the payment of a small bribe. In one small village where he works, a traditional agreement called a Dina, forged among every member of that village, helped strengthen norms against theft and attacks. (The penalties of the Dina, despite operating outside the government's law enforcement system, have proven so successful that they are now sanctioned by the government). BIANCO has also helped. "It gives a village a sense of being protected. If gendarmes work with thieves, for example, BIANCO will now prosecute them."

Virtually every president since independence has tried to reallocate the power of the provinces vis-à-vis the capital. In an effort to gain rural support, they all promise to give more power to the coasts, and yet primary control still resides in Antananarivo. The national constitution says local communes must provide development solutions in the provinces, Arivezo told me, but the central government is always reluctant to cede power to the regions. And while they encourage the regions to develop their own projects they don't give them the means to implement them. "They often don't ask local or regional leaders to be involved when they come up with a new development project, so the projects they fund are not suited to local conditions. Here in the north, our development priorities should be tourism, mining and environmental preservation. We need to build and improve a road around Amber Mountain [one of the region's top ecotourist sites]. There are chronic water shortages here, so we need to protect our clean sources of water around Diego and improve access to them. Instead, the central government gave us a fish factory! It employs dozens of women, that's true, but at very low wages and it does nothing to develop the region as a whole."

Arivezo believes that Madagascar is slowly moving to renewable energy sources, but needs much more. Diego itself has abundant sunshine and wind, and the sea tides are another renewable source, but other regions are not so lucky. "We are not a poor country in terms of resources, in fact we have so many, from vanilla to cocoa to minerals and beaches and forests. But corruption takes a terrible toll on our economy. The first question from the central government when an investor wants to start a development project is, "Where is mine?" meaning what is my percentage of your profits? The gold mines here in the north are a prime example. The government only announces a small fraction of the gold that's mined here. Most of it is sold on the black market by people who have paid off the government to look the other way."

Africa is urbanizing at an incredible rate, and cities in Madagascar are likewise becoming more crowded every day. Arivezo told me that urbanization has accelerated during the past 10-15 years. "Before when people came from the villages it was only young people looking for education, now it is also producers looking to sell their goods at a market. You know, the roads we built to rural areas ten years ago were intended to help move products to cities, but it eventually brought the people themselves, some of whom became attracted to modern conveniences in cities like electricity (especially young people). We in the local development community have tried to give them reasons to stay in the village, by bringing development projects like electricity to them there, but the trend is becoming clear as more and more people arrive." Cell phones and solar panels in the villages have also given people fewer reasons to leave, but still they come. "The influx into Diego has not been overwhelming, at least not yet, but in Tana as I'm sure you've seen, it's brought tremendous change. Personally, I can only stay in Tana for four days and then I have to leave. There are so many people in the street now! In fact, Tana is no longer Tana as you and I once knew it; it's become a melting pot for the six provincial regions of the country."

The newcomers vary in their places of origin. Some come from other towns and cities along the east coast who are looking for work, while others are from rural villages a few hours from Diego; according to Arivezo they already know they don't have the skills required to work in the city and arrive simply to sell their products to a larger market. Sometimes they are confused by very basic infrastructure. "New people here try to assimilate to the culture in the city, but many of them hold onto their customs as well," Arivezo believes. "Sometimes you will see a group of three or four women, for example, sitting down in the middle of the paved street to have a chat, not realizing the street is reserved for cars!"

* * *

If Arivezo is the local savant regarding small scale, rural development projects in the northern regions of the country,

Vahiny Victor Angelo Rodilson is the government functionary responsible for implementing the Rajoaelina government's development projects in the North. Technically, he is the Regional Director for the Ministry of Agriculture, Fish and Livestock, but he described his role as something broader, more akin to a regional development director. I liked Rodilson immediately. Where most Malagasy are small in stature and typically reserved in temperament, Rodison was a great bear of a man, with hulking shoulders and a booming voice that could be, and often was, heard outside his office door. He grew more exuberant as our conversations grew longer, often slicing the air with his hands to emphasize an important point or walking over to a large map on the wall to show me exactly where a project was located, before returning to his desk and resuming his analysis, sometimes out of breath.

Rodilson echoed Arivezo's sentiments about Madagascar's potential almost verbatim. The country is rich in so many natural resources, he said, and especially in the region of Diana, where Diego sits. Diana has become a center for agriculture, ecotourism and industry, all of which will be vital to Madagascar's development. The first two are the most important to Diego's growth, he told me, although it also has a couple of industries like the shipbuilding facility and the fish factory outside of town. "Diana is a rich region," he said. "There is no famine. People live stable lives here with most of their resource needs met. There's plenty of rice, manioc, bananas, potatoes to go around."

Up to 75% of the people in the region work in agriculture, so that's tremendously important, he continued. Vanilla, cacao, coffee and cloves are the major export crops here. The big distributors, who are a mix of Malagasy and Indians, reap the most benefit. The city of Diego and the island of Nosy Be, where tourism is strong, earn a lot for the region and the country. Interestingly, he told me the foreign currency that tourists bring to these places goes into the state's coffers, but the Ariary the tourists receive in exchange and then spend all go to local merchants, providing a big stimulus to the economy.

Rodilson explained to me that the provinces now have more power than ever before to guide their own development, thanks to decentralization over the years. "Twenty years ago it was always the national government who imposed their ideas onto the regions. Now we come up with our own regional development plan in consultation with the local population and international experts. The plan then goes to the national government for funding by the state and international donors, then back to us for implementation. This is the way the system should work."

Like Arivezo, Rodilson worried about the growing pressures on Diego and its surrounding areas from migrants arriving from poorer areas. "Right now it's not a huge problem but in 10 years it could be," he said. "It could get like Antananarivo. Most of these people go to the country to plant crops. They face no backlash or discrimination there, because Malagasy people are very welcoming of foreigners and those from other regions of the island." Similarly, urbanization is another problem on his radar. "Diego is a small city in terms of population and geographically. It's now expanding into a kind of sprawl that brings a bit of chaos in terms of management. The land surrounding the outer edge of the city is owned by the army and people are starting to encroach onto military land, who send them back into the city limits. So we're starting to see a situation where large numbers of people don't have their own land."

Crime concerns him, too, as farmers begin to plant more vanilla in the wake of the crop's sudden rise in price over the past decade. While rightfully viewed as a boon to local economies, vanilla can also bring its own set of hazards, principally related to crime. In the neighboring region of Sava farmers grow more vanilla and thus face more problems surrounding security than in Diana. He sees the murders and crop stealing in Sava as a precursor to what might happen to his region. "We're afraid the same will happen here in Diana now that we've started to grow more vanilla. We've got to start partnering more with the police to safeguard the lives and property of those who work in this sector."

Despite his claims of ample resources available for everyone, Rodilson confided to me that clean drinking water is probably his biggest concern right now. "Fifty years ago there were 77 sources of fresh water coming down from Amber Mountain; now, as a result of deforestation and environmental destruction, there are only five. Add to that the fact the city's infrastructure was designed for a city of 10,000 people, and now the population is 800,000. Those with money are starting to build more cisterns to keep as much as possible for themselves. Those without it have to wake up in the middle of the night to go look for it. If the state doesn't find another water source for people here, this will be the biggest problem in the future." My thoughts drifted back to Gladonia's middle-of-the-night searches for water as he said this.

Another big problem for government officials in all of Madagascar's cities is youth unemployment, something that everyone from police chiefs to development experts had told me. For Rodilson as with others, the responsibility for the high urban unemployment rates lies with the government, while praising the new president's efforts. "The state is simply not creating enough employment opportunities for young people," he said. "They end up stealing, going into prostitution, or other bad things. This is the responsibility of the state to remedy, they're the ones who create jobs. Industry isn't developed enough to absorb all the people looking for work. President Rajoelina is making a real effort to finance new programs for people who want to start their own small businesses selling something they make, which is often the only option here. I believe he understands the problem well and has made it a priority."

* * *

If Madagascar is ever to escape its history of low growth and chronic poverty it will have to find opportunities for its people to move from subsistence agriculture to more formal sectors of its economy, including in its manufacturing and service industries. And to do that the country's hopes will rest on highly educated young people with college degrees – still well under 10% of the relevant-age population. These university graduates are the ones who will become leaders in their society, in government, in the professions, in business and in civil society organizations. And yet they too suffer from a tragedy of numbers: the number of college graduates is rising at a much faster rate than the market for their skills, forcing them to navigate a tortuous path between chasing their dreams and making ends meet. I traveled to the northern port city of Diego Suarez to meet a group of recent graduates from the University of Antsiranana to get a sense of the opportunities and challenges for highly educated young people in the country.

Ismaya Said is a 21-year-old student in her third year at the University of Antsiranana, in the Department of Law, Economics, Accounting, and Political Science, where she hopes to earn a degree in economics. Ismaya was born and raised in Diego. Both of her parents went to college but she was raised by her mother, who worked in a fish factory outside of town.

Ismaya is everything those who want Madagascar to succeed could hope for from its next generation. Smart, articulate, and motivated, she nevertheless wears her education easily, maintaining an engaging and self-deprecating style of conversation. She makes friends easily and is open about her life in a way that is rare in Madagascar. She has had a fortunate upbringing in some ways, with a mother that loved and encouraged her, but the absence of her father, and his rejection of her and her mother, has clearly scarred her. Her vulnerability shines through as much as her ambition. When she wants to make an important point she looks straight at you and shakes her head ever so slightly for emphasis, in an authoritative manner that belies her youth.

Her story begins with her family, and the influence they have had on her since she was young.

It was always obvious I would go to university. My grandfather gave me the desire to learn, my mom too. Everyone in my family is educated, except my grandmother. So I guess you could say I never had a choice. [37]

After graduating from high school and earning her baccalaureate in 2016, Ismaya went to the capital, Antananarivo, for one year to continue her studies, and to see her father, who was visiting from France. (Her father is Malagasy but became a French citizen before she was born). She wanted to study chemistry, but arrived in Tana just after the university's registration period had closed for the year, blocking her enrollment. She decided to take an English class for four months instead, but quickly came to feel as if she wasn't being productive. On top of that, she had trouble adjusting to life in the capital. "I didn't like Tana, I felt lost there," she told me. "It was my first time away from my mother, and that was very difficult for me." She ended up staying a total of seven months, living with her cousin. She saw her father only occasionally, usually at her aunt's house. He told her he wanted to stay in Tana for a year with her but soon left without much explanation. "I was sad but I wasn't really surprised," she said. "I am one of those who believe most men make promises they don't keep, and my father is an example of that. I saw him for the first time when I was eight years old, after begging my mother to let me meet him. Since then he always encouraged me to study in France and said he would take care of all the paperwork, but he never did. He just doesn't take his responsibilities seriously. Now I think girls who grow up without a father are more vulnerable to the seductions of men they meet because they are so desperate for a man to love them."

After seven months in Tana she came back to Diego on an extended vacation. One day she was talking about college with a family friend and he encouraged her to study economics, telling her that she would have a better chance of finding a good job with an economics degree than one in chemistry. And he was right, she soon realized. "A career in chemistry here just isn't realistic – I think it's more a profession for the developed countries. Anyway, I realized I didn't really want to return to Tana. The seven months away really made me appreciate my life here."

So Ismaya enrolled at the state university in Diego. Still dreaming of traveling to France to study and reunite with her father, she couldn't focus much that first year and had trouble accepting that she was back in her hometown, probably for several years. She knew that the universities in Antananarivo are considered the best, with the universities in the provinces regarded as a little bit beneath them, and this disheartened her as well. The economics program was strong, however, if a little confusing to her as well. "I didn't understand it at all at first. It wasn't the professor's fault, it was just an entirely new discipline and there were times I felt so confused I didn't even know what questions to ask. And I'm one of those people who like to be perfect in everything, so this was really hard for me to struggle with initially. I was a perfect student all the way through high school. I'm never happy with any grade less than a 15 [out of 20]." Ismaya devoted herself to her studies after the first couple of months and ended up with a 16 for the first year.

College in Madagascar is surprisingly competitive. In contrast to university life in the United States, where the lion's share of students expect to graduate, and usually do if they show up to class and do a minimal amount of work, students here face relatively intense pressure to perform well and competition is sometimes fierce. A substantial percentage of students don't even make it past the first year, with language fluency often posing a key obstacle. Ismaya's class as a whole posted mediocre grades, and she believes the language barrier was a key reason. "I think a major reason was because all of our courses are in French and many of them didn't speak French well. Some were very weak in fact, which makes you wonder how they ever passed the *bac* to get into college; that's a question that hangs in the air around our university." There were 100 students in her class the first year, but by her second year the enrollment had dropped to 40. The university requires each student to pass an exam each semester to continue, and the other 60 were those that failed and had to repeat a semester, chose to drop out or were simply excused. Now, in Ismaya's third year, there are just 30 students left.

Like many college students, it took her some time to learn how to balance the demands of the university with the new freedoms she discovered as a young woman. Several times during our conversations Ismaya hinted at a certain disdain for other students who were too serious about their studies to find time for a social life, something that was clearly important to her.

My second year at university my life was different, because you understand better what you're doing, where you're going. Most students also begin to have more of a social life and that outside life begins to impact your university life. That's what happened to me, anyway, and I let my love life affect my studies. I've always had an active social life. Not a lot of friends, mind you, but very close friends, and I enjoy going out and doing things. I've also had a lot of guy friends, I'm not sure why, but maybe it's because female friendships can become petty sometimes. I got a boyfriend and I spent a lot of time with him and neglected my classes to the point where it became a problem. But looking back I have no one to blame but myself, it was all my fault. The relationship started at the end of my first year and lasted almost all of my second year. My last semester of second year was the worst semester of my life – I think I even got a 10 (out of 20) in Statistics! My average dropped from 16 my first year to somewhere between 14 and 15 for my second year. Even though it hurt I think the breakup, when it came, was the best thing that could have happened to me.

Some of my classmates are bookworms who study all the time, but I think that's a mistake. Getting a good job takes more than good grades, you have to learn to communicate to work together, and people who study all the time by themselves don't realize that. Grades don't indicate how valuable you will be to an employer. And generally our class is lazy; most of us don't work very hard, although some manage to still get good grades. Me, I could do better, study harder, but I'm happy with where I stand today.

I asked her how often she heard from her father during that time and she just shook her head: not very often, she said. But the lure of France and the chance to see him more often never left her, and after her second year she decided to make one last effort to follow him. She went back to Tana between her second and third years to check on her immigration status with the French consulate. She had submitted papers to become a French citizen – based on her father's citizenship – all the way back in 2008, but had never received a response even after 10 years. During her meeting at the consulate they told her that because her father had not become a French citizen until 2001, a few years after her birth rather than before, she was disqualified from receiving French citizenship. "They told me I would still receive a final, official response, but that hasn't arrived yet and I've actually stopped thinking about it. I've tried to move on and just focus on my future now – a future without France in it."

After that disappointment she returned to school for her third and final year. But when she and her classmates showed up at the beginning of the semester, they were told by the university to go back home for a month or two because the university wasn't ready for them yet. University administrators then announced they would combine the next two semesters into one to try to make up for lost time. With the third year of university in Madagascar traditionally considered the hardest anyway, this packed schedule promised to make Ismaya's last year even more stressful. But she remained on schedule to graduate with a degree in economics in 2020 or 2021. Her goal is to eventually get a Master's degree and then a doctorate in economics, but with no university in Diego offering graduate programs in economics she will have to look elsewhere, perhaps abroad if she can earn a scholarship. She wants to get some work experience first, and while she seemed well aware of how challenging it might be to find a good job, her optimism was still palpable.

After graduating next year I will work first before going for my Master's degree. Most of my colleagues will do the same. For me it's because I want to take a break and because I want to help earn some money to help my mother, who is all alone. Several of my friends plan to work in a bank after graduation. I'd like to work in tourism. To graduate I have to write a short book, at least 50 pages, on a subject in my major. During my first year I decided to write one on the economic aspects of tourism, after I saw what happened one time when tourists on a cruise ship arriving in Diego refused to disembark because several cases of the plague had hit the city. That had a big impact on the local economy. The book is still in the planning stages. As I write it I hope it will guide me as I start to think about a career. I'd like to start my own business in the tourism sector someday.

The thought of having a boss and working for a company sounds unpleasant to her – she would much rather start her own company – but she realizes she will probably have to find a routine job in order to get some experience. Maybe at a bank, she told me, though that doesn't interest her much either. "I'm not sure what all my options are at this point. If they ask me to teach first year economics at the university, I would do that too. I also want to do something for Diego. I want to help others in my work. Everyone has a responsibility to do that; why live if not to serve others, to be useful? If you don't help your community or your country, who will?"

Ismaya confided to me that all of her classmates are afraid of the future. She knows the options for new graduates in Madagascar aren't plentiful, especially in the wake of the Coronavirus. Occasionally she meets taxi drivers who have university degrees, reminding her how difficult it will probably be to find something in her field. That's why she wants to start her own business, believing it might be the only option she has. "But I see the glass as half full; I think I will be successful. You are what you believe, you attract what you think and what you project. I know it won't be easy. But my mom needs me, and I need me too, so I really have no choice but to succeed. And succeeding also means being a good citizen. There's a quote I like from Albert Einstein: the world is a dangerous place, not because of those who do evil, but because of those who look on and do nothing."

I asked her how difficult it was to pay for college and how prohibitive the cost made higher education for students who were qualified and wanted to go. At a state university like the University of Antananarivo, you just pay once, when you register. Tuition ranges per year, but averages at less than $100 annually. A private college could cost as much as $450 per year. Her mother has always paid the fees for her, which makes Ismaya feel guilty because she knows it's difficult for her mother to afford now without a permanent job. She says her friends' parents also pay their children's tuition, since none of the students have jobs. "And that's why we want to work after getting my degree – to help our parents and earn a little money of our own," she said.

So while financial concerns are by far the biggest obstacle to most students' ability to go to college, there are cultural obstacles as well, especially for girls. After a certain age, most girls realize they either have to marry or work for the rest of their lives. Ismaya found those choices unsettling. "Most girls I know decide they're going to depend on a man to support them financially, and most times it's with a foreigner, since they usually have money. Poverty imposes that choice on a lot of women here. It's sad, but it's one of the results of the economic situation here. I could never do that – sell my body to a man or marry one just for money. It's my education that prevents me from doing that. But I understand that others don't always have a choice so I can't judge them for seeking out a foreign man to support them. I'm just lucky because I have a mother like my mother, who taught me to be strong even after all the trauma my father caused for us."

In a few of our discussions we ventured away from her personal experiences and talked about the future of Madagascar and the forces that always seem to keep the country poor. She said her class discusses the future of our country often and are sometimes asked to give an opinion, so they've all pondered it.

Most have taken a negative attitude, concluding that Madagascar is unlikely to develop quickly or smoothly. She told me it's hard to identify the real problem in Madagascar; there are so many it makes it hard to prioritize them. National leaders and corruption rank high on her list, however. "Politicians promise everything, and we always believe them! So the problem is them, but it's also us for allowing them to get away with things." And as for corruption, her cynicism about progress was colored by too many of her disheartening experiences:

Corruption dominates everything here, and that holds us back so much! It is a huge problem it is because we've normalized it. It's become banal. I'll give you an example. I got my driver's license last year (2018), but after passing the exam I still had to wait four or five months to get the permit. That's the way it is for almost everyone. Then I heard that a few people had paid someone off and gotten their permits in just a few days. And you know what, I wasn't even mad, because it's all become so normal to me! We complain, sure, but that won't do anything. We're corrupt from head to toe here. It's not impossible to change the culture but it's going to be extremely difficult.

She also pointed to other cultural impediments to progress. Ethnic distrust, or "tribalism" as she called it, holds the island back tremendously. Ismaya hasn't seen much change over time. A mix of several tribes, she considers herself a Northerner more than a member of any tribe, but this is unusual and she recognizes it. Her resentment to the perceived superiority complex of the highlands was always just below the surface when we talked about it, as it was with dozens of people I met along the costs. One story she told me revealed her frustration:

After he left the presidency Marc [Ravalomanana] said

Tana is 'the portal' to Madagascar. Like everything has to go through them for it to become important here or even real. That angered me and a lot of us here, because by saying that he was putting the rest of us below the Merina. But it goes both ways: there are some places in Madagascar where the Merina can't even go because they aren't welcome. And sometimes on Facebook I see insults going in both directions – from the Merina to the coastal people and from us back to them. Some families here won't accept a Merina into their family because there's just too much baggage, too many bad feelings from the past. We grow up here to believe that the Merina want to control all of Madagascar's resources, even if they won't admit it publicly. That scares me for the future.

She told me about a cousin who consistently received grades of 18 at the University of Antananarivo, but saw the final average on her record changed to 15. Why is that, she wondered? Her family thinks it's because she isn't Merina, and perhaps because she wears a headscarf for religious reasons. Ismaya believes that politicians from Tana give privileges to people from the highlands, and that her native people simply don't have enough opportunities because of it. "You know, a country is like a family," she said, "and when one group is held back it holds all of us back."

At our last meeting, Ismaya was presenting for a presentation later that night and was a little distracted. She was still as charming and thoughtful as ever, but her mind was clearly elsewhere, and I eventually asked her if she wanted to take a break and practice her presentation with me. "Yes! Then we can get back to solving all of my country's problems," she said with a laugh. She was eager to practice her presentation with me, and as I listened to her speech about the ways in which the government's investments in a better tourist infrastructure could raise living standards of regular Malagasy across the island, it occurred to me that she might have a future in politics. Eventually we got back to her college experience and whether she felt prepared to move on.

> The university did the best they could for us, with the professors and materials they provided. I feel like I'm prepared for the career I want now. But on the other hand, we only learned theory, there was no practical component to it, so I'll have to learn on the job too. The biggest thing is that I've gained confidence because in all our classes we have to give our opinions on different topics. Some of my classmates have had experience working before. But they're not ready either. Our professors have told us our class is graduating at a low level of competence compared to other classes, so maybe we're in for a big surprise when we go out into the world and realize we're not ready.

The future of the island will undoubtedly be led by those will college degrees, but Ismaya didn't want to hear that. A college degree was just the start for her, and by itself it seemed to mean very little.

> We who have graduated from college are not special, even though we're a small percentage of people in Madagascar. Three extra years of education after the *bac*? That's nothing! Why should we feel special? The big difference I think comes with getting a Master's degree. Now that's something. That will get you a good position somewhere. Yes, I know that today's college graduates are the future of Madagascar. But I'm not sure that the country will change simply because of a change in the generation leading it. We've always said that and look where we still are. Sometimes I think we're going in circles. So I can't say that my generation will be any better than the ones before ... Our professors ask us what we're

going to do after college, and we all lie. We all say something overly ambitious, something that's impossible, something that's a dream. I believe most of us want to do something for the country, but first you have to take care of your own house, as they say. That's what I plan to do, then find a way to help others, because I know our country needs more of that.

It's possible Ismaya will have a more challenging road to success than a man with her skills and education would have. The World Bank's *Face of Poverty* report, however, found little evidence of discrimination against women in the country, and Ismaya echoed their conclusion. It's not more difficult for women generally to succeed here, she told me. She acknowledges that most top positions still go to men, and a few administrative positions are unofficially reserved only for women, like secretarial work, but she believes a woman can accomplish just as much as a man in Madagascar, and she made it clear to me that she intends to.

Victor Hugo said women have a singular power: that they are made from a reality of strength and an appearance of weakness. I think that's true. Men are afraid of an intelligent, independent successful woman, in fact. That's why those types of women here have problems finding a serious relationship, because men are intimidated by them. But I'm going to be one anyway and I'm not afraid of the consequences, because those kinds of men aren't serious anyway, they're not what I'm looking for. My mom always told me: you must shine through your mind, not your body.

I don't know if we'll ever see a female president in my lifetime. I actually haven't thought about that much. Maybe we need one though! I don't mean that as a criticism of the current president, maybe he will turn out to be really good. If, that is, he and the other politicians in Tana start to realize there is more to Madagascar than the capital city. I think you already know how I feel about that.

As we wrapped up our last conversation I asked her to tell me what she thought her future would look like in five years.

By that time I will have finished my Master's degree, I will have started a tourist company, I will have traveled abroad I – hopefully to Australia to see the kangaroos I – and my mom will lack for nothing. That's the most important thing to me. Maybe I'll be married by that time too. You know, I can see an image in my mind of the other things but for some reason I don't have a picture of what marriage will look like. I'd like to get married, I think, but maybe it's more important just to find the person I love and who loves me in the same way. I want to know what love really is, because I've never had that with a man. In fact, it's been just the opposite – I've been really hurt by them. But I have to be confident, hopeful, or none of it will happen. The bad experiences I've had in my life have given me strength, and my mother has given me strength too. So I'm scared of the future, but I don't have a choice: I have to succeed.

* * *

Everyone who goes to college thinks that once they graduate they will embark upon a successful career. This is as true in Madagascar as it is in the United States or anywhere else. In Madagascar, too, a degree confers a certain degree of respect on new graduates, perhaps even more so in a country with so relatively few of them. And yet with more and more high school graduates clamoring for ways to go to college, Madagascar's economy is much too sluggish to provide jobs for all of them, leaving thousands of young people looking for something meaningful to do with their lives.

This crisis facing young, educated Malagasy has been building for decades. Social science research reveals a significant drop in socioeconomic status among college graduates on the island, in part because the state has been hiring fewer of them. One survey found that the starting salary for young civil servants fell 70% in the late 1990s compared to the period from 1975-81. The benefits of a college degree have rightfully been called into questions in Madagascar, where, contrary to developments in advanced economies, inequality has actually fallen between those with and without college degrees.[38]

Nasser Amady is 34 years old already and has had a university degree for a decade now, graduating in 2010 with a degree in Environmental Science from the University of Antsiranana. He is now working on a Master's degree in the same field and from the same university. We met for coffee one weekend in one of the restaurants along Rue Colbert, the main street in Diego Suarez.[39]

"My university experience was really the start of my career and my adult life," Nasser told me. "I moved away from home the first time. I learned to live on my own. And it's because of my university experience that I am where I am today."

But he has mixed feelings about the value of his university degree. From 2010-15 looked everywhere for a job in his field but was continually told there was nothing available, that he lacked the right experience, or that a position had already been filled internally. Eventually he settled for work as a teacher in a secondary school, which in Madagascar does not even require a college degree. "I sent at least 25 resumes over those years and got nothing," he told me. "Only those who know someone in government or business find jobs right away."

There are a few thousand college graduates each year in Madagascar, 150 from the state university in Diego and another

250 from private colleges in the area. Diego is a charming city with wide streets that are safe to walk even late at night; a warm, windy climate; and a laid back atmosphere that shuts down for a couple of hours every afternoon to allow everyone to take a siesta; but it has very few industries that employ more than a handful of people. There is no possible way for Nasser and his hundreds of classmates to find work there, as he discovered soon after graduating. His wife, Osna, had a similar experience. She graduated in 2011 from the same state university, also in Environmental Science. After four years of searching for work in her field and finding nothing, she took a job in a photocopy shop until their first daughter was born in 2015, at which point she simply gave up on a career.

Nasser told me that in addition to navigating an anemic economy, young graduates are forced to contend with an employment system riddled with corruption. "For some jobs, you have to pay the employer to hire you," he said. "For example, to work in the custom's bureau you have to pay 20 million Ariary, while a job as a police inspector requires a payment of 12 million. Sometimes the bribe requested is even more than the salary offered. And what really bothers me is that those that can pay for jobs are often the ones who are least competent to do them."

Thus the labor market is almost as crooked as everything else in Madagascar, and the government knows it and has always tolerated it, according to Nasser. But like several other young people I met in the northern region of Diana, he supports the president's efforts to fight corruption: "We're on the right path now with corruption," he said. "Now the police can go to prison if they're corrupt. That wasn't the case before."

Whether in the United States or Madagascar, there will always be examples of individuals who achieve outsized success without a college degree, prompting some to question whether higher education is really worth it. In Madagascar this is a legitimate question, at least from a purely economic point of view. Nasser is not sure that those who go to university end up with a better career than those who start working earlier, work hard and move up on their own. "Maybe all that young people with a university education really get is a superiority complex," he mused. "Only a few of them have better jobs." This is depressing to hear, but until the economy starts generating higher paying jobs, it will be the reality.

And yet what's inspiring on some level is the desire to go to college nevertheless. "The college entrance system is very challenging," he told me. "It's very hard to get in with so many applicants. That's one reason for the huge growth in private colleges, to accommodate the surge in young people wanting a university education." But corruption exists at the examination level as well. "If you fail the entrance exam you can still go to college if you pay the right price. It's rare but it happens."

There is no doubt that he and his wife will send his two daughters to college someday, and it inspires him to work harder even if his own job prospects remain dim. "I will encourage my daughters to go to university because it's expected of us and of them. Sine my wife and I are both well-educated my children must be as well. Now I'm working hard to find a job for myself, yes, but also to be in a position to help them find work when they're old enough so they don't have to go through the same experience I did. If I reach a high enough position I can help them find jobs more easily," he said, acknowledging something I had heard throughout Madagascar, that family connections, more than anything else, may help his children find work one day."

Nasser understands that the situation will potentially get worse with more young people flooding the educational system over the next two decades, and here he appeals to his country's leaders to improve the economy in time to accommodate them. "The employment rate depends on the government, they have to find a solution. But everyone here knows the future depends on education. We must educate everyone to a certain level, even all the peasants in the small villages, to get them away from traditional methods of farming and even traditional ways of thinking. That is the only way to make Madagascar a modern country."

I caught up with Nasser six months after our first meeting and was delighted to hear that he had successfully launched his own vanilla exporting company in Sambava, a mid-sized town outside of Diego, with €7,500 he received from an environmental fund based in Germany. He and a friend from Sambava got the idea after working and doing research in Sambava over the past few years. His environmental science degree had been only indirectly helpful in launching his new career, by providing him with an introduction to Sambava through his part time work and research there, which allowed him to make contacts in the vanilla industry. Other than that, he said, it wasn't really useful. He still plans to finish his Master's degree in the near future. Meanwhile, with his colleagues in the program still struggling to find leads for employment, he considers himself lucky to have found an opportunity in a potentially lucrative business. Even more, he is proud of himself for taking the entrepreneurial risk.

Justin Sanamo has a similar story. Now in his mid-thirties, Justin has been looking for meaningful employment for almost ten years. He earned a bachelor's degree from the University of Antsiranana in 2010, then took four years off to look for work. Finding none, he went back to school for his Master's degree in Biodiversity and Ecosystem Preservation, earning his degree in 2018. During both stints at the university he did various internships and certifications but was unable to find any full time work, living with his parents so that he could save enough money to pay the annual tuition of 200,000 Ariary per year.

When he received his undergraduate degree in 2010 he started his job search right away. "There is a place in Diego where job openings are posted," he told me. "I went there every week after I first graduated. Every year I sent at least 25 resumes, but only got about seven interviews over four years, with no offers." Of the 54 members of his class, he estimated that only ten found jobs, with only three of those related to the student's area of study. The other seven became gendarmes or police investigators or found other work that did not require a degree. For Justin and the other 43 members of his class who found nothing, life became incredibly frustrating. "It was embarrassing," he told me. "We spent a lot of time studying and had nothing to show for it years later." He believes there are simply not enough businesses or organizations offering employment to meet the demand. Like Nasser, he witnessed a lot of recruitment of family members for open positions, and believes the employment system is still based more on connections than merit. "The system doesn't work at all," he said.[40]

Olin Serazaka, the president of the students' association at the University of Antsiranana, concurred. Olin is studying architecture and has just one year left before graduating. Up to 90% of graduating students won't be able to find work in their area of study, he told me, leaving them no choice but to accept jobs that pay very little. "Students here just accept the situation, they know there's nothing they can do," he said. "And another problem with many firms is that you have to pay them first before they will hire you. Sometimes it's 25% of your monthly salary."[41] As shocking as handing over a down payment on your job might sound to Western ears, I heard it over and over from students I met in Madagascar.

And yet, despite all of the reasons *not* to go to college in Madagascar, the dream of a university degree is only growing stronger, prompting tens of thousands of young people on the island to seek it out every year. Perhaps even more than in other parts of the world, a degree here sets you apart from the masses of undereducated people around you. As Marie Rose Rasoavololona, a French major at the University of Antsiranana, told me, "Even if there is no work for us in our field of study, I and all of my friends will still be happy to get a university degree because of the pride it will give us. There is a certain respect you receive when people know you are a university graduate."[42]

But Anissa Volatiana Mahazatsakila, studying for her Master's degree in Marine Science, wants more than respect for her years of hard work. She dreams of a job working in marine conservation even though she has no illusions that it will be easy to find. All of the employers she's talked to want someone with a lot of experience, which she doesn't have. She has resigned herself to the fact that if she can't find work studying the oceans she will have to accept the best job available. Anissa agreed with virtually everyone I met who said the lack of work is the biggest problem for young people in Madagascar. "Most students think they'll have a good job after graduation but the reality is they won't. Many graduates, once they realize the situation, immediately return to school for a Master's degree if they can afford it, thinking that will get them real work. But continuing your education gets expensive and puts off earning money, so it's a tough decision."

Even with all of the obstacles for young graduates, she wouldn't hesitate to make the same decision again. "I would still go to university knowing the job market is not good," she told me. "You meet a lot of people there and make contacts for later. And in the long term, the job prospects are better. The respect factor is there too, but more people back in the village will respect me for the good job I get than the degree itself. I am still optimistic I will find a good job once I finish this year."[43]

Anissa had many thoughtful ideas on how to make the higher education system more efficient and beneficial for students like her. First, she said, the state should designate more positions for recent graduates when it allocates funds for development projects across the provinces. That would provide an immediate boost to morale among young people. And like other students I met in Diego, she believed the system is deeply unfair to students outside of Antananarivo. "There is a test every year open to all university graduates in Madagascar who want to work for the national government, but most jobs still end up going to students from the center [the capital]," she said. Whether that's because schools and universities in Antananarivo have always been better or because of the persistence of discrimination against coastal tribes is unclear, but there is a strong feeling among Anissa and her friends that it is the latter, and that the state should designate a certain number of government jobs to students from each region.

* * *

Some young Malagasy didn't have the means or the opportunity to pursue higher education, and of those people some chose to start their own business. Entrepreneurship is becoming more common in today's Madagascar, undoubtedly helped along by the fact that, according to the World Bank, it now takes only eight days to start a business on the island, compared to 67 days as recently as 2018.

One of those people is Dodo Razafindrakoto, who along with his French girlfriend Malo opened a popular burger joint in Antananarivo, along with a startup chocolate factory outside of the city. In his small restaurant high above the teeming market stalls of Analakely, Dodo could be seen doing everything from grilling meat, tending bar, accepting food deliveries and dressing down lazy employees. I became one of his best customers during my months in Tana, and he and Malo became two of my good friends.

His story is nothing less than one man's attempt to return

home and remake his native city, for Dodo was born and raised in Antananarivo. He left at age 24 and spent over a decade abroad before coming back to Madagascar in 2016. His journey abroad took him first to Paris, where he spent a year at a university before declaring it a waste of time. After another year spent working odd jobs in the French capital he grew homesick and called his old boss in Madagascar to ask if there were any open positions with his construction company. His boss didn't need help in Tana but, remembering Dodo as a model employee, sent him a ticket to Mauritania, where Dodo worked for several tears in the logistics and supply chain industries, traveling all around West Africa. Dodo thrived in his new environment. "Unlike in Paris, people in Africa were smiling and warm. It reminded me of home," he told me. Some of the countries like Mauritania were majority Muslim nations, and on several occasions members of the local mosque tried to convert Dodo, who respectfully declined each time. "I knew I wasn't going to be a Muslim but it wasn't annoying when they asked, actually it was interesting to talk with them about it," he said.[44]

In addition to encountering new languages and new religions, Dodo also experienced new cultures, not all of them attractive. He found the people in West Africa much more violent than the Malagasy, who, he believes, are basically peaceful and often fail to carry through on their threats. Violence in mainland African cities was much more serious, and he knew several friends who were beaten or stabbed. During all the years in Africa he didn't really pay attention to what was going in Madagascar, but he did take notice of a constitutional crisis in 2010 in the Ivory Coast, where Laurent Gbabgo and Alassane Outtara both claimed victory after a disputed presidential election. "When I saw this happen it reminded me so much of what we went through in Madagascar in 2002," he said.

He recalled those days vividly:

In 2002, people were fed up with Ratsiraka, and we were all getting poorer and poorer. The people were desperate for change. The international community came out in support of Marc and that really encouraged us to make sure he won. But Ratsiraka blocked everything from the East coast, so hundreds of thousands of people started marching on Tana and there were strikes everywhere. It was difficult to understand what was happening. You could hear gunshots, not every night but almost. The great thing I remember is that people here really helped each other – we gave each other food, supplies, all those things. It was actually a pretty organized system that the people of Tana set up on their own to get through the crisis. We even formed our own security patrols in bad neighborhoods so the crime wouldn't take over the city.

He explained the recurrent crises in Madagascar as a symptom of inexperience with democracy. "Africa isn't like the West, which has laws and enforces them," he said. Here in Madagascar, if someone doesn't like the outcome of an election he thinks he can just shut the country down until he gets his way. People like Ratsiraka become addicted to power. Even Marc [Ravalomanana] became that way. He dominated so many businesses in the country – even while he was President – and tried to get richer and richer. He created even more advantages for his businesses and blocked competitors from competing with him. This caused a lot of anger, especially among the Karana [Indo-Pakistani] community."

Dodo came back to Madagascar in 2016 because he missed his friends and family and wanted to try to help rebuild his country. He and Malo work long hours trying to manage and grow their two businesses, but they are thrilled to be part of the new dining scene in Tana. "When I came back I started working for my old construction company again but people told me to try to do something bigger. I found it wasn't that hard to start a business here. The EDBM [small business agency] was really supportive and I think they're trying to make the process shorter for everyone so the economy will improve."

"I love being back here," he said. "I have my own business and I'm my own boss. I've never done anything like this before but I think we all have experiences and common sense to draw on, and that's what I use to run my business. So I'm happy to be back in my country, but there are of course some things I'm not happy about." He cited the pollution in Antananarivo as his biggest nuisance and implored all of the city's leaders to do something about it. He was dismayed by the level of corruption still present in Tana but hoped the new president was serious in his statements to end it. And he was bothered by other evidence that the tragic plight of so many people in other poor, crowded cities was now a reality in his hometown. "Seeing young girls selling themselves to old white men is also disgusting to me, but I also think those girls are in an impossible situation because it's so easy for them to make good money that way. I just don't want to see Madagascar end up with a reputation like Thailand; I want tourists to come here for the food, the culture, the beaches and the national parks and forests, not for sex."

And yet with all of Antananarivo's troubles and the modest growth in his businesses so far, he remains an incorrigible optimist. "Think positive and things will get better," he tells himself. "I believe things are slowly getting better. But change must come from individuals. I want to do the right thing for my country and I think everyone should have this mentality. It's not up to the president to solve everything for us; each person must bring his own brick to rebuild Madagascar. For me it's about running an honest business that will make people happy."

Dodo places a lot of faith in his generation and the one that follows to change the narrative about the capital city and the island at large. Madagascar has lots of potential, he told me. "We have so much land, a young population and natural resources. But we must educate our children. The biggest problem here is a lack of education. The lack of education today means we don't have enough qualified people to manage things. We have to change that. Education means schooling of course but it also means learning respect and understanding different kinds of people. Education is not just about books and diplomas but also understanding one another. Young people here have completely lost respect for their elders, which was so important to Malagasy people in the past. This loss of respect – you see it in everything in daily life. And people here must learn to open doors for themselves and not wait for our political leaders to give us everything. Education also means learning from about the mistakes we've made as a county in the past."

As a proud member of the Merina ethnic group, Dodo has never wanted to live anywhere else in Madagascar other than in Tana, but he realizes the distrust between ethnic groups haunts the island as much today as it did in the past. The tension between the highlanders and the coastal people is a real problem, he told me.

We try to live together. We respect them. But like all of human history there is a legacy here of one people ruling another people, and that leaves a lot of anger with the people who were colonized, for lack of a better word. You know they ruled over you and you think they still want to. That history is still with us even after 200 years and you can't forget it. So I understand the anger coming from the coasts. But I have no doubt we can overcome it. Look at Rwanda! The hatred there was much worse there – so bad they had a genocide – and now their story of recovery and building trust is amazing. I give Paul Kagame a lot of credit for that. But we all need to understand where the anger comes from. When you're at the bottom you resent those who are above you, even if they're no longer ruling over you. And politicians keep the ethnic problem alive so they can get support from their tribe by constantly bringing up ethnic solidarity and saying, "Look what I've done for our tribe, now you all must vote for me."

Dodo follows politics closely but, for such a thoughtful and well-spoken man, was surprisingly agnostic over the Ravalomanana-Rajoelina rivalry. He was rooting for the new president to succeed not because he particularly admired him or his policies but because he believed the island yearned for stability above all. "I don't know yet if the new President will be good or bad. We're still desperate for good leadership like we've always been. But unfortunately most of the people still follow their favorite politician blindly: whoever has the best banner or gives out the best t-shirt, we vote for him. But I think we have to let Rajoelina try to succeed, just like we did with Marc in 2002. I am hopeful he will succeed. Let's give him two years to see if he keeps his promises. More than anything the people here don't want to see another *coup d'etat* – that just sets us back by 100 years each time it happens. I think we've learned our lessons from 2002 and 2009, when all the chaos caused so many people to lose their jobs and poverty increased."

Dodo believes the next five years will be crucial to the island's progress. Stability and economic growth would set Madagascar back on the right path. More political crises and pervasive corruption, however, may send the country into a downward spiral from which it may never recover. Perhaps because he is an entrepreneur whose credo is self-reliance, he refused to put all of the responsibility for Madagascar's future on its political leaders. "It's up to everyone," he told me. "Let's give the president a chance to achieve some stability here. He must bring foreign investment back to get things started, then it's up to us as individuals. But we can't expect the president to do something magical. We must all work hard. I'm one of those people who doesn't believe in relying on the government to survive or even think we should give anything to beggars on the street, because it only creates dependency. With time, we can change the culture of corruption in Madagascar, but that will only come through education. If we can find a way to educate everyone across the whole island, things will change for the better."

* * *

I thought more about Dodo's insights when I returned to the northern city of Diego Suarez. I remembered that nearly all of the students in Diego had mentioned to me the possibility of opening their own business, just as Dodo had done in Tana. With so few job prospects available even for the highly educated and with governmental assistance for small businesses almost nonexistent, it's no surprise that many young people see venturing out on their own as their best option. But is this a viable strategy for development? Most of those I talked to here said no.

Professor Jaony sees a lot of opportunity for new businesses in the north of the island where he teaches economics. Bright students come to him all the time with good ideas for new businesses, but in most cases he is forced to tell them to temper their expectations, for four reasons. First, they probably won't be able to find financing for their ideas. Banks and other microfinance lenders demand collateral first, and are highly reluctant to take any chances on someone without a proven track record of business success. He did, however, credit President Rajoelina for creating a fund of 200,000,000 Ariary for young people interested in forming a startup. This produced some initial excitement among new graduates and led to 200,000 applications, but most of them are still waiting for a response. The second problem Professor Jaony sees is the lack of a market for anything but very basic goods. In a classic chicken-and-egg conundrum for developing countries everywhere, new businesses have very few consumers with the disposable income to buy their products, but it's hard to create those consumers unless more people can find gainful employment. And only a tiny percentage of aspiring businessmen and women have contacts abroad they can turn to for sales. Third, he said, the island lacks people with professional or technical skills that most new businesses require, so even the best ideas often can't be implemented. And finally, he faulted the government for its national development plan centered around agribusiness. That can only be operated by big businesses, so it's not a realistic possibility for startups or young people. He would prefer to see the government funding many small projects rather than one huge sector.

McGordon Ranaivo Arizezo, the rural development expert in Diego, agreed. "The bottleneck for startups here is funding. We have commercial banks, not development banks, so they don't loan to young people unless they have collateral, which they don't have. The banks help those already involved in business, not those without experience."

When I asked him about the president's new fund for startups, he, like Professor Jaony, expressed ambivalence. Under the new fund, he said, the president pays 10% of the 11% interest charged by banks (and when he said "the president" he meant that literally, claiming that the true source of the 10% donation was unknown and, incredibly, may even be from the president's own personal funds.) "We thought the announcement of support was just propaganda at first," he said, "but the first projects have now been funded in Tana and Antsirabe, so we're hopeful it will continue. But no one was surprised when Rajoelina gave the first grant to a potential competitor to Ravalomanana's dairy business."

He believes a market for startups exists if entrepreneurs will choose to sell things people need. There are small markets for new products here in Madagascar, but elsewhere in the Indian Ocean there are even more markets, so long as the quality is high enough to satisfy the expectations and requirements of those countries. There is also a cultural problem with producing large quantities of new goods: people in Diego tend to work alone, but need to band together to satisfy the large demands from nearby countries. "Tana has more experience working in groups. Maybe because the level of security here is better," he mused. "So we have to learn to work together, especially young people. People here think more about being their own boss rather than working in an office, and that's generally a good thing, but we also need startups that grow into offices that employ many people. If a few succeed, that could inspire others, especially in rural areas." McGordon summed up the island's needs succinctly. "Water, roads, and energy should be the three biggest priorities for this government," he said. "If people have those, and enough security to go out and feel safe, people here will work and the country can develop."

During my final few days in Diego I thought about everyone I had met there over the past ten weeks. The more I thought about them the more I kept coming back to two people who stood out for me: Ismaya and Gladonia, two young women of the same age but worlds apart in their life situations and future aspirations. I thought again of Nasser's question about whether college was really worth the time and effort in Madagascar if most graduates ended up with so little to show for it. Of course it is, I realized. Just look at Gladonia and Ismaya: one will remain stranded in poverty all her life, voiceless in the swirl of change taking place around her, while the other will eventually find a good job and become a leader in her community, well connected to the others in this closed society of the educated and the talented. Reducing the high rate of poverty and building a middle class in Madagascar will be the job of Rajoelina and his party in Parliament, yes, but it will also take the drive and ambition of people in distant regions of the island who, if by no other manner than through the example they set, inspire others to follow them on their path to success.

Chapter 5

Where Will All These Kids Work?

Economic decline has been the consequence of a profound malaise rather than its cause. At the heart of Madagascar's difficulties has been population growth of staggering proportions – as in continental Africa, probably of a scale and speed unique in human history.

Solofo Randrianja and Stephen Ellis

Madagascar: A Short History

I was sitting on the grass inside the soccer stadium in the southern city of Tulear, resting after running for an hour around the dirt track that encircled the field. Since it was a weekday afternoon and no match was taking place, the stadium was empty except for three boys who were also lounging on the field about twenty feet away from me. They glanced over at me a few times, and after their curiosity finally got the best of them they tentatively walked over to say hello.

As the boys approached I noticed a few things about them. First, they all looked to be about ten years old, though one was noticeably taller than the others. Second, none of them were wearing shoes. And third, they were all wearing English language t-shirts that, like thousands of others I saw on the island, had somehow made their way to Madagascar either by way of some charitable contribution or through a secondhand market for used clothing. As they gathered around me and we greeted each other in Malagasy I read the messages emblazoned across each of their chests. "Not A Morning Guy," one said; "The End Is Only Beginning," blared another; and "We Should All Be Feminists," was the advice worn by the taller boy.

I quickly determined that they had no idea what the words

on their shirts meant, and after considering whether to try to explain the messages to them I decided to ask about their families instead. They told me their names, but I had already differentiated them by their shirts, and even begun to attribute certain motives and beliefs to each of them based on the printed messages appearing before me. I soon learned that one of the boys had three brothers and sisters, one had four siblings, and the third – the Anti-Mornings Kid, as I recall – had six. I asked him to tell me what their names were.

"Jessica, Christian, Alain, Natasia, Joseline, and..." His expression clouded over and he squinted off into the distance, trying to remember the last name. "Jessica, Christian, Alain," he repeated again, counting on his fingers this time. When he stopped again at five siblings the other two boys began to tease him.

"Ha, you forgot one of your brothers!" The Doomsayer cried.

"Wait until I tell your sister you don't remember her!" The Feminist said.

Eventually he remembered the last name, of course, but for a minute I thought he wouldn't be able to, and in that minute I felt incredibly sorry for him. It had never occurred to me that one of the unintended consequences of having large numbers of children might be their eventual unfamiliarity with one another.

* * *

Sub-Saharan Africa is the only region of the world where the rate of population growth is still increasing. This has led to some consternation among the optimists of international development who foresee nothing but steady progress in the reduction of extreme poverty around the world, but who acknowledge that, at some point, unchecked population growth has the potential to eat away at economic gains. Even those who don't see population growth as a problem per se view its rapid increase in Africa as a cause for concern. And yet very few will come out and say that population growth is as dangerous to the continent's future as other perils, like climate change or ethnic conflict. But the evidence is becoming crystal clear: sub-Saharan Africa will soon have too many people to develop the way it wants to, and tens of millions more people will be mired in poverty and suffer from malnutrition simply because there will be too many of them for their economies to accommodate. Madagascar will suffer the same fate and for the same reasons unless it miraculously begins to undergo a dramatic reduction in the number of children being born. Absent that, the slow-growing nightmare of overpopulation will drain the island of nearly all of its precious potential.

But before we talk about Madagascar's incredible growth in people, some context is helpful. Almost everyone knows that the world's population has been growing nonstop for well over a century. What has been remarkable is the world's ability, thanks to modern science, to absorb the huge growth in numbers with very few catastrophes, be they famines or other disasters. Thomas Malthus famously predicted that, with the world's food supply growing arithmetically while the population increased geometrically, millions of people would eventually starve to death until the population was reduced to a sustainable level, when the population would begin to grow again and the cycle would repeat itself. This didn't happen, at least not on a large scale. In fact, in defiance of Malthus, as world population quadrupled between 1900 and 2001 (from 1.6 billion to 6.1 billion), grain production increased fivefold, from 400 million to 1.9 billion tons. And yet there have been enough historical examples of countries outgrowing their resource base and witnessing their populations cut back down by horrific famines that experts agree on the continual need for a balance between population and resources.[1]

This balance is about to be tested like never before, and the tension between the inexorable rise in the human population and the limited supply of Earth's resources seems to be reaching a breaking point. Neo-Malthusians are back, becoming louder and more prominent each time we cross another billion-person milestone. As the debate over whether the world is (or will be) overpopulated, there will be a few key points to keep in mind. The first is that the global population will continue to increase for the rest of the century, but the rate of population growth is steadily declining, so much so that at some time around the turn of the 22nd century the number of people will finally peak and start to decrease. The second is that almost all of the population increase for the rest of this century will take place in the developing world, precisely in places like Madagascar. The big questions are whether the planet can survive in anything resembling its current state over the next 80 years with billions more people living on it, and whether all those additional people can also survive. Even in 2100, when the population has peaked and starts its slow descent, will the crisis truly be over, or will it last another 50 years until the number of people finally reaches some optimal level?

Here is what the numbers tell us. In its 2019 forecast, the UN's Population Division predicted that the global population may stop growing completely by 2100. But before that happens, the global population of 7.7 billion in 2019 will increase to 9.7 billion by 2050 before reaching its peak of 10.9 billion at the end of the century. (This last number is actually a reduction from the 11.2 billion at century's end predicted by the UN in 2017.) The prediction that total growth will stop in 2100 is an approximation, but the important point made by John Wilmoth, the director of the division, is that "it will eventually stop growing." In addition to the overall rise in numbers, the UN identified several key population trends, including the declining global fertility rate (the 3.2 births per woman in 1990 fell to 2.5 in 2019, and is predicted to fall to 2.2 by 2050), and the emergence of people 65 and older as the fastest growing segments of the global population (more on this in a moment). However, the report noted that fertility rates remain high in some regions, particularly sub-Saharan Africa, where the population could double in the next 30 years. Wilmoth said this represents a challenge for achieving the UN's Sustainable Development Goals, including the elimination of poverty and hunger by 2030. "This reinforces that the most rapid population growth is happening in areas where it is difficult to accommodate that growth," he said.[2]

What's fascinating about global population trends is not just the overall rise in numbers but the concentration of growth in just a few areas of the world, with other areas already heading in the opposite direction. In fact, nine countries – India, Pakistan, Nigeria, Democratic Republic of Congo, Ethiopia, Tanzania, Indonesia, Egypt and the United States (the only developed country on the list) – will account for more than half the population growth between now and 2050. Conversely, during that same time span, 55 countries will see population reductions of at least 1%, including 26 that could see reductions of 10% or more.[3] Those countries are aging at a rate never before seen in human history, as falling fertility rates and longer life expectancy are combining to cause parts of the world's population to live well into their 80s and beyond. In 2018, people aged 65 or older outnumbered children under five globally for the first time. And the UN predicts that by 2050, one in six people will be older than 65, up from one in 11 in 2019, while the number of people aged 80 or older is expected to triple by that time. This aging trend has troubling implications for countries with growing numbers of retirees, as experts question whether those societies will be able to support their older generations as the "population support ratio" – the ratio of working age people to those 65 or older – continues falling around the world.[4] So for those living in South Asia and Africa, a surge in population will be a fact of life, while for the rest of the world the problem, if there is one, will be the decline in birthrates and how to care for an increasingly aging population. Widespread confusion over demographic trends is likely as the chattering classes go from discussing a population boom in one breath and a population bust in the next – both of which could be considered true – to describe what might be called demographic whiplash.

* * *

The emergence of these countervailing forces has caused a split between those observers who believe overpopulation is a serious problem threatening the health and welfare of billions of people, and those who think the rise in numbers is better viewed as a temporary condition that will eventually pass without great harm as the global population ages and eventually starts to decline. This divide in population studies represents a sharp distinction from the wholly justified alarm expressed over climate change, where a consensus has emerged that the effects of a warming planet are an existential danger to all of humanity. As we'll see in Chapter 6, this consensus has never been stronger. But no similar agreement exists among development experts that the world has too many people, and this makes it perhaps a more surreptitious threat.

Neo-Malthusians who adamantly believe that hundreds of millions will go hungry in the future have been fighting an uphill battle ever since the publication in 1968 of Paul Erlich's book, *The Population Bomb*, which predicted a slew of major population-driven crises that never came to pass. Undaunted, this group believes that now, the 21st century, is when the bomb will explode. Eugene Linden echoed this sentiment recently in his assessment of Lesotho, which was one of 18 African nations that suffered drought in 2018:

Lesotho is a case study in how rapid population growth can nullify development efforts that might otherwise let an emerging nation endure periods of abnormal weather... Did Lesotho ever have a chance? Some setbacks can be traced to crop failures, political turmoil or the 2008 recession. But when 50 years of development efforts don't produce meaningful gains, something other than bad luck is probably at work ... Lesotho's biggest problem was, and is, the obvious: too many people. In 1974, the average woman in Lesotho gave birth to six children. It's possible to imagine an economic miracle that would have let such a woman both feed her family and improve her material prospects. But it would be much easier to imagine that outcome if the woman had given birth only to two or three children back then. And so we have Lesotho today – echoing Malthus, not the future intended by aid agencies. Everyone should pay attention. As Europe faces huge waves of migrants, those masses are dwarfed by the number of poor families seeking refuge within their own or nearby countries. In Somalia, more than a million are internally displaced, while some 885,000 have migrated to neighboring countries with displaced populations of their own.[5]

In an accompanying article in the *New York Times*, Bill Marsh called the problems caused by overpopulation "an unfolding catastrophe."

Mass migration, starvation, civil unrest: overpopulation unites all of these. Many nations' threadbare economies, unable to cope with soaring births, could produce even greater waves of refugees, beyond the millions already on the move to neighboring countries or the more prosperous havens of Europe. The population crisis is especially acute in Africa ... but it spans the globe.[6]

Though alarmist in tone, people like Linden and Marsh have latched onto something important, which they call the "The Malthusian Moment Postponed." While the population growth rate is declining, the absolute number of people continues to rise, "with millions more at risk when things go awry." The implication is that, at some point, things *will* go awry, sweeping away the relevance of slower growth rates and amplifying the reality of millions more people vulnerable to disease or famine. A quick calculation demonstrates what these writers are talking about: while in 1967 the population growth rate was 2.1% and the increase in population was 73 million, in 2016 the growth rate was only 1.2% but the numerical increase was 80 million. This growth adds the population equivalent of a new Iran or Germany every year. The combination of globalization, which increased economic output and raised living standards globally, and the Green Revolution, in which scientific advances produced astounding increases in crop yields in many parts of the world, managed to produce enough food and jobs in the midst of soaring populations to offset the doomsday scenarios envisioned by Erlich and others. But if they don't continue to deliver the same results, it is no exaggeration to say that hundreds of million more people will suffer than ever before.[7]

The Coronavirus laid bare this fact unlike any other event of the past fifty years. The World Health Organization estimated the pandemic was likely to double the number of people facing acute hunger in 2020. About 265 million people in low- and middle-income nations were expected to face starvation by the end of that year, a doubling of the 135 million who already faced acute food insecurity in 2019. Covid-19 wreaked its devastation in often unpredictable ways, not only shuttering national economies around the globe but upending the global food supply, with lockdowns and social distancing mandates impacting everything from agricultural production to levels of nutrition and tourism. For people who only eat once a day or when they earn a wage, like millions in Madagascar, the virus has caused a sudden loss of income and pushed them over the edge. The world has never faced a hunger crisis like this, according to food security experts like the chief of the World Food Program, who said the world was on the brink of a "hunger pandemic." As with famines of the past, there is no shortage of food globally, but the supply chains in developing countries are so labor-intensive that they become much more vulnerable to disruptions caused by shocks like the virus. Food security is likely to deteriorate significantly worldwide for years to come, and the worst crises are likely to occur in Africa.[8]

Some neo-Malthusians take a more nuanced view of the issue, avoiding phrases like "hunger pandemic" while reaching many of the same dire conclusions. As population growth begins to rise again as a major topic in development circles, several books over the past decade have succeeded in taking the issue off the back burner and putting it where it now belongs: as a core development issue to be addressed as a corollary to climate change. Though none of them mentions Madagascar, the crisis they identify threatens to upend the island just as much as any other country. Threading its way through each work are three beliefs: first, that the world's food supply won't be able to keep up with the rising demand for food from three billion new people; second, that time is of the essence to reverse the inexorable upward trend in numbers, since all of those additional people will be born this century; and third, that sub-Saharan Africa will be on the front lines of the coming crisis.

Alan Weisman has long warned of the perils of more people. In his book *Countdown,* he goes further than most by advocating for an actual reduction in the total population rather than settling for slower rates of growth. Reducing our numbers has become imperative, he writes, citing the 1993 estimate by the Erlichs and Gretchen Daily that the optimum global population to preserve biodiversity for future generations is two billion people, the world population in 1930. The slower rate of growth we're seeing isn't good enough, because of what he calls population momentum: even if today's parents are having fewer children, the fact that their parents had so many still results in a million more people on the planet every 4.5 days.[9] And even if we somehow manage to bring population growth under control, global carbon dioxide emissions will continue to rise because of humanity's rising consumption levels. We may need to actually reduce global population to keep the planet livable, he believes.[10]

Although sub-Saharan Africa will be most affected, Weisman posits Pakistan as a test case for measuring the impact of the population explosion. It will soon surpass Indonesia (which has a stellar family planning program) as the most populous Muslim nation, and could have 395 million people by midcentury – far more than the United States, when Pakistan is only the size of Texas. South Asia is where the Green Revolution was first implemented, but with rivers and wells already giving out, 30% of Pakistan's children are now malnourished and 60% of the country is under 30 years old. The country will be a vastly different place by 2050 simply because of the population pressures it will face.[11]

Global food security will come under incredible stress not only in Pakistan but all across the globe, and the biggest reason to worry is that there is simply no more land available to increase food production for the billions more people on the way. We're already using all the cropland we'll ever have, Weisman says, and we need to feed two billion more people in the coming years using that same acreage. When you add the anticipated consumption demands of Asia's growing middle class, it means we will have to double the world's food supply by midcentury. To do that in the absence of more land becoming available, we will need to triple today's crop yields, a highly unlikely prospect. There are already a billion undernourished people in the world and by 2100 there will be one billion more. The effort to solve this dilemma will be what Weisman calls "the biggest challenge humanity has ever faced." He ends with a searching question: wouldn't reducing global population be a better solution than trying to again squeeze more food from the same exhausted land?[12]

Joel Bourne is even more concerned with the enormous stress that future population growth will place upon the world's food supply. The Green Revolution, when farmers and scientists managed to keep up with the fastest doubling of the population in human history – from three billion people in 1960 to six billion in 2000 – was a modern miracle, he writes in his fascinating book, *The End of Plenty*. The number of chronically malnourished people fell from 30% of global population in 1950 to 12% in 2015. Grain production nearly tripled during the same period, mostly from steadily increasing yields on lands already in production.[13]

But like Weisman, he believes that producing food for more than 10 billion people without destroying the planet will be "by far the greatest challenge humanity has ever faced." The world is running out of food for a very simple reason, he writes: because demand is outstripping supply. And population growth is the classic driver of food demand. The unprecedented population levels we're about to witness will leave us with a staggering task over the course of the century: in order to stave off widespread hunger, misery, violence, and ecological destruction, he writes, we will need to grow nearly twice the amount of food we currently produce by 2050.[14]

Three things contribute to per capita food production, according to Bourne: the total area harvested, the total annual yield per hectare, and the total population. Ninety percent of the increase in food over the next 40 years will have to come from land already in cultivation. And the amount of agricultural land per person is falling as population rises and commercial development continues. So if available farmland is a finite resource we will soon exhaust, the X factor is yield growth, which currently offers few grounds for optimism. The world hit "Peak Grain" in 1986, after which per capita cereal production started to fall due to rapid population growth, and the world may soon be in the same place we were in before the Green Revolution took off. The Green Revolution, therefore, may come to be viewed as simply a one-time miracle rather than a long-term phenomenon.[15]

And here is where Africa, and Madagascar, enter the scene. Africa is the only region in the world where the Green Revolution did not take hold – food production per capita actually decreased during this period. The reasons were mostly political, coming both from within and outside the region; environmental concerns emanating from the West and corrupt rulers at home conspired to keep modern fertilizers away. As a result, yields in Africa today are the same as they were in 1960 – just 1 ton of grain per hectare, and with population growth in Africa expected to explode in the coming decades, the continent could face steep declines in per capita cereal production levels, with East Africa only able to feed 44% of its population in 2030 through domestic cereal production. Now, based on current projections, Africa will need to more than triple its food availability by 2050 for everyone to be adequately fed, in large part because 23 of the 25 countries where the average woman has more than five children are in Africa. This will be the real crisis area, according to Bourne.[16]

So while the challenge of adapting to food scarcity caused by climate change is almost always framed in terms of improving agricultural output, reducing population growth would be a more direct and achievable solution, he believes. Again, the demand side of the problem must be addressed along with the global supply of food. Ethiopia will be a good test case for how the world will manage several challenges at once: average temperatures in Ethiopia are rising, rainfall is more erratic, maize yields are projected to decline steeply in coming decades – and population is expected to double by 2050. The developed world must do its part too. While helping poor, malnourished countries slow their population growth through family planning is important, developed countries must begin to limit their consumption patterns to offset the expected rise in living standards and greenhouse gas emissions in Africa and Asia.[17]

David Rieff wrote *The Reproach of Hunger* in response to an unprecedented spike in food prices around the world in 2008, which increased food costs for people in poor countries by up to 40%. The rise in prices came as a surprise to most development experts, and while the causes are unclear, he believes that overpopulation is one of them. There are now three billion people living on less than $2 per day, and if the cost of food staples continues to rise (or even stabilizes at high prices), the effort to feed all of them will be infinitely harder.[18] The food crisis in 2008, he writes, swelled the ranks of the truly poor by 130-150 million, and for the first time in human history, the number of chronically undernourished surpassed the billion mark.[19]

Rieff's target throughout the book isn't any policy or even trend but the groupthink that has developed among development experts as to the inevitability of progress. He takes a decidedly more pessimistic, contrarian view and thinks a Hobbesian world of "all against all" is more likely, though not certain, than a world of peace and prosperity. Despite the fact that famines have been the norm rather than the exception for all of human history until 1945, optimism rules the day and realists (not to mention pessimists) who question whether the end of poverty or hunger is actually possible are seen as heretics. This is a dangerous development for the analysis of any system, but especially one involving the fate of billions of people.[20]

Unchecked population growth is one reason why the

optimists might be wrong. The problem with such optimism, according to Rieff, is that it fails to take into account the very real prospect that major wars, health epidemics, environmental catastrophes and exploding population growth will become reality. The success in eradicating extreme poverty to this point has largely been the result of China's economic success. If the population increase in countries like Uganda and Ethiopia does not start to come down fast, there will be a severe aggravation of poverty, not an end to it.[21] He doesn't mention Madagascar, but that will be another test case.

Rieff and others believe that the nearly century-long era of cheap food is coming to an end, and that food is going to be more expensive in the first half of the twenty-first century than it had been in the second half of the twentieth. Foreign aid focused on agricultural development fell in the decades before the 2008 food crisis, and has only recently begun to catch up to align with the scale of the problem. More expensive food and a growing global population mean one of two things is going to happen: either we will find a way to grow more food with less environmental and economic cost, or hundreds of millions of people will go hungry.[22]

Rieff poses two basic questions: What if, because of rapid population growth and the simultaneous worsening of global warming, we fail to produce enough food to feed 10 billion people? And will producing more food necessarily mean the poor will have access to it? After all, more than enough food is produced today to feed the seven billion people on the planet, yet two billion suffer from chronic malnutrition or undernutrition. "Population is a somewhat taboo subject but must be addressed," he writes. Sub-Saharan Africa's population went from 100 million in 1900 to 770 million in 2005, and could go to 1.5 –2 billion by 2050. There is a legitimate question as to whether the demographic transition to fewer births now beginning in many African countries will take effect before it is too late.[23]

In the past it would have been easy to dismiss these three authors as just the latest acolytes of Malthus and Erlich. But something is changing in the literature, and now even the optimists agree that unchecked population growth is a serious threat to global development. The development expert Steven Radelet acknowledges that Malthus's prediction of population growth quickly outstripping global food supplies captured exactly what had happened up until that point, but what Malthus couldn't foresee was the Green Revolution and the ability of humanity to find solutions to support seven billion people. But ten or eleven billion is a different story, he says, and past success may not be replicable under even greater pressure in the future. In the end, Malthus could be proved right, and the world's poorest countries would bear the greatest costs and suffering.[24]

Jeffrey Sachs also believes that if future fertility rates don't come down quickly, the planet could be in trouble. The most important challenge of sustainable development, he believes, is how to reconcile the continued growth of the world economy and the risks to the Earth's ecosystems and biodiversity. And almost everyone agrees the global economy will continue expanding: Sachs estimates that the world economy will undergo more than a threefold increase by 2050 (from $82 trillion to $272 trillion). If this occurs using today's technologies and business models, humanity will completely burst through the planet's capacity to sustain it. The challenge, he writes, is to find a way to develop the world economy in a fundamentally different way in the future.[25]

Far from rejecting Malthus, Sachs sees the rapid increase in the global population as an old problem in a new form. The challenge of feeding the planet is with us again, he believes, but now the issue is even more complicated than in Malthus's time, for four reasons: (1) a significant portion of the world today is malnourished; (2) the world population continues to grow; (3) climate change and other environmental changes threaten future food production; and (4) the food system itself is a major contributor to climate change and other environmental harms. Taken together, these factors will make global food insecurity worse before it gets better, as it will be continually destabilized by climate change and other environmental crises, not to mention rising demand for grains and meat.[26]

The answer to raising global living standards, or one of them according to Sachs, can only be found if the astounding rise in population growth is finally brought under control this century. Like others, he sees the absolute number of people as a growing problem notwithstanding the fall in the rate of population growth. Even though the growth rate is falling, the arithmetic increase is still huge, increasing by 75-80 million people per year, the same as in 1970. Fertility rates therefore have to fall even faster. The UNPD's most plausible scenario projects a global population of 10.7 billion by 2100, but if current fertility rates continue it will be much higher. By contrast, under the low-fertility variant, the population would peak at 8.3 billion in 2050 and decline to 6.8 billion by 2100; this would be a much safer outcome for the developing world.[27]

Sachs also focuses on another aspect of population growth that will have to be managed: the growth of cities and the number of people who live in them. Urbanization is the wave of the future, he writes, and a key challenge for sustainable development. The world's population will reach eight billion by 2025 and nine billion by 2040. All of that increased population is expected to be in urban areas, and the proportion of people living in urban areas will increase from 53% in 2013 to 67% in 2050. As a consequence, the number of megacities (those with more than 10 million people), which has already climbed from 10 in 1990 to 23 in 2015, will grow to 36 by 2025, and only seven of them will be in the high-income world. Overpopulation will be primarily an urban problem.[28]

Even those who don't worry as much about population growth globally agree that it will be a problem for Africa. Sarah Harper's book, *How Population Change Will Transform Our World*, focuses on the changes in the age structure of the population and how they will impact future development. For her, the defining demographic issues for the world are less likely to include "population explosions" and more likely to be about the trend in declining births and stabilization in population size. The key challenge will not be how to feed 11 billion people but how to accommodate a ratio of working–age people to older people that will go from 5.0 to 2.9 by 2050.[29] The world is undergoing an unprecedented change in its age composition, she writes, as a result of a process known as the demographic transition, when death rates start to fall followed by a decline in birthrates.[30] By 2050, for the first time there will be the same number of old people (over 60) as young (under 15).[31]

But for a book ostensibly devoted to the effects of the change in age structures, Harper has a lot to say about the danger of overall population growth in sub-Saharan Africa. African countries, like those of other less developed countries, have an average total fertility rate of 4.27, a high proportion of child dependents and an age structure with 40% of their populations under age 15. The high proportion of child dependents is what concerns Harper the most, since these dependents, combined with the continuing rates of high fertility in the region, delay a benefit known as "the demographic dividend" that would normally accrue to a developing country with a growing number of workers. Even more troubling is that the pace of fertility decline in the region is weak, and may even be stalling: almost two-thirds of the countries in the region experienced no significant decline in the first decade of the 21st century. This phenomenon, occurring principally in Africa, may push global population projections for the rest of the century upward.[32]

With the average woman in sub-Saharan Africa still bearing over four children and with a population so young and already so large, the continent may face decades of rapid population growth and high child dependency rates even if the pace of fertility decline picks up, according to Harper. The UN's medium growth scenario predicts African childbearing rate will fall to three children per women by 2050 and to replacement levels sometime this century, resulting in a population of 4 billion by 2100. But if, as she believes, the decline in fertility rates has actually stalled, the number could end up significantly higher. On the other hand, if Africa achieved replacement level fertility rates by 2050, its growth in food demand would be reduced by one-third.[33]

It is clear to Harper and others that the large number of child and adolescent dependents in Africa is holding back economic growth and reducing the potential impact of the demographic dividend. In an echo of Sachs, who talked about the importance of even small changes in fertility rates, she maintains that per capita incomes will be much higher in 2040 if Africa achieves the UN's medium fertility variant and avoids the high fertility variant. And there are three major ways to reduce fertility, according to Harper: reduce infant mortality, increase family planning programs, and empower women. Education has a positive impact on all three, she believes. And yet half of African girls do not complete a primary education.[34]

* * *

Each of these authors understands that the problems of overpopulation are only compounded by the coming devastation of climate change. Global food supplies around the world, but especially in Africa, will face unprecedented challenges in the decades ahead at exactly the time when more people need to eat. A basic rule of thumb for staple cereal crops holds that agricultural yields decline by 10%. with every degree of global warming. So if the world warms by five degrees by century's end, when projections suggest we may have at least three million more people to feed, we may also have 50 percent less grain to give them. Even with four degrees of warming, corn yields in the US, the world's top producer of maize, are expected to drop by almost half, which would almost certainly imperil food security in places like Africa. Overall, the UN estimates the planet will need nearly twice as much food in 2050 as it does today.[35]

Climate change also means more severe drought in much of the Global South. Drought may be the biggest problem as the world's food supply tries to keep pace with global population growth, with some of the world's most arable land turning quickly to desert. Without dramatic reductions in emissions in the years ahead, southern Europe will be in extreme drought by 2080, and several places which today supply much of the world's food (the Middle East, densely populated parts of Australia, South America, Africa and the breadbasket regions of China) would no longer be reliable sources going forward. Africa is already straining to feed one billion people, a number which could surge to four billion by 2100, and if global emissions do not come quickly under control then places like southern Madagascar won't be able to support their growing populations.

Rapidly increasing numbers of people are also likely to exacerbate water shortages across much of the world's driest regions. Half of the world's population depends on seasonal melt from high elevation snow and ice, deposits that are now dramatically threatened by warming, which means that as soon as 2030, global water demand is expected to outstrip supply by as much as 40 percent. And demographers predict that most of the world's population growth is expected in regions like Africa that are already strained by water shortage. In many parts of Africa, people are expected to get by on as little as 20 liters of water each day – less than half of what water organizations say is necessary for public health. As many as 250 million Africans are now threatened with water deficiencies due to climate change. Water demand is expected to increase significantly around the world in coming decades, and the World Bank has found that water insecurity alone could significantly reduce GDP in hotter regions.[36] All of which makes rising population totals in places like Madagascar all the more worrisome.

An example of what happens can be found right next door to Madagascar in the impoverished nation of Comoros, a cluster of islands about 570 miles from the Great Island. Here the effects of unchecked population growth and deforestation are on full display. The population of Comoros has more than doubled since 1980, to just under one million people, putting extreme pressure on its forests. From 1995 to 2014, 80% of the country's remaining forest cover was cut down in what became one of the fastest rates of deforestation in world history, causing fertile soils to erode and lose vital nutrients. The islands get more rainfall than Europe, but the clearing of relentless clearing of forests and the impact of climate change have caused at least half of its rivers to stop flowing in the dry season. With so many trees and plants cut down, the water that islanders in Comoros would normally collect and feed back into the ground and rivers is disappearing, resulting in thousands of families struggling to meet their domestic needs and farmers finding it hard to irrigate their fields. Crops have suffered considerably, and tens of thousands of people are now trying to leave the country for Mayotte, a nearby French territory. The UN estimates just 13% of the population now has access to the clean water it needs.[37]

It's important to note that the experts cited above may still be a minority in the debate over whether the developing world is becoming overpopulated. In fact, many economists believe that more population growth, not less, is what developing countries need to keep their economies humming. Ruchir Sharma wrote an influential essay in *Foreign Affairs* lamenting the slow rate of economic growth since the Great Recession and concluded that much of the blame lies with a slowdown in the growth of the labor force, which is driven mainly by the increase in working age people. Between 1960-2005, he found, the global labor force grew at an average of 1.8% per year, but since 2005 the rate has dropped to 1.1%, and will likely slip further as fertility rates continue to decline. He acknowledges that the labor force is growing rapidly in places like Nigeria, the Philippines and other countries; but it grew just 0.5% per year in the US for the past decade and is already shrinking in some countries like China and Germany. "The implications for the world economy are clear: a one percentage point decline in the population growth rate will eventually reduce the economic growth rate by roughly a percentage point…The world should brace itself for slower growth and fewer economic standouts."[38]

Sharma discounts Neo-Malthusian fears surrounding the predicted rise in the world's population and the fear that agricultural productivity won't be able to keep up. He claims that while the absolute number of people will rise, the slowdown in the population growth rate will be driven largely by the thinning ranks of working age people. Slower population growth reduces the pressure on the food supply, as does the aging of the population, because elderly people consume up to a third fewer calories than young people. And such demographic decline is nonetheless toxic for the economy, he claims. The primary threat most countries now face, in his view, is not too many people but too many young workers.[39]

Sharma points to 1990 as the time when "population growth fell off a cliff," going from around 2% a year before to 1% a year since. Like others, he credits longer life spans and lower fertility rates for the recent decline. The average human life span increased from 50 in 1960 to 69 today at the same time as the world experienced a "global baby bust," with the average number of births per woman falling from 4.9 in 1960 to 2.5 in

2015. In part, the fall in fertility rates is due to rising prosperity and educational levels among women, many of whom decided to have fewer children. But according to Sharma the decline has mostly been the result of aggressive birth control policies adopted in the developing world in the 1970s. China went from 3.6 to 1.5 births per woman, while India went from 5.9 to 2.5. The result is that nearly half of all the people on Earth today live in one of the 83 countries where the fertility rate is below the replacement level of 2.1 births per woman.[40]

To further his case he looked at the 56 historical cases where a country sustained economic growth of at least 6% for a decade or more. The average rate of population growth was 2.7% during these booms, suggesting that the rise in the number of workers was instrumental to the economic miracles that ensued. And he settles on 2% as the necessary rise in the working age population to portend an economic boom; a country is unlikely to experience sustained economic growth of 6%, he says, if its working age population is growing slower than 2%. As of the 1980s, 17 of the 20 largest emerging market economies were above that threshold, but now only two are: Nigeria and Saudi Arabia. Over the next five years, the working age population growth rate in other emerging markets will likely fall below the 2% threshold as well. In Brazil, Indonesia, India and Mexico, it will fall to 1.5% or less, while in China, Poland, Russia and Thailand, the working age population is expected to shrink. (So the chances of China sustaining 6% economic growth rates going forward are very small.).[41]

But Sharma's own evidence calls for caution before concluding that future economic growth is highly dependent on maintaining high rates of population growth. First, in a quarter of the cases he studied the countries attained long stretches of economic growth without reaching the 2% threshold for population growth, including such major economies as Chile, Ireland, Japan, and Spain. Second, Sharma admits that in most cases, population growth doesn't automatically translate into an economic boom. In 698 decade-long periods going back to 1960, he found that 60% had working age population growth rates above 2%, but only a quarter of those population booms led to economic growth rates of 6% or more in the same decade. Leaders still need to ensure the conditions necessary to attract investment and generate jobs, he says. The Arab world is a perfect example of a region where millions more people yielded next to nothing in return: growth rates in the working age population were over 3% from 1985-2005, but the region never experienced an economic boom, and youth unemployment is today at 30% in some countries. So in those populous countries like Bangladesh, Kenya, Nigeria and the Philippines where the working age population is still growing at or near 2% per year, nothing is assured without enlightened leadership and smart policies.[42]

The large exceptions to Sharma's rule weaken his core argument considerably and have significant implications for countries like Madagascar, where the economic benefits of population growth have been conspicuously absent. Historically, there is no doubt that such growth had a crucial impact on Madagascar's development in both the 20th and 21st centuries, but not for the reasons Sharma describes. The French colonial period and independence were obvious markers in the rise and fall of the island's sovereignty, writes one historian, but "the most important historical developments actually occurred between these dates, notably with the beginning of a major population growth that shows no signs of levelling out," and the establishment of a bureaucratic state committed to improving the condition of so many people.[43]

The precipitous rise in the population in Madagascar has even graver repercussions today. As the historians Randrianja and Ellis have written, the periods of the late 20th and early 21st centuries witnessed major crises, economic decline and recurrent political instability on the island. But "at the heart of Madagascar's difficulties has been population growth of staggering proportions – as in continental Africa, probably 'of a scale and speed unique in human history.' The astonishing increase in the number of people has resulted in a very youthful population and the burgeoning of towns and cities."[44] While they don't draw a direct link between the population explosion and the various crises, it's hard not to see the connection.

But Sharma is far from alone in ruing the sharp declines in fertility rates around the world. Zachary Karabell, writing in a 2019 essay in *Foreign Affairs*, also believes fewer people will eventually lead to smaller rates of economic growth, before reaching an even more troubling conclusion: the population contraction could be such a revolutionary transformation as to end capitalism as we know it.[45]

Karabell traces the rise in global population over the centuries to show just how historic today's falls in fertility are. The number of people in the world went from one billion in 1800 to two billion by the late 1920s, three billion in 1960 and four billion in 1975. It has nearly doubled again since then. But now, most parts of the world are now witnessing sharp and sudden contractions in either birthrates or absolute population, he says. Only longer lifespans are keeping some countries from shrinking more quickly. And the consequences will be enormous:

A world of zero to negative population growth is likely to be a world of zero to negative economic growth, because fewer and older people consume less. There is nothing inherently problematic about that, except for the fact that it will completely upend existing financial and economic systems. The future world may be one of enough food and abundant material goods relative to the population; it may also be one in which capitalism at best frays and at worst breaks down completely … Capitalism as a system is particularly vulnerable to a world of less population expansion; a significant portion of the economic growth that has driven capitalism over the past several centuries may have been simply a derivative of more people and younger people consuming more stuff. If the world ahead has fewer people, will there be any real economic growth? We are not only unprepared to answer that question; we are not even starting to ask it … The demographic future could end up being a glass half full, by ameliorating the worst effects of climate change and resource depletion, or a glass half empty, by ending capitalism as we know it.[46]

The effects will not be the same everywhere, he writes, and countries like Madagascar could suffer the most. Currently, the decline in population growth is occurring mostly in affluent countries that are able to withstand slower economic growth rates using the accumulated wealth they have been built up over generations. Countries like the United States and Canada, he believes, are able to temporarily offset declining population with immigration. But he puts forth an entirely different set of fears for the poorer regions of the world. "As for the billions of people in the developing world," he writes, "the hope is that they become rich before they become old. The alternative is not likely to be pretty: without sufficient per capita affluence, it will be extremely difficult for developing countries to support aging populations." While he recognizes that sub-Saharan African countries may face a separate demographic crisis than the advanced economies (and even China and India now), he sees no need to dwell on the population concerns of Africa because it too will soon set off on a path toward lower fertility rates. "In those places, as well," he writes, "it is only a matter of time before they catch up, given that more women are becoming educated, more children are surviving their early years, and more people are moving to cities."

But this is a fundamental misreading of the situation in countries like Madagascar. First, to hope that the island's population becomes rich before it becomes old is a fantasy. As we'll see, Madagascar's population will grow so rapidly over the next 80 years that it will quadruple to almost 100 million people, and there is no hope of it becoming rich when it can barely cope with 25 million now. Second, it is not just "a matter of time" before the nations of sub-Saharan Africa catch up to the richer parts of the world in terms of lower population growth or contraction. The next few generations of Malagasy and their brethren in other African countries will emerge into a fundamentally different world than their peers in advanced economies that have already seen their birth rates decline sharply.

* * *

Madagascar is in the early stages of the demographic transition, a broad term that essentially refers to the stage of a country's development when death rates start to fall followed by a decline in birth rates. Population tends to grow rapidly between these two trends before the effects of declining fertility rates start to kick in. In advanced economies like Europe, where the transition is now complete, the percentage of young people in the total population is already low and still declining. But in places like sub-Saharan Africa where mothers are still having well above the 2.1 children considered replacement level, the percentage of children and young people is very high. Such a high number of children portends a large population increase in the future, unless the next generation of mothers has much fewer. As we'll see, this is unlikely to happen in Madagascar anytime soon, and the question facing it and other African countries is whether the demographic transition will occur before it's too late.

Indeed, you can't truly appreciate the threat that population growth poses to Madagascar until you look at the forecasts for its rise during the rest of this century. Here are the country's population figures from the UN Population Division's World Population Prospects 2019 Report:

Year	Total Population	Annual % Change	Total Fertility Rate	% of Population Under 20	Urban Population
1960	5,099,373	2.34%	7.30	51.4%	10.6%
1970	6,576,305	2.65%	7.30	55.7%	14.1%
1980	8,716,553	2.90%	6.95	56.6%	18.6%
1990	11,598,663	2.88%	6.25	56.3%	23.5%
2000	15,766,806	3.19%	5.80	55.6%	27.1%
2010	21,151,640	2.90%	4.83	54.3%	31.9%
2020	27,691,000	2.67%	4.11	50.9%	38.5%
2030	35,622,000	2.45%	3.63	47.8%	45.2%
2040	44,471,000	2.14%	3.25	44.8%	51.6%
2050	54,048,000	1.89%	2.96	41.5%	57.9%
2060	64,059,000	1.63%	2.73	38.5%	N/A
2070	74,035,000	1.39%	2.54	35.8%	N/A
2080	83,598,000	1.16%	2.38	33.2%	N/A
2090	92,343,000	0.94%	2.23	30.8%	N/A
2100	99,957,000	0.74%	2.10	28.5%	N/A

Several things jump out from the table. First, 100 million people by 2100! That is also when the fertility rate declines to replacement level and demographic transition will be nearing completion. But how in the world the country will manage a fourfold increase in just 80 years has to be at the top of the list of problems to solve for policymakers. It won't be, of course, but it should. Second, the rise in the urban population to over half of all inhabitants by midcentury will put major stress on the infrastructure of cities throughout the island. Creating full-time employment for so many young people migrating out of their villages and into urban areas will be an enormous task. Finally, over 40% of the population will still be under 20 at midcentury, meaning any failure to reduce the island's fertility rate toward the 2.1 figure predicted by century's end could have catastrophic consequences.

The rate of population growth on the island now puts Madagascar among the world's fastest growing countries. It has moved up 22 spots in the list of most populous countries since independence, and figures to rise higher in the coming years. Its total fertility rate in 2018 was the 35th highest in the world, its population growth rate was 24th highest, and its median age was 34th lowest. In 2018, almost 40% of its population was under 15 and only 3.35% were 65 or older. By contrast, the US had 18.6% of its people under 15 and 16% who were 65 or older. Madagascar's population is still so young – over 60% were under the age of 25 in 2018 – that it will continue to grow even if fertility rates come down faster than expected. But that doesn't seem likely, given its total fertility rate of more than four children per woman.

There are four likely impacts from the island's rapid growth in population. First, and most importantly, is the possibility of a humanitarian crisis that will only worsen the problem of undernourishment and leave millions of Malagasy hungry. Second, in a nation that is desperately trying to raise incomes for its struggling citizenry, it will make the challenge of poverty reduction infinitely harder. Third, the quality of life for those living in urban environments will inevitably decline, even for those who earn enough to eat and raise their families. And finally, the pressures from so much growth will push Madagascar's pristine natural environment to the breaking point.

As some local and national leaders were quick to point out to me, Madagascar's population problem is not a lack of space on the island for everyone to live. The island actually has a very low population density (42 people per square kilometer) with very few desert areas that categorically rule out human settlement.[47]

Madagascar is not Rwanda in that sense, where an exceedingly high population density contributed to a genocide between its two largest ethnic groups. Instead, the burgeoning population in Madagascar will lead to a humanitarian crisis of a different order – one that will include joblessness, migration, hunger and environmental destruction. The problem with such a rapid rise in absolute numbers, in Madagascar and elsewhere, is that it puts highly vulnerable economies in a perilous position when things don't go as planned. In the event a recession or drought hits, the human consequences become terrifying. As Bill Marsh wrote in the NY Times, "When conditions worsen, the numbers are staggering, and Malthusian concerns come back with a vengeance."[48]

The highest birthrates are found in rural areas, where most Malagasy live and where cultural norms are still very traditional. I discovered this myself during my informal inquiries. Few people in the cities I visited had a friend or relative with more than four children, but as soon as I set foot in a small village they became common. And there are cultural roots to this phenomenon: according to various sources, many young Malagasy girls in these areas are withdrawn from school, marry early (often under pressure from their parents), and soon begin having children. This causes more problems: early childbearing, coupled with Madagascar's widespread poverty and lack of access to skilled health care providers during delivery, not only contributes to higher population levels but also increases the risk of death and serious health problems for young mothers and their babies.[49]

To cite one example, a 2019 UNICEF report found that nearly half of all teenage girls in Atsimo Andrefana, the southern region that includes Tulear, are now mothers. A newspaper editorial tried to put a positive spin on it by highlighting the admirable work being done by a local NGO to try to change the culture through education:

According to a UNICEF report, 48% of girls aged 15-19 have already given birth to at least one child in the Atsimo Andrefana region. Indeed, the high number of teenage pregnancies is a plague that no one can ignore in Madagascar. To combat this phenomenon, the Malagasy government and private organizations have long been united to inform and help young people.[50]

In this context, the Center for Art and Music (CAM) in Toliara dedicated the Alahady Festival in August to this theme "Let's fight against early pregnancy". This festival took place from August 16th to 18th. For three days, the subject was at the heart of all the recreational, sports and artistic activities on offer.

Although sex education is often considered a taboo subject on the social and cultural level of Madagascar, all groups of CAM have been able to address this theme to make it accessible to the public through theatrical, musical, circus, dance performances, and sports. Emphasis was also placed on the consequences of premature pregnancy. Thus, the public was fascinated by the use of art used for information and education, especially for young people, on this theme.

One can only hope that such festivals and dance performances will someday produce a cultural shift in the minds of young Malagasy. But until that happens the onus will be on Madagascar's government to devise a more comprehensive response to the crisis. Putting aside the question of how all of the island's newborn children will become productive members of society when they grow up, Madagascar has trouble enough keeping those infants alive. An October 2019 report by UNICEF revealed that 59 children out of 1,000 now die before age five. Half of all children under five suffer from chronic malnutrition. Two-thirds of children in rural areas don't have access to treated water. In the realm of education, half of all children ages 13-15 hadn't completed primary school, and only 17% are able to read in French or Malagasy.[51]

What does 100 million people look like for a country that is unable to cope with so many? Just consider at Egypt, which stands as a fine example of a country whose population explosion is dooming its future. In early 2020 the country's population reached a hundred million, and was on pace to reach 128 million by 2030, officials estimated. Fertility rates have risen since 2008, to 3.5 children per woman, according to the UN, and the population is growing 1.8% annually, a rate that adds one million citizens every six months. Egypt's government has acknowledged the scope of the problem, with President Abdel-Fattah al-Sisi describing population growth as a threat on par with terrorism, yet has been mostly powerless to stop it. The construction of a huge new dam in neighboring Ethiopia only increased Egypt's growing concern about the country's continued reliance on the Nile river to support everyone. And their reliance on the famous river cutting through the heart of Egypt only amplifies the country's population crisis: 95% of the population lives on about 4% of the land, a green belt along the Nile.

As in Madagascar, fertility rates in Egypt are not uniform throughout the country, having risen to higher levels in rural areas, where a large family is considered a blessing. But their impact is felt most keenly in Cairo, where a city of 20 million has already spilled into the surrounding desert and farmland. Suzanne Mubarak, wife of former President Hosni Mubarak, pushed for a reduction in fertility rates in the 1980s and 1990s that made modest inroads, pushing rates down from 5.2 to 3.0 in the 1990s and 2000s. But rates rose again around the time of the Arab Spring in 2011 and have skyrocketed ever since. Egypt's fate is not irreversible, however; other large developing countries with soaring populations have successfully brought birthrates under control. Vietnam, where the population rose from 60 million in 1986 to 97 million in 2018, has reduced its rate of increase to 1%. Bangladesh, with a population of more than 160 million, has done the same. In Egypt, though, the rate of growth is nearly twice as high, reaching 1.79% in 2018-19. This translates into 700,000 young Egyptians entering the job market every year, an unsustainable number that will only funnel more young people into violent extremism. It also means a dearth of decent housing prospects for Egypt's poor, as well as a rising poverty rate that exceeded 32% in 2019.[52] This is what Madagascar has to look forward to as it races toward 100 million people across the island.

Population pressure is such an obvious threat to Madagascar's development that I couldn't help but make it a focus of my research. And yet my inquiries about its effects were often met with bewilderment, amusement, or worse. Overpopulation, I learned, is a delicate subject to discuss with strangers around the world, in part because it implies a judgment made about an entire culture of childbearing. Several times when I raised it my interlocutor would pause and fix me with a certain stare, as if to say, "Who are you to come here and tell us we have too many people?" I began to wonder if and when the government would speak out about the problem. Finally, in August 2019, no less than the country's Finance Minister used the occasion of the release of the official census to address the inexorable rise in numbers.[53]

The census, the first of its kind in decades on the island, put the number of Malagasy at almost 25.7 million people. It predicted that the figure will double in the next 20 years, based on the average increase of 3.01% per year on the island between 1993 and 2018, compared to 2.7% for sub-Saharan Africa as a whole. The Finance Minister, Richard Randriamandrato, said the government, specifically the Ministers of Economy, Population and Education, would put programs in place to respond to the situation. Among his proposals were an increase in social infrastructure spending on one hand and the implementation of a birth control policy – only vaguely described – on the other.

The census also confirmed that the majority of the Malagasy population is rural, with 20,676,428 inhabitants living in rural areas and an urban population of just over 5 million people. Other information included the finding that Malagasy are unequally spread over the island, with more than half (52%) living in six regions. The overpopulation of Antananarivo is striking, with a density of 210.3 inhabitants per square kilometer, compared to a national average of 43.7. The most troubling finding, however, was how quickly the Malagasy population would add millions more people in coming years.[54]

It was good to hear a senior member of the government speak out about what will be a crucial issue in the island's future development. But as an editorial in *Midi Madagasikara*, one of Madagascar's leading newspapers, pointed out, the report was likely to be ignored by most people in the country unless the government made it an urgent priority:

The figure [of over 25 million people] on the big island, announced a few days ago, is enough to make you dizzy. And the announcement says the number will certainly double in the next [thirty] years if we don't organize a birth control program. The problem would not be so bad if the country enjoyed harmonious economic development, but in the current circumstances it is still difficult to think of getting out of this poverty anytime soon and joining the pack of emerging nations.

The growth of the population is undeniably a possible source of wealth, but it can also become a handicap if the environment in which it evolves is flawed. The country has enormous potentialities, but they are not exploited properly and the country does not enjoy favorable economic conditions to live decently. The vast majority of 25.4 million Malagasy people live below the poverty line. And the situation could become even more dramatic if the rate of population growth remains the same. The solution advocated by the Minister of Finance when presenting the figures of the last census is a limitation of births through birth control. This recommendation is a step in the right direction, but it will be necessary to mobilize enormous resources to convince the vast majority of the population that still reacts unfavorably to birth control measures. The report that was made earlier this week has not caused a stir in public opinion, and yet it is alarming. The state must be on the front lines if it plans to wage a real battle against a galloping population. A family planning campaign will soon be launched, but doubt already exists in the minds of actors on the ground. All Malagasy must be made aware that a real sword of Damocles hangs over them.[55]

One way to understand how more people can lead to more poverty in Madagascar and other poor countries is to consider the growth of extremely poor people relative to the total population. In many countries the population of "the most impoverished" (people living on less than $1.90 a day) has grown to exceed their total populations from decades ago. Madagascar's population grew from seven million people in 1970 to 24 million in 2015, but 20 million Malagasy were among the most impoverished by that time. This ratio of almost three to one is the worst in the world, but there are a dozen other examples almost as distressing (Mozambique: nine million people in 1970 and 28 million in 2015, of which 20 million are the most impoverished).[56] With so many people barely able to meet their daily needs, the potential for a catastrophe impacting millions of people when things go wrong is always present.

But the threat of overpopulation is not just a Malthusian struggle for survival. It's also about quality of life and whether the greatest impact of crowded metropolises on everyday citizens is to make them more miserable. Indeed, the past few decades of adding millions more people have already left Madagascar struggling for ways to adapt. The capital city alone is bursting at the seams. A 2019 editorial in Madagascar's leading newspaper discussed how population pressures were impacting Antananarivo, a city whose name translates as "The City of The Thousand" but one that now holds more than 1.3 million inhabitants:

Antananarivo has all the flaws of a modern megalopolis with its polluted air and monstrous traffic jams. The capital of Madagascar remains at the center of the location reserved for it by colonial administrators and which successive governments have kept since independence. It is high time for Tana to evolve and for new cities to be created. In any case, the nightmare in which its habitants now live is untenable. On the eve of Independence Day it is time to give a healthier living environment to this overpopulated city.

The celebration of World Environment Day the day before yesterday has pinpointed the problems facing the inhabitants of the capital. Tananarivians suffer the effects of pollution and the hassle of overpopulation with a certain inevitability. But the breaking point is almost reached. In recent days, traffic jams have put the nerves of motorists to the test. Being stuck in a line of vehicles for an hour and sometimes even more without knowing the reason is annoying. Especially when there are police officers to regulate traffic at each junction. The causes are numerous: the narrowness of the streets, the large number of cars that circulate, the road repairs that are necessary and the presence of carts continuing to circulate despite the recent decree. The authorities are aware of the situation and are trying to manage it the best they can, but they know it is time to give more space to this growing population. And that what's happening now needs to be remedied. The regime is planning the construction of Tanamasoandro, a new city, but it will take time. For the moment, it is an issue of education and the establishment of a certain discipline that is necessary. Tananarivians are patient people, but they need to be guided. With good will, we will be able to decongest our capital, which is no longer the city of a thousand, but the city of a million.[57]

High numbers of births in rural areas causes its own set of problems, but urban hyperdensity makes a place like Antananarivo almost unlivable. An editorial appeared in *Midi Madigasikara* the day after World Environment Day pleading for the government to do more to protect the health of its citizens by taking steps to reduce the air pollution choking urban areas, especially the island's capital. To drive its point home the paper even reprinted a column written in October 2018, during the first world summit on air pollution in Geneva:

The air pollution rate in Tana is now three times higher than the tolerable threshold set by the WHO. This pollution that rages in the City of A Thousand places the Malagasy capital just in front of the megalopolis of Shenzhen in the People's Republic of China, which ranked as the 15th most polluted megalopolis (cities of more than 14 million inhabitants) in the world. Even worse, in Antananarivo, this air pollution during the day can reach even higher, to a mind-boggling level exceeding even the annual average of New Delhi, the most polluted city in the world! These are alarming figures that have alerted some political leaders and the WHO to the urgency of finding solutions and measures to begin to combat air pollution, whose consequences are cross-cutting and disastrous.

The high level of atmospheric pollution in Antananarivo

originates from a number of contingent factors, but the three most important factors identified by national and international experts are the recurring problem of an upsurge of bush fires that causes emissions and intoxication; lead poisoning, particularly from industrial plants; and finally the "astronomical" number of cars constantly bottled in monster traffic, with the direct pollution that is caused by their escape. Moreover, this atmospheric pollution is increased tenfold by global warming, a direct effect of climate change, which affects Madagascar and contributes to the high-speed degradation of its unique environment (deforestation, gradual disappearance of mangroves, etc.).

If these causes of air pollution in Antananarivo are trivialized both in practice and at the political level, its equally serious consequences are unfortunately underestimated. In Antananarivo, as in other cities hit by air pollution, children are the first victims. In Madagascar, 11% of children under 5 suffer from acute respiratory infections such as pneumonia. On the first day of the World Summit on Air Pollution and Health in Geneva, the WHO has relaunched a study it completed on the subject, which found that 600,000 children die prematurely each year because of atmospheric pollution. Elderly people are also affected, with a clear correlation among strokes, high blood pressure and air pollution.[58]

The rise in air pollution in Madagascar only mirrors what's happening around the world. The negative health effects for billions of people living in both industrialized countries and countries trying to industrialize are now overwhelming. Already more than 10,000 people die from air pollution daily. In the developing world, 98% of cities are enveloped by air above the threshold established by the WHO, and 95% of the world's population is breathing dangerously polluted air. By the end of the century, as many as two billion people globally will be breathing air above the WHO "safe" level.[59] Political leaders in Antananarivo are well aware of these trends and will have no excuse for failing to make their city a healthier place to live.

* * *

Millions of people from around the world have journeyed to Madagascar in recent years to witness the spectacular flora and fauna that lies in almost every region of the country outside of the capital. Five percent of the world's species are found on Madagascar, and of those, 80% are found nowhere else. And yet the pressures put on the land by the island's own growing number of people is slowly destroying several of its main attractions. Ecotourism forms the backbone of the country's $390 million tourism industry, but deforestation and rampant logging are already threatening it. At least 90% of the nation's natural ecology – unique after being separated from other landmasses for 160 million years – has already been destroyed so far. To reverse the trend, Madagascar's government has imposed multiple logging bans in recent years, but conservationists say a lack of enforcement still leaves the forests at risk. One says over 500,000 hectares of natural forests – 4% of the island's total – were destroyed in 2017 alone.

President Rajoelina has also come under intense criticism for his handling of the environment. Prior to the election in 2018, several environmental writers wrote that the election of Rajoelina would be a disaster for Madagascar's budding conservation efforts. After Rajoelina's coup in 2009, William Laurence wrote, illegal logging and exporting of wood soared under the new president and continued under Hery Rajaonarimampianina, his hand-picked successor. Such logging is destroying the habitat of the country's famous lemurs; there are 111 species on Madagascar, yet nearly all are on the brink of extinction due in large part to deforestation, making them the most endangered primates on Earth. A few timber barons became enriched by

Rajoelina's willingness to look the other way after the coup, as did the president himself, according to Laurence. Ravalomanana was less than perfect on the environment, but he managed to triple protected areas when he was president, which then reached 10% of the island, and banned all commercial logging in them. Another Rajoelina administration would set the country back by a decade, Laurance implied.[60]

The new president attempted to answer his critics soon after taking office, at least on the issue of deforestation. Madagascar is now trying to end the destruction of forests that has made the country a poster child for environmental degradation and actually "reforest" much of its denuded land. Madagascar has lost about half of its forests since the 1950s, and they continue to be razed at an alarming rate. High rates of poverty cause much of its rural population to resort to slash and burn agriculture and illegal mining, each of which depletes the soil and causes more forests and species to disappear. These practices are particularly tragic in Madagascar, with so many plant and animal species found nowhere else on Earth. Some hope that an era of political stability will result in better environmental protection. In March 2019, President Rajoelina told the UN Environment Assembly that Madagascar would reforest over 40,000 hectares of land every year. This was actually a slightly less ambitious goal than the one Madagascar had previously agreed to under the Bonn Challenge, when the country committed to reforest four million hectares of land by 2030. In any event, he has tasked Alexandre Georget, a founder of Madagascar's first Green Party in 2008, with implementing its new reforestation policy.

Environmentalists remain skeptical of the new president's vows to tackle the problem and claim he will prove to be a poor steward of the land for two reasons: first, because of higher priorities crowding his agenda, and second, because of the level of corruption tied to illegal logging, corruption which the president has been linked to for years. But there are some bright spots from Rajoelina's first two years. The sale of precious timber from Madagascar became illegal under the Convention on International Trade in Endangered Species of Wild Flora and Fauna (CITES), but enforcement was never robust. The Ravalomanana administration had even petitioned the CITES Secretariat to be permitted to sell off its remaining stockpiles, valued at potentially hundreds of millions of dollars. Georget withdrew that request soon after taking office, however, instead pledging no domestic use and no export of its endangered timber. He even pledged to import wood to save Madagascar's trees.[61]

The precarious state of the environment is becoming a more frequent topic of conversation on the island these days, especially in Antananarivo, where government officials now understand the importance of maintaining their country's natural beauty as one of the surest ways to increase revenues from international tourism. An editorial in Madagascar's leading daily newspaper captured the environmental challenge facing the country and the possible benefits of reforestation.

Intensive farming and industrial livestock farming have proven to be harmful to the environment. In Madagascar, initiatives to expand farmland are nibbling at forest areas, aggravating the phenomenon of deforestation. The conclusions of the report of the Intergovernmental Panel on Climate Change are incontrovertible: land use has a major impact on climate change. The report indicates that the world's population uses nearly three-quarters (72%) of the total area of land that is not covered by ice. Land use activities constitute pressure on the planet, exacerbated by climate change, which increases degradation, loss of biodiversity and food insecurity. In addition, the agricultural sector is responsible for 75% of deforestation worldwide … Madagascar is affected by this problem of land use. Indeed, the main cause of forest loss is the conversion of forests to farmland. According to World Wildlife Fund in Madagascar, the Big Island will have to rectify the destruction and make optimal use of its cultivated land, while the expansion of agricultural land should be done in a concerted and carefully managed way that ensures sustainable production and respects nature, keeping in mind that the Malagasy population is growing rapidly: to more than 55 million people in 2050, according to the United Nations estimate … The solution [to these problems] lies in environmentally friendly agriculture.[62]

Rajoelina's pledge to make Madagascar greener is an ambitious and laudable goal in light of the island's tragic losses to its biodiversity. Bushfires and the abusive exploitations of natural resources have now dropped Madagascar to third, behind Mexico and Indonesia, in its rate of disappearing species. If the president is successful, reforestation will help restore Madagascar's biodiversity and maintain its status as a first-rate ecotourist destination. Rajoelina has enlisted others in his administration to promote reforestation, including former Prime Minister Christian Ntsay, who said in 2019 that it was no longer just an environmental matter but also a political one. He claimed the government has finally adopted the necessary resources to tackle the problem, and that Madagascar's success could inspire other nations to follow suit.[63] But in a reminder of how difficult that would be, the country's Environment Ministry conducted a study to determine the extent of bush fires still burning on the island at one time. It found 9,144 fires burning at one time during just one week in late October 2019. Little, if anything, had really changed.

* * *

Almost everyone I met in Madagascar agreed that another 10 million people in the next ten years will pose insurmountable problems for the country. As Professor Jaony at the University of Antsiranana told me:

> The potential of the country is great. The resources are there to support a country the size of Madagascar. But all the resources are controlled by the rich. And population growth will become an economic issue soon. The South has the highest level of poverty and the highest birth rate, which is unsustainable. Population growth eats away the economic growth of the country, and we simply can't support 35 million people anytime soon.

McGordon Ranaivo Arivezo, the local development expert in northers Madagascar, began working on the population issue early in his career, when he worked for an organization focused on environmental conservation.

> The problem is a burden not just to the nation but to families themselves. Poor communities are the ones having more kids. When they are poor, many families want to have as many children as possible in the hope that one will succeed and be able to support them later. And that they will all help with the field work when they are young. We tell them two children are better than many because there is a better chance one of them (if only had two) will go to university after schooling. I often look at a field full of children playing somewhere and ask myself, Where are all those kids going to work?

Even those inside the government are now acknowledging the scale of the problem. Anja Hobiniaina Ratovomamonjy is the Director General of the Social Protection Department in the

Ministry of Population, one of three Departments in the Ministry. Like many countries in Africa, Madagascar has a Ministry of Population not to tackle overpopulation concerns but rather to oversee social welfare issues. The Ministry of Public Health, by contrast, manages the country's family planning program, which includes education on contraceptives and administration of them, in the form of shots and pills. But Anja had his feet in both worlds, and was keenly aware of the population pressures facing Madagascar. He was also one of the busiest public officials I met during my eight months on the island. We met at a downtown restaurant one day with a mutual friend to discuss population issues, and his phone hardly stayed silent for more than thirty seconds throughout our two-hour lunch. "My boss won't leave me alone," he moaned to me at one point. "Can I take a picture with you guys to send her some proof I'm at a business lunch and not off sleeping somewhere?" We dutifully posed for a group selfie and he fired it off to his boss, giving us a brief respite until a minute later, when someone else tried to reach him.

Anja confirmed for me what the national census had already foretold about Madagascar's exploding population. The number of people has grown by 2.8% per year over the last 10 years, according to his ministry's figures, and projects to have 30.9 million people by 2030, which is close to the UN's estimate. The problem of overpopulation is especially concerning in the South, he said, where women were still having 6-9 children each. Child marriage in various regions (particularly in Anosy and Androy) has led to higher rates of childbirth, but throughout the coastal areas the rate is higher than in Antananarivo. But he didn't agree – at least initially – that the problem was a serious threat nationwide. "Madagascar is so vast that we can create other living spaces, new cities for people to live, so it shouldn't be a major problem," he said. His bigger concern was creating employment for all those people. "And we must find a way to limit the number of children being born so the nation's infrastructure can keep up," he said.[64]

Anja's work at the ministry focuses on protecting the most vulnerable sectors of the population. One of his department's biggest initiatives is the Safety Net Program, which gives direct cash transfers to the island's poorest citizens. Recipients are means tested and required to spend the money on health, education and food; spending it on anything else voids a recipient's eligibility immediately. Each family receives about $8.50 per month. "We have a poverty rate of 71.5%, and an extreme poverty rate of 52.7% according to our statistics," he related. "The objective is 15% extreme poverty by 2023." When I pressed him on how realistic that is given the island's rapid population growth, he quickly relented: "I am pessimistic about meeting that target," he admitted.

In a striking example of how dependent the country is on foreign aid, his department received $75 million for its operations from the World Bank from 2015-19, but only about $1 million from his own government. Part of this is a result of Rajoelina's austerity program: ambassadors once received $30,000 per month, but now receive only $14,000. And the president's stated reason for closing the Senate is to raid its $34 million budget and split that money between new education initiatives and support for regional governments (partly to further his decentralization plan). But Anja acknowledged that ending the country's reliance on foreign aid will be a lot more difficult in the midst of rapid population growth.

He said the same thing about the initiative to "make people more productive," a phrase the government uses to mean increasing employment, creating a national health insurance system, and bringing its citizens into the formal economy so that they contribute revenue to the state in the form of taxes (90% of Malagasy currently work in the informal sector). "The Bureau of Labor wants to make people more productive, but I agree that it's going to be a lot harder when the country adds millions of people over the next ten years," he said when I asked about it.

The longer we talked the more obvious it became that the success of all of his initiatives hinged on the population question. Trying to reducing extreme poverty and reduce unemployment across the island in the midst of surging total numbers each year was like running a race into a strong headwind. As so often happened when I discussed this issue, our conversation eventually turned from plans and statistics to the reality of culture. "Our family planning program began in 2006 and it's starting to have an effect," he said at one point, "but children are seen as a sign of wealth here, so it's hard sometimes to change the culture of having large families. A benediction given to newlyweds on the wedding day is 'May you have seven sons and seven daughters,' and we still say that. But at least in Tana, where education is greater, we have seen a big change. Now, doctors here will reprimand young parents when they come in with more than three kids because they know it's hard for poor families to give adequate care to so many children."

As optimistic as Anja was, he knew the challenges ahead for his country if the population growth rate didn't come down soon, and this was typical of almost every member of the government I met. Only one person really denied that it was a major problem for the island. Vahiny Victor Angelo Rodilson, the charismatic Regional Director for the Department of Agriculture in Diego, said there was plenty of farmland in Madagascar to support 25 million people. "Even 50 or 100 million people, or 200 million," he told me.

There is a lot of available farmland, he told me. "Madagascar should be the breadbasket of the region, with enough surplus to export food to the rest of the Indian Ocean and even parts of Africa where they don't have enough." But the problem remains one of technology. "We don't have the machines to cultivate enough of it," he said. For example, the island has plenty of spades and shovels but not enough tractors. The "mechanization of agriculture" is what the country required, he said, one that would allow it to catch up to the twenty-first century. Then he ticked off a wish list that would conceivably alleviate any threat from overpopulation: "We also need a better system of registering land, because many peasants are unsure of who owns the land they work and won't cultivate more than a small patch of it for fear that someone else will reap the profits. On top of that we need better irrigation systems, because right now there is not enough water to cultivate all the land. And of course we need better access to the land – there aren't enough roads and too many of them are in bad shape. If the country develops and we get all that, we will have no problem being self-sufficient for food, even with 50 million people."

Rodilson confirmed that the South, where I was headed next, was where the real problems lie. The climate is the biggest challenge there, he said, meaning the devastating droughts that have begun to afflict the region over the last decade. There is plenty of land to cultivate, but no water, he advised me. "But just because it's a desert doesn't mean you can't grow food. Look at Israel, the Arab countries. They live in a similar climate and there is no shortage of food there. The South is fertile, we just need to find ways to extract the water from underneath their soil."

Rodilson said the government is trying to limit population growth through various family planning initiatives, at least until the economy starts to catch up and the country can be assured of feeding itself. The statements above about having more than enough land were his own personal opinions, he said. He doesn't believe food security is a problem yet for the island. But he acknowledged that there is a growing problem in the *brousse*, the countryside, where large numbers of children are being born and there isn't enough land for their parents to divide among them. That forces many young people into the cities, where they lack the skills or confidence to cope. "We have a proverb or blessing that we still say to young couples: May you have 14 children, seven boys and seven girls," he said, repeating an admonition that Anja had shared with me, one which clearly does not bode well for reducing the island's population pressures anytime soon.

* * *

I would regularly meet women with large families during my travels throughout the island, and I always found their stories both illuminating and tragic. For those of an earlier generation, I found, the lack of birth control options effectively doomed many women to a life of poverty. For those still having many children now, the reasons are more complex, but to what extent they feel they fully control the number they bear is a legitimate question.

Three things stand out from the interviews I conducted. First, there has been a sea change in the availability of contraception from one generation to the next, and women are overwhelmingly relieved to have more options to control their family size. But serious concerns remain over the contraceptives themselves, with often severe side effects that can lead women to avoid them, even if they don't want more children. Second, all of the women are well aware of the financial difficulty they themselves have endured as a result of bearing so many children, and of the very challenging prospects their children will face in the future as a result of the high number of births in their villages over so many years. And lastly, while most of the women I met would counsel their daughters to have fewer kids, they recognize that changing a culture where the presence of many children is seen as a sign of good fortune may not happen easily.

Isabelle Razaiarisoa, 55, is a perfect example of a woman who grew up entirely unaware of all but the most rudimentary birth control options. To arrive at her house I took a dirt track that veered off from the university in Diego Suarez and led to one of the cliffs overlooking the sea. After a few inquiries I found Isabelle's house, a tin shack supported by narrow wood beams that afforded a beautiful view of the emerald water and the beach across the bay.[65] Isabelle arrived in Diego with her seven children in 2009 as a single mother. She had never married, and her children were fathered by two different men. "There was no family planning then, so when you were in a relationship with a man, kids were part of the deal," she told me through an interpreter. "I wanted three kids, after that I didn't want more, but I didn't know any birth control so I had four more with another man. The men didn't want more than three either, but that's what happens in Madagascar. I finally decided to stop at seven."

"There were many women I knew like me," she continued. "We didn't know how to protect ourselves, to stop having kids. It wasn't the men pressuring us to have them, we just didn't see an alternative. Men didn't like to wear condoms then, and they still don't. Three kids would have been much easier. It was really difficult to pay for seven kids as they grew up. With seven I was always busy and there was not enough time to work to support them all. There were plenty of days when there wasn't enough for everyone to eat. I had to make some very difficult choices about who to feed and when. I thought my children would be able to help me when I was older, but they haven't been able to do that as much as I'd hoped. So my life is still hard, but it's not as bad as before when were all living together and I had to pay for all of them.

Things are different now here. You can have kids when you want them because everyone knows what precautions to take. I'm not sure if it's easier today for women even though they know how to avoid having so many children. Sure, they have fewer kids, but life is just as hard because if they live in town they have to buy everything and it's still expensive, even if you just have two. I would advise girls today to follow their parents' advice closely, to do what they say, and to plan your life well and learn what precautions to take to not get pregnant every year. Life gets harder here every day, so think about how hard it will be with many children."

In the same village I met a woman named Zaramany, age 39, who has five children ranging in age from six to 15, all by the same father. She has only one name, like some Afghans and Brazilians I had met, and since it was somewhat rare in Madagascar to come across someone without a last name I asked her about it. She told me she used to have two names but when she realized at age 16 that it had been left off of her birth certificate by mistake she decided to stop using it, and the lack of a surname has never caused her any problems.

Zaramany has never been married. Unlike Isabelle, she doesn't know any women her age with more than five children, and this is probably because she came of age almost two decades later. "I wanted to have two children," she said, "but there was no family planning in my village so they just kept coming. My boyfriend wanted three. Family planning is easy here in town, I just get a shot once every three months. Most women I know do that now, and it's free. Before there was no chance of that in small villages, but now the new technology is available everywhere. But life remains very difficult because of all the things I have to pay for. School fees for five children are very expensive – almost 100,000 Ariary per year for each child. I will tell my daughters to have only two children to avoid the situation I am in."[66]

Isabella and Zaramany lived on the outskirts of Diego, close to the city but not quite in an area considered rural. One day I decided to visit a small village further away to get a better sense of attitudes in the countryside. A rickety bus took me far from the city, and after getting off I walked for twenty minutes down a red-dirt road toward the village of Maromagniry, passing a herd of zebu and a few goats as I went. Just outside the village I came across a group of men and women seated on the ground about ten feet apart, each pounding large rocks into smaller stones that could be sold in Diego for landscaping. It was a beautiful sunny day, and as I entered the village I could see Amber Mountain off in the distance and the sun glinting off the blue water of the bay below. It wasn't the first time I had marveled at how extreme poverty could exist in such picturesque settings.

I met my guide, and after meeting a few women I quickly discovered that attitudes were markedly different here. I sensed a greater fatalism toward childbirth and family size: women seemed to believe that greater birth control options gave them greater control over the number of children they bore, but only to a point. "It's up to God how many children I have," is a refrain I heard over and over again.

I was introduced to an attractive woman named Giselle, age 32, who like Zaramany uses only one name. She lives with her eight children and their father in a two-room shack in the center of the village. She has six boys and two girls, and her children range in age from three to 16. She and the children's father are not married, which is not unusual in rural settings like this one, where a formal ceremony is often viewed as too expensive.

Giselle told me a different story from most of the other women I met. She claimed she always planned to have many children. "I wanted to have many children because it's the custom here and many children is considered a great gift. I'm very happy I have eight children. I never had a definite number in mind but I always knew it would be more than five. I know a lot of women here in the village who have more than five." Her mother had 10 kids, and encouraged Giselle to have many children, although maybe not eight.

But like the other women she was quick to point out the extreme financial burden it places on their family. Like the cluster of men and women I had seen when I entered Maromagniry, both she and her partner hammer rocks for a living, which is what most people in the village do for work. "It's very hard on us because it's so expensive to raise them. It's harder now than ever before because the school fees have gone up and are more expensive than ever. Sometimes there is not enough money for food or school for everyone."

She uses contraception now, an injection she receives every three months that recently became available in the village. "I just learned about it over a year ago. It was probably available before then but I wasn't interested because I wanted more children." And yet despite her expressed happiness over her large family she would advise her daughters not to follow the same path. "I don't want them to have so many kids. I hope they will start using contraception earlier and have only two children." She believes it will be more difficult for her children as they become adults because there may not be enough work for all of them. "But it's up to God how many children they will have when they grow up."[67]

Not far from Giselle's house I came across Elizabeth Soa, age 35, who had ten children, including one who died in childbirth. The nine surviving children range in age from two to 16. She is not married although she lives with the father of her youngest three children. "I never planned to have so many, it just happened over time," she told me. "I was aware of contraception but didn't understand it very well. The fathers didn't want so many kids either, but that's what happened." Six months ago she started receiving the contraceptive injections every three months in the village. "God has given me so many children," she said. One thing she said that I heard from others was a real wariness over contraception. Not that it didn't work, but that it caused side effects that some women couldn't tolerate, leading them to skip it.

Elizabeth told me that while both she and her partner work, it doesn't bring enough to pay for all of her children. "Sometimes there is not enough food," she said. The rent of her two-room shack is 30,000 Ariary/month, which takes up most of her income. She also believes there will probably not be enough work for all her children when they grow up, and when I asked her about a generational change in attitudes toward large families, she was skeptical. "The culture is not really changing," she said, "so my daughters will probably have many children also."[68]

Before leaving the village I met with two young women who already had five children and were considering more. Dieudonne Ravoana, 31, said she never planned to have five children. "God gave them to me; he decided," she said. The contraceptives she tried, both pills and the injection, made her sick, so she stopped receiving them. "Life is very difficult, with not enough money for school fees or even food somedays," she told me.

Lucia Raharivololina, 26, was one of the few who attempted an explanation for the different attitudes in Diego and her village. Part of it centered on the rejection of abortion in the village. "In Diego, many abortions occur whenever a woman wants one. In the village, no one gets an abortion because they see the child as God's will." She believes women would like to have fewer children but that the contraception options can cause problems. "When I was 17 I didn't know about contraception; I only learned it at age 20 after I got pregnant with our third child." She started receiving the injection, but it caused her period to last for weeks, so she stopped. She is still very thin and isn't sure what is causing her to be so sick. "I only wanted three kids originally but now I'm happy with five, and we're thinking about having one more before stopping. I come from a small family and I always wanted to start a large one that will grow bigger with each generation." But she conceded that employment opportunities for all of her children and others in the village will be problematic. "I don't know what they will all do for work later," she acknowledged.

Those women were all in the northern regions of Madagascar, but I found the same attitudes in the South, where life was much harder and the struggles to raise multiple children even more obvious. Two engaging women I met personified the island's attitude toward childbearing perfectly. Rano Ben Florentin is 51 years old and has nine kids between the ages of four and 35 from three fathers (and would love to have more!). Rano Lazal is 40 and has eight kids aged between three and 25 from the same father. The fathers of these children also wanted large families, the two women claimed.

Both women told me they wanted so many kids primarily to help them when they got older. That's a part of Androy culture in the South: as children grow up they are expected to help their parents in everything from harvesting crops, tending livestock, and doing household chores. In that sense having a large family is seen as a financial investment in a couple's future, one that occasionally pays off for these women, as their children are already starting to give them food when they have extra.[69]

But it was very difficult to feed all of them, both women acknowledged, and it still is. Sometimes they had no food for three days, forcing them to feed their children boiled water to fill their bellies and help them sleep. All of their children over a certain age grow crops in the village, and the young ones are already learning. And then they made an astonishing admission: each of them told me that only their firstborn child went to school (and for just a few years); the rest never went at all.

Ben is happy to have so many children, but sad their fathers had all left. Lazal is happy too. Her kids all work the land together on a plot given to them by their parents, but there is not enough land or food for all of them, so she ends up giving them some food from time to time. As a financial investment her large brood turned out to be one with a low return. Ben and Lazal said there is family planning in the village, but both of them stopped taking pills when they became sick and heard rumors that they could kill you. The younger generation of women take it now (via shot or pill), they told me, but still complain about the side effects. And after all of their professed contentment with their large families both women said they would advise their daughters to have just two or three children because it's too hard to feed more than five.

One member of that younger generation, a young woman named, Rano Soa, 23, seemed to be following that advice. I sought her out because I heard she didn't have any children yet, which turned out to be true, but not for any family planning reasons. In fact, she hopes to have five kids someday, but she and her husband (a night watchman in Faux Cap) haven't been able to conceive yet. As the two older women had told me, Rano Soa wanted a large family primarily to have someone to help her when she's older. And she acknowledged how unusual she was to be childless at 23; her friends started giving birth at 14, and most of them want two or three kids, but some still want eight or ten. There's just a wider range now, she told me. Some accept the family planning services that come to the village from time to time, but some don't. "There's already not enough land to feed all of the kids in the village, and adding many more children would make the situation impossible," she said.

* * *

As Madagascar races toward 54 million people by mid-century, it's hard to fathom how the island will cope. Most of the population increase will occur in cities, and those urban areas will become sprawling seas of chaos as more people push them past their original boundaries and into outlying areas. The urban poverty now so vividly on display in Antananarivo will become the norm in places like Tamatave, Antsirabe, and even Mahajanga and Tulear, where the economy will likely be unable to keep pace with the influx of young people looking for work. In rural areas, millions more will be undernourished as climate change dries up the western and southern regions of the island. The tragedy is that it didn't have to be this way. Even the modicum of a family planning policy by the island's first leaders after independence would have helped reduce the population growth rate to manageable levels. While the current regime's vow to institute such a policy in the near future is a welcome sign, it will inevitably be too little, too late. Madagascar has enough remaining farmland and natural resources to avoid catastrophe, but the country should plan on at least 10 million people being added to the 20 million already living on less than $2 a day, due solely to an unprecedented explosion in numbers.

Chapter 6

The Great South

The struggling people of Madagascar are caught between their own corrupt, ineffective government, which denies the scale of the crisis, and overseas governments that don't want to curb carbon emissions.
Nicholas, Kristof, *The New York Times*

To travel into the Great South of Madagascar is to venture into another world. Gone are the lush hillsides and the terraced rice fields of the central highlands and the eastern escarpment. Here the land is hot and dry, flat stretches of red dirt road and desert broken up by random outcroppings of rock. An occasional baobab tree stands sentry over the cactus desert, while thousands of tall, thin octopus trees bend eerily toward some unknown gravitational force. Towns and small cities rise up out of nowhere, and within a few minutes the traveler can go from desolation to burgeoning villages that envelop any vehicle stopping for a break. Once you've left these small towns, the emptiness returns and an ominous stillness reigns over a setting harshly beautiful. Some landscapes around the world are so bleak they almost prepare you psychologically for the human suffering that lies within them. Southern Madagascar is one such place.

Zebu, the humpbacked cattle of Madagascar, outnumber people in large swathes of the Great South. They are a traditional source of food for the five tribes inhabiting this region, but even more important, of status. Men are expected to give a few zebus as dowry to their bride's family when they marry, and any celebration or funeral requires a feast centered around the ritual slaughter of at least one bull for a feast. The elaborate tombs of the Mahafaly and Androy tribes dot the region every few miles as colorful tributes to the ancestors.

Traveling through this region is not easy. Every person I met in the South lamented the poor state of the roads in the region, but they did not need to tell me how bad they were. I had just traveled them back and forth for a month, in every vehicle imaginable, from an old Dacia pickup truck to the long truck-buses known as *taxi-brousses* that get crammed full of people. Tenuous welding and questionable suspensions afflicted all of them. I liked riding the overnight buses, usually paying a little extra to sit up front with the driver and his assistant to see all the sights along the route. My presence on these voyages as a foreigner – the only foreigner I ever saw riding the buses in this part of the country – was a constant state of interest, even excitement. On one redeye trip I rode in the main hold and sat in the seat behind a woman who had fallen asleep before I got on, her head lolling back to face me as she slept. When the bus started back up she opened her eyes and saw a white man, upside down, staring back at her. She must have thought it was part of some dream, or nightmare. She let out a sharp cry, her eyes grew big and her jaw literally dropped at the sight of me. I placed a hand on her shoulder to reassure her that I was no ghost, and she laughed at her startled reaction, but she continued to look back at me the rest of the night to verify that what she had seen was real.

On another trip the bus broke down and had to be repaired for several hours while we waited. Some people stayed on and slept while others got off and talked, or walked, or stared up at the night sky. As dawn approached I took a stroll outside down the length of the bus and saw a young boy and girl, brother and sister, awake next to the window, looking down at me. I reached out to shake their hands through the open window and the boy reciprocated enthusiastically, reaching across his sister with a wide grin on his face. The young girl, however, was clearly afraid to touch me. She stared at my outstretched hand as if it were a snake. I dropped my arm after a few seconds and apologized for upsetting her. Before I could turn away, however, the young boy began cajoling his sister to accept my offer. I couldn't understand what he was saying, but he was both mocking her fear and talking to her earnestly trying to convince her to trust me. Finally, after a few more attempts by me and constant goading from her brother, the girl tentatively took my hand for a brief moment. When she let go she immediately gripped her wrist and stared at her hand as if it might fall off. I learned later that some people in the Androy region tell their children that shaking a white man's hand will turn their own hands white.

Crossing from the Mahafaly lands into the Androy region was to enter an even harsher, more isolated environment. In Betioky, a major Mahafaly hub, I was welcomed as an esteemed guest. In a small *hotely*, or café, where our bus stopped to eat in the middle of the night, the woman working behind the counter gasped at the sight of me entering her restaurant and disappeared into a back room. When she emerged she was carrying a baby boy, not yet a year old, and rushed over to me to have me kiss the baby's forehead. One of my traveling companions explained to me that some Mahafaly still consider a white man's kiss a harbinger of good luck to newborns. But I received a much chiller reception when I entered Androy territory. Enduring yet another travel delay to repair an overloaded bus, I walked outside at dusk and saw a mother and two children approaching me down the sandy path next to the road. They were a beautiful family in traditional dress, and I approached slowly, saying hello and gesturing to my phone to ask if I could take a picture. The mother stopped about ten feet away from me and stared, and I could see her breath start to come more quickly. She uttered one word to her children and they took off on a dead sprint through the bush, making a wide circle around the bus before carefully emerging back on the road about forty feet ahead of us. I stood in place, shocked at the panic I had just caused. Several people laughed when I told them that story and told me that rumors dating from the mid-20th century of white people murdering the Androy for their organs still lingered deep in the bush here. These kinds of things never happened to me in any other part of the country.

But the Great South is not only the most isolated region of the island, the place where colonialism left its weakest footprint and where traditional ways still predominate. It is also where disaster looms in Madagascar. Throughout vast stretches of the South, drought has left millions of people in a permanent state of nutritional deficiency that can at times border on famine. Wells have dried up and forced entire towns to search for new sources of water. Banditry, though declining, still persists, as desperation and the quest for cattle drive hundreds of young men to rob buses passing on the highways, tourist caravans traveling to the coast, or entire villages who happen to be in their path.

It is here also that the population is increasing the fastest, in a scenario straight from Malthus. Tens of thousands of people leave the region in search of better opportunities and more fertile farmland every year. Millions more who stay face chronic food shortages, and at times, near-famine conditions. The South is kept alive almost entirely by foreign aid, without which the region would soon become uninhabitable. When it becomes too hot and dry to grow even a minimum of food, it may have to be abandoned at some point anyway, prompting an enormous internal refugee crisis. The Great South, always an outlaw region of Madagascar, is quickly becoming its dustbowl. And it is all because of one global phenomenon that is coming to define the 21st century more than any other.

* * *

Climate change has come to dominate headlines around the world in recent years, but the science predicting man-made weather catastrophes has been around for decades. In fact, world leaders have been unforgivably slow to react to the mounting evidence of human caused planetary warming. The UN Framework Convention on Climate Change was agreed upon in 1992 at the Rio Earth Summit, but not until the Paris Agreement, adopted by 195 nations in December 2015, did they identify a verifiable target for slowing the growth in temperatures. Two degrees Celsius above pre-industrial levels became the agreed-upon maximum beyond which temperatures must not rise, and limiting the increase to 1.5 degrees was fixed as an even more desirable goal. But by that time it was almost too late; more carbon had been released into the atmosphere since 1989 than in the entire history of civilization preceding it.

The 2-degree target is admittedly somewhat arbitrary, but the focus on one number helps galvanize a global cross-section of governments and activists around the world. We now understand that "2-degree warming" would be a problematic but grudgingly acceptable outcome while "4-degree warming" would be an outright catastrophe. With this understanding, not to mention all of the science and momentum behind finding a cure for climate change, you would think that the world would already be well on its way to staying close to two degrees. And yet little is being done to curb emissions on a meaningful scale. Nathaniel Rich recently summed up the civilizational stakes involved and the consequences of falling short:

> The world has warmed by one degree Celsius since the Industrial Revolution. The Paris climate agreement – the nonbinding, unenforceable and already unheeded treaty signed on Earth Day in 2016 – hoped to restrict warming to two degrees. The odds of succeeding, according to a recent study based on current emissions trends, are one in

20. If by some miracle we are able to limit warming to two degrees, we will only have to negotiate the extinction of the world's tropical reefs, sea level rise of several meters and the abandonment of the Persian Gulf. The climate scientist James Hansen has called two-degree warming "a prescription for long-term disaster." Long term disaster is now the best case scenario. Three-degree warming is a prescription for short-term disaster: forests in the Arctic and the loss of most coastal cities. Robert Watson, a former director of the UN Intergovernmental Panel on Climate Change, has argued that three-degree warming is the realistic minimum. Four degrees: Europe in permanent drought; vast areas of China, India and Bangladesh claimed by desert; Polynesia swallowed by the sea; the Colorado River thinned to a trickle; the American Southwest largely uninhabitable. The prospect of a five-degree warming has prompted some of the world's leading climate scientists to warn of the end of human civilization.[1]

Where are we on that spectrum? The answer is stark and depressing. While rightly viewed as an admirable diplomatic achievement at the time, the Paris Agreement's goal of two degrees warming is looking more and more like wishful thinking. In the immediate aftermath of the accord climate watchers were somewhat optimistic that emissions would start to decrease within a few years. They could not have been more wrong. Despite all the momentum building from the Paris Agreement, carbon emissions increased by 1.5% in 2017 and 2.1% in 2018. Global emissions only rose 0.6% in 2019, but the important point is that they were still rising. Meanwhile, global temperatures in 2019 were the second highest on record, according to the Copernicus Climate Change Service, only a fraction less than the record set in 2016.[2]

So despite a pledge by 80 countries in 2019 to ramp up their climate commitments ahead of schedule, the world is currently

on pace for four-degree warming by 2100. We've already covered
what that will look like. We're in the process of missing our
target so badly because as of 2018 not a single major industrial
nation was on track to fulfill the commitments it made in the
Paris treaty. Of course, those commitments only get us down
to 3.2 degrees; to keep the planet under 2 degrees of warming,
all signatory nations have to significantly better their pledges.
As David Wallace-Wells writes, "If the best case scenario is now
between 2 and 2.5 degrees of warming by 2100, it seems that the
likeliest outcome sits at about 3 degrees, or just a bit above."[3]
That forecast, written in 2019, has now been narrowed further,
with the latest research predicting a range of between 2.6 and
4.1 degrees of warming.[4]

A handful of countries are responsible for almost all of global
carbon emissions. In terms of historical responsibility, the United
States bears by far the greatest share, accounting for one-third
of all emissions to date as of 2019. The climate scientist James
Hansen has estimated that developed countries are responsible
for 77% of all carbon emissions between the years 1751 and 2006.
China is now the world's largest annual emitter, spewing 27%
of the global total, while the U.S contributes 15%, the EU 10%,
and India 7%. India also had the world's highest growth rate in
2018. China's rise to its position as the world's biggest polluter
by far answers the question as to whether its heavy investments
in renewable energy would offset its continued reliance on coal-
fired power plants to boost manufacturing at home and in new
markets like sub-Saharan Africa; they didn't.[5] Some good news
was that the US and EU both managed to cut their emissions in
2019, while India's emissions grew more slowly than expected.
And global emissions from coal, the worst polluting of all fossil
fuels, unexpectedly declined by about 0.9%, although that drop
was more than offset by strong growth in the use of oil and
natural gas around the world.

Aggregate emissions by country are interesting, but

emissions by each individual in those countries are even more revealing, putting the consumer culture of the West on full blast. As of 2017, the U.S. emits over 5.3 metric tons of carbon dioxide per year, or 16.2 metric tons per person. EU emissions total around seven metric tons per person. The average for all lower and middle-income countries taken together is only 3.5 metric tons per person. China, the largest offender of any country in the aggregate, emits 7.4 metric tons per person, while India emits only 1.7 metric tons per person. Over one billion people in Africa emit just 0.8 metric tons per person, less than 1/20th the US number, and account for just 2% of the world's energy-related carbon dioxide emissions. And yet they and their brethren in the Global South will bear the brunt of most of the warming.[6]

The consequences of 3-degree warming – now the most realistic scenario by century's end – cannot be overstated. As we saw in the last chapter, experts agree that feeding 9 or 10 billion people by mid-century in the face of a rapidly worsening climate is likely to prove the greatest challenge in human history. The UN projects 200 million climate refugees by 2050, and possibly one billion by the end of the century. Every part of the world will be routinely hit by floods, droughts and heat waves that damage crops. Salt water intrusion from sea level rise will threaten some of the richest agricultural deltas in the world. Ocean warming, acidification and overfishing may severely deplete the amount of food available from the sea. If we stay on our current emissions trajectory and allow global temperatures to reach 4 degrees Celsius above their pre-industrial level, we will quickly surpass the limits of human adaptation in many parts of the world. In addition to Rich's parade of horribles, we will see worsening Dust Bowl conditions in many arid regions, sea level rise of over 6 feet, massive species loss, much more extreme weather, and increasing food insecurity, as the global population approaches 10 billion and agricultural yields decline.[7]

Let's not forget that even 2-degree warming is probably too much. In October 2018 the UN's Intergovernmental Panel on Climate Change (IPCC) issued a report that sent shock waves through the climate change community. The report essentially warned that small global temperature increases can have enormous consequences. For example, the half-degree difference between 1.5 and 2 degrees of total warming has outsized real world effects: climate problems will simply metastasize in the hotter scenario. Two degrees would consign twice as many people to water scarcity, put ten million more at risk from sea levels rising ten centimeters higher, and plunge several hundred million more people into poverty as lower yields of key crops drive hunger across much of the developing world. The size of global fisheries will drop by 50 percent in the 2-degree scenario. Twice as many species will lose their habitat. Nearly all of the planet's coral reefs will be lost, versus 10-30% that could survive if warming was limited to 1.5%. Tens of millions more people will be exposed to deadly heat waves, water shortages and flooding. And the difference between 2.5% and 2% is even greater than between 2% and 1.5%, since the damages mount exponentially as temperatures rise.[8] As *The Atlantic* put it in their review of the report, "the battle to prevent climate change entirely has already been lost. But the battle to blunt its effects, and to choose to a better, cooler future, has just begun."[9]

The most alarming thing about the IPCC report wasn't its explicit rendering of the dire consequences from just a half degree of warming; it was its admission of how unlikely we are to avoid them. The report warned that significant hurdles exist to limiting global warming to 1.5 degrees Celsius over pre-industrial levels. Such progress would require "rapid, far reaching and unprecedented changes in all aspects of society," changes that many experts are skeptical we can make any time soon. Limiting warming to 1.5 degrees would require global net human caused emissions of CO2 to fall by about 45% from 2010 levels by 2030, reaching net zero around 2050 (meaning any remaining emissions would need to be offset by removing CO2 from the air). By contrast, allowing the global temperature to exceed 1.5 degrees would mean a greater reliance on techniques that remove CO2 from the air to get us back below 1.5 degrees – techniques that are unproven and may carry unacceptable risks for sustainable development.[10]

Moreover, limiting warming to 1.5 degrees would require humanity to abandon coal and other fossil fuels in the next decade or two: an economic transition so abrupt that "it has no documented historic precedents." The report's plan calls for the annual level of carbon pollution to begin to fall immediately, but as we saw, emissions hit a record high last year. By 2030, the world would need to halve its annual emissions, and we're not even close to achieving that. By 2050, the world must get 80% of its electricity from renewable or nuclear power, but only 20% comes from those sources today. The need to start removing more CO2 from the atmosphere than we emit by 2050 is, again, a longshot at this point. Coal must account for no more than 7% of global electricity by 2050, down from 40% today.[11]

The obvious way to reverse these trends and put ourselves on a path to reaching these goals is to start reducing emissions now. To have a better than 50% chance of keeping total warming below 2 degrees, we need to cut the emissions of CO2 and other major pollutants by more than 50% by mid-century, so that, by 2100, the world's total net emissions can drop to somewhere close to zero. To be equitable, many experts believe wealthier countries should take the lead, reducing their emissions by 80%-90% by mid-century. China and the US, who together account for 40% of global emissions, must take the lead.

The mechanisms and methods to achieve such drastic cuts in emissions are actually relatively straightforward. What's missing is the political will to achieve them. The argument against them usually centers on their allegedly high cost and the unacceptably sudden brakes they would put on economic growth. Some conservative pundits have claimed that implementing a robust package of climate change measures will inevitably lead to recessions in the world's major economies, already buffeted by the Coronavirus. Most independent economic analyses of the costs of such measures, however, have concluded that they would be quite low; for example, the UN found the result of full implementation to be a reduction in median annual economic growth of just 0.06%, and this estimate does not even take into account the benefits of avoiding the enormous costs that would be imposed if we don't stay below a 2-degree rise.[12] The bottom line is that, according to the IPCC, we have just 12 years to cut global carbon emissions in half. And the longer we wait, the harder it will be. If we start today, when global emissions are still growing, the challenge will undoubtedly be great. If we delay another decade, it will require us to cut emissions by 30% each year, which most experts think would be impossible.[13]

The steps required to prevent catastrophic climate change are many and varied, ranging from a tax on carbon to more fuel-efficient cars and better agricultural practices. Many studies show that dietary changes across the globe are critical to achieving the 2 degrees target, as greenhouse gas emissions from meat and dairy productions are comparable to the emissions from the global transport sector. But significant dietary changes are unlikely to take place on their own. Rather, the reality of insufficient land and fresh water to sustain 3 billion more people by 2100 could compel the world to forego a meat-intensive diet, if only to avoid mass starvation. We may not have any choice.[14]

All of this was confirmed in the UN's annual emissions gap report for 2019, which also found that average temperatures are likely to rise 3.2% over the baseline temperature at the start of the industrial age, even if every country keeps its commitments under the Paris Accord. It concluded that "deeper and faster cuts are now required," and that the world's 20 richest governments, responsible for more than 75% of worldwide emissions, must take the biggest, swiftest steps to move away from fossil fuels. In order to avoid the most severe consequences of climate change, global CO2 emissions would need to steadily decline and reach roughly zero well before the end of the century. To avoid the worst effects of climate change (droughts, storms, widespread hunger), the report said emissions must decline sharply, starting in 2020, and continue declining by 7.6% every year through 2030.[15]

Suffice it to say the situation is getting worse, not better. The atmospheric concentration of carbon dioxide, the main greenhouse gas, now exceeds 410 parts per million, the highest level in 800,000 years. Global average surface temperatures are 1.2 degrees Celsius higher than they were before the Industrial Revolution. Humanity still has around 20 years before the chances of limiting global warming to 2 degrees will become essentially impossible, and most projections show that the world will exceed it. As temperatures rise to three degrees above that level, and even beyond, the distribution of climate phenomena will shift and the tail risks will become even more extreme.[16]

The scariest part may be that we are already witnessing some of those phenomena, events that climates scientists considered fringe scenarios twenty years ago. Antarctic ice sheets and Arctic permafrost are melting at a faster rate than once considered possible, sea levels are rising and becoming warmer more quickly, and extreme weather is causing more havoc than anyone imagined. In Bangladesh, for example, up to 18 million people face displacement by 2050 from sea rise alone. For decades, most scientists saw climate change as a distant prospect. But many worst-case scenarios outlined in the 1990s have now become reality, while the costs of underestimation have proven to be enormous. Not until 2017 did UN experts acknowledge that 3% warming was more likely than staying close to 1.5%, and this came nearly 30 years after climate change became a mainstream issue. It's unclear how well governments around the world understand that sudden, rapid climate change is the new normal.[17]

In a cruel twist of fate, children will be among those most severely affected by rising global temperatures, according to a November 2019 report by *The Lancet*. The report found that failing to limit emissions to well below 2% would lead to health problems caused by infectious diseases, worsening air pollution, rising temperatures and malnutrition, principally because children absorb more air pollution relative to their body size than adults. Air pollution killed seven million people in 2016 alone, with children disproportionately affected. One author said that without changes the rise in temperatures could reach 4 degrees by 2090, a date most children born today will live to see. "We roughly know what that looks like from a climate perspective," he said. "We have no idea what that looks like from a public health perspective. But we know it is catastrophic."[18]

That's admittedly a lot of science and global data for a book ostensibly about modern Madagascar. But there's no way to understand what's happening in a place like the Great South without understanding the global forces wreaking havoc on its climate. Sadly for the people of the region, there is little reason to be optimistic about the world's ability to forge a solution before the two-degree target becomes an impossibility, in part because, as an article in *Nature* recently found, the world is warming more quickly than most climate models predict. And that's not even considering the deluge of emissions that continues to pour unabated into the atmosphere each year. In 1990, humankind burned more than 20 billion metric tons of carbon dioxide. By 2017, the figure had risen to an obscene 32.5 metric tons, another record. As Nathaniel Rich laments, despite every action taken since perils of climate change became common knowledge – the billions of dollars invested in research, the nonbinding treaties, the investments in renewable energy – the only number that counts, the total quantity of global greenhouse gas emitted per year, has continued its inexorable rise. The only hope now of staying under two degrees Celsius is to somehow find our way to "negative emissions," extracting more carbon dioxide from the air than we contribute to it.[19]

In December 2019, in a fitting coda for the demise of the once-inspiring Paris Accords, UN talks on climate change ended with the US and other big polluters blocking even a nonbinding measure that would have encouraged countries to adopt more ambitious targets for reducing greenhouse gas emissions next year. The conference was "widely denounced as one of the worst outcomes in a quarter century of climate negotiations," according to the New York Times. Rather than using the forum to advance climate talks, the Trump administration pushed back on a range of proposals, including a way to compensate developing countries for losses related to more severe storms, droughts, rising seas and other effects of global warming. Just one more example of the vast gap between the steps that scientists urge us to take and what the world's most powerful countries will agree to.[20]

* * *

For dry, desert regions of the world like southern Madagascar, global warming is akin to a death sentence. Drought stalks the bottom third of the country known as the Great South like never before. As crops dry up, the caloric intake of most people living in the region goes down, often alarmingly so. And water becomes a commodity more precious than gold.

Madagascar will not be alone when its looming water crisis finally explodes. Water shortages have now become global and perennial. Nearly half the human population is now living with water scarcity, inhabiting places unable to fully meet their drinking, cooking and sanitation needs. A recent study found that countries that are home to one fourth of the world's population now risk running out of water. Seventeen countries are already under extremely high water stress, meaning they are using almost all the water they have, according to new data from the World Resources Institute. Represented among those countries are several major cities that require huge supplies of water but have faced acute shortages recently, including Sao Paulo, Chennai and Cape Town, which in 2018 narrowly avoided what it ominously called Day Zero, the day when municipal water sources are unable to meet demand. Among cities with more than three million people, 33 of them, with a combined population of over 255 million people, face extremely high water stress, with repercussions for public health and social unrest. Those numbers will increase to 45 cities and 470 million people by 2030, with Madagascar inevitably among them. As with most environmental crises, the poor are impacted disproportionately. Around the world, inadequate water and sanitation kills 780,000 people each year. [21]

Climate change is of course the culprit here, as it is in so many issues involving food and water scarcity. Its impact on the world's freshwater supplies will vary by region, but the negative effects in arid and semi-arid parts of the world will outweigh the benefits in other regions. And the warming of the planet will inevitably make it thirstier: a one-degree rise in temperatures results in a 3-4% increase in water demand overall, which, because of its magnifying effects on agriculture, could increase the demand from agriculture by almost 100% by 2050. This would be almost impossible to meet. [22]

Two investigations of water crises in other countries already suffering from severe water shortages offer a glimpse of what could happen by mid-century in Madagascar. Although the science is still evolving, more and more evidence leads to the inescapable conclusion that global warming can make extreme weather events, including drought, more frequent and more intense. India is Exhibit A, both because of its large desert areas and enormous population. Piped water has run dry in Chennai, and 21 other cities are also facing the specter of Day Zero. Last year, Chennai, a city of 8 million, had 55% less rainfall than normal. Prime Minister Modi has promised piped water to all Indians by 2024, but about half of the 6,000 water bodies that once supplied Chennai and its two neighboring districts are now gone, and rampant development has destroyed the spaces that were natural sponges for monsoon rains. The Indian government's newfound faith in desalination ignores the fact that it takes tremendous amounts of energy to transform saltwater to freshwater – and India is already struggling to get power to its growing population. This is a lesson Madagascar, with its keen interest in desalination to solve its own water crisis, should heed. Finally, the lack of water is fundamentally derailing economic growth in Chennai, another example of how ignoring the environment can actually hinder the economy.[23]

Closer to Madagascar is Zimbabwe, a southern African country whose governmental corruption and mismanagement over the past few decades makes Madagascar look something like Denmark. Zimbabwe faces a situation just as dire as India's, though with a much smaller population. In the capital city of Harare, more than half of the city's 4.5 million residents now have running water only once a week, forcing them to wait in lines at communal wells, streams and boreholes. Zimbabwe's acute water shortage in 2019 was the result of a particularly bad drought that year, a symptom of climate change. And poor water management has wasted much of the water that remains. Two of Harare's four reservoirs are empty from lack of rain, but about 50% of the water that's left is lost through leakage and theft, according to the city's mayor. The shortage of water has become an annual problem in Zimbabwe, with rainfall this year now 25% less than the annual average. In response to the crisis, Zimbabwe's government is in the process of securing a $71 million loan from China to renovate the nation's water system. The government's record of maintaining that system, however, not to mention ensuring widespread access to it, is far from encouraging. So residents are drinking less, washing less, and relieving themselves less, in a system of coping that will only lead to more health problems.[24]

But the stories from India and Zimbabwe are, if anything, an oversimplification. There is a paradox surrounding water crises in the age of climate change, as some countries become inundated by water while others suffer from a lack of it. Drought in both the Horn of Africa and the continent's southern countries have put millions at risk of thirst and even starvation. Somalia, for example, saw 260,000 deaths in 2011 after a particularly severe drought and subsequent famine. Climate change, through rising temperatures and shifting rainfall patterns, will subject some regions to inadequate and irregular rains, leading to harvest failures and insufficient water for human needs, but other parts of the world will suffer similar effects from flooding and rising sea levels.[25]

For those countries like Madagascar wondering whether intensifying droughts in the Great South will cause their water supply to evaporate someday soon, desalination is a tantalizing prospect. An island surrounded by so much water, many Malagasy officials believe, must have some way of turning the oceans along its coasts into a source of drinking water or at least irrigation. In a somewhat surprising outreach to a part of the world they have little to do with, or that has little to do with them, Malagasy leaders have recently turned to Israel for help in devising a way to desalinize water along the island's coasts to irrigate its parched southern region. The Israelis are viewed as experts in water issues by countless people I spoke to within the region.

Other countries have similar ideas. Globally, desalination is increasingly seen as one possible answer to problems of water quantity and quality that will worsen with global population growth and the extreme heat and prolonged drought associated with climate change. The Middle East and North Africa are at the center of the growth of desalination plants, since renewable water supplies in these countries have fallen well below the UN definition of absolute water scarcity, which is about 350 gallons per person per day. A 2017 report from the World Bank suggests climate change will be the biggest factor increasing the pressure on the water supply in the future. Yet no one is sure where else desalination will take hold. In low income countries like Madagascar, it has barely begun, and the primary reason is cost. Because of the enormous amounts of energy it requires, desalination remains expensive, which has so far limited its implementation to affluent countries, especially those with fossil fuels and access to seawater. The United States, Spain, Australia, and China are all in this group. There are environmental costs to desalination as well, with large greenhouse gas emissions one byproduct of the energy consumed and a concentrated, toxic brine another. As a result, desalination only accounts for 1% of the fresh water found in the world today. Saudi Arabia, one of the most water-starved nations on Earth, is the world leader, accounting for one-fifth of the total; desalinated water makes up about half of the fresh water supply for its 33 million people. But even they struggle to make it economical. Scientists in Saudi Arabia are trying to make the reverse osmosis process used in almost all new desalination plants cheaper and more efficient, but the older thermal plants found throughout the country are harder to modernize. In 2009 the Saudi minister for water and electricity estimated that one-fourth of all oil and gas produced in the country was used to produce the country's fresh water and electricity. This does not bode well for a very poor country like Madagascar, which has just a fraction of those energy reserves.[26]

* * *

The link between global warming and the severe droughts now becoming increasingly common in certain parts of the world is still tenuous. Yet enough research exists to show that rising carbon emissions are an incontrovertible cause of severe weather patterns from the southeast coast of the United States to flooding in South Asia and droughts in southern Africa. Climate change is generally thought of in the developed world as a euphemism for higher temperatures, but in Africa it has come to be identified with something altogether more dangerous: less food.

A hotter planet is inextricably linked with food insecurity, for several reasons. First, the idea that global warming will merely shift agricultural production from currently warmer lands to cooler ones as temperatures rise is proving to be a myth. In fact, it's becoming increasingly unlikely that loss of production in currently arable lands will be offset by greater yields in colder regions of the world, so total food production might actually fall by 2050. Part of the reason has to do with rising water levels in tropical and subtropical regions of the world, which already pose significant problems in chronically malnourished areas of the world.[27]

Second, global grain stocks are down to their lowest levels since the 1970s, meaning the world will have to increase grain production by 70%-100% by 2050 to keep pace with the demands of a rising population. This would be an incredible challenge in normal times, and if the global rise in temperature reaches more than 4 degrees Celsius by 2100, which some experts think is possible, half of the world's farmland would become unsuitable for agriculture, dashing any hopes for such a dramatic rise in production.[28] And the irony is that agriculture, as currently practiced, is itself one of the greatest contributors to climate change, pumping out a quarter or more of the world's annual greenhouse gas emissions. As Joel K. Bourne has written, "We are literally farming ourselves out of food."[29]

Two recent reports affirmed how climate change is making the challenge of feeding the planet increasingly daunting. The World Resources Institute published an analysis in December 2018 that said the world's agricultural systems will need to make drastic changes in the next few decades in order to feed millions more people without triggering a climate catastrophe. Agriculture already occupies about 40% of the world's land and is responsible for over a quarter of the world's greenhouse gas emissions, and with the population expected to grow to almost 10 billion by 2050, the environmental impact will grow dramatically, especially with millions of additional people consuming more calories as incomes continue to rise. The WRI report found the world will need to produce 56% more calories in 2050 than in 2010, based on current consumption trends and population projections. That will be infinitely more difficult if rising temperatures reduce crop yields. Moreover, if that demand is met by clearing away forests and other ecosystems for farmland and pastures, as Madagascar has done, an area twice the size of India would be transformed, which would make it nearly impossible to stay at 2 degrees warming, since so much forest destruction would release huge stores of carbon.[30]

The IPCC produced a similar report in August 2019 that highlighted the difficulty of ensuring food security for 10 billion people while simultaneously solving the climate crisis. The world's land and water resources are being exploited at "unprecedented rates," the report found, which, combined with climate change, is putting enormous pressure on the ability of the world to feed itself. And the window to address the threat is closing rapidly. Already, more than 10% of the world's population remains undernourished, and hunger in much of sub-Saharan Africa is rising, with malnutrition rates reaching nearly 20%. A half-billion people now live in places turning into desert, the report said, and soil is being lost at a much faster rate than it is forming. Climate change will make those problems even worse, as floods, droughts, storms, and other types of extreme weather threaten to disrupt, and over time, shrink the global food supply. If emissions continue to rise, food costs will increase as well, and food crises could develop on several continents at once. This is the nightmare scenario experts fear most, especially since food shortages would probably end up impacting poor regions of the world far more than rich ones, according to several authors of the report. And higher concentrations of CO_2 will also reduce food's nutritional quality, even as rising temperatures reduce crop yields and harm livestock.[31]

Tragically, the world's poorest countries will suffer the most harm. Five billion people will live in the tropics and subtropics by 2100, an astronomical number of humans, many of whom are already dealing with drought to some degree. If temperatures rise by 4 degrees Celsius, areas affected by drought would increase from 15% of global cropland to 44% by 2100 (and 35% of African cropland will become unsuitable for cultivation if temperatures rise by 5 degrees). One study found the median poor country's income will be about 50% lower than it would be without climate change. Food prices could skyrocket in the next 20-30 years, when more taxing demands from growing middle classes are rising. So the best case scenario – limiting the rise in temperature to 2 degrees Celsius – avoids many of the most serious consequences for poor countries like Madagascar. But as we saw, limiting the rise to 2 degrees would require a cut in global emissions to 80% or more below current levels, a level of sustained commitment for which the world has shown no appetite.[32]

The significance of this failure for developing countries cannot be overstated. By 2070, 3.5 billion people, or roughly one-third of the global population, will live in areas considered too hot for humans (84° Fahrenheit). In 2020 it's mostly the Sahara that endures such high temperatures, but in fifty years the extreme heat will become a fact of life for most of the areas now known as the Global South, encompassing a much larger part of Africa, most of India, the Middle East, Southeast Asia, South America and Australia. There are so many problems associated with subjecting so many people to extreme heat, from migration issues to recurrent drought, but perhaps the biggest economic loss of all will be a plunge in global labor capacity as it becomes too hot to work for many months of the year. And it bears repeating that the parts of the world that are growing hotter are precisely the ones where populations are growing the fastest.[33]

Some experts have begun to speak of global warming's disproportionate impact on poor countries as a "problem of environmental justice."[34] The injustice they cite is being borne out globally, where, with one exception – Australia – countries with lower GDPs will warm the most. That is notwithstanding the fact that most of the global south has not, to this point, defiled the atmosphere of the planet all that much. One study found that the world's richest 10 percent are responsible for up to 40% of global environmental damage, including climate change. The poorest 10% account for just 5%.[35] And yet the poorest countries continually bear the brunt of the effects of hotter temperatures and rising sea levels, with countries like Bangladesh witnessing the submersion of up to a third of their territory. The gap in per capita income between the poorest and richest countries is 25 percentage points higher than it would have been without climate change. Between 1961 and 2000, climate change throttled per capita incomes in the world's poorest countries by up to 20% or even 30%. Nigeria, the most populous country in Africa, would have been 29% richer without it.[36]

Climate change will therefore undermine not only the promise of economic growth that so much of the world now takes for granted; it will also, by punishing the poor much more dramatically than the rich, lead to an increasingly stark income inequality between rich and poor countries and, according to some analysts, lead to negative economic growth in the world's poorest countries.[37] Madagascar already has enough self-created obstacles to growth; allowing its entire southern region to dry up as a result of carbon emissions released overwhelmingly by rich nations constitutes a tragedy in large part because the island will be powerless to stop it.

* * *

As we've seen, drought is devastating countries by destroying their arable land. Madagascar actually witnessed a 70% increase in its farmland over the last fifty years, but this came about by relentlessly clearing away forests in order to grow crops.[38] Forests, of course, are a great bulwark against climate change; globally, they take more than a quarter of the carbon released from human activities out of the atmosphere every year. The problem in southern Madagascar is that the rainy season, when farmers grow their staple crops like manioc, corn and beans, has shrunk to just a few months, not nearly long enough to last most families for the rest of the year. From 2014-17 the island suffered through a catastrophic series of droughts that caused severe malnutrition to spike across the southern half of the island, and in some cases resulted in scores of people starving to death. The country's largest aid partners, led by the UN's World Food Program and the European Union, ramped up food and financial assistance to their highest levels on record, with the EU unlocking 300 million Euros in 2019 for UNICEF to aid the hunger crisis in the South, but even these efforts made only a modest impact relative to the scale of the crisis.

Conditions in Madagascar received international attention in 2017 when drought became so severe in southern Africa that over a million children in the region suffered from acute malnutrition. The *New York Times* reported that families in Madagascar were slowly starving because rains and crops had failed for the past few years, and had been "reduced to eating cactus and even rocks or ashes." The UN estimated at the time that nearly one million people in Madagascar alone need emergency food assistance.[39]

When severe droughts persisted in the Great South in 2016, farming production plummeted. Five years of droughts have now ravaged the region, causing a 60% decrease in staple crop production in 2018. About 1.3 million people are now deemed "severely food insecure" in the south, and nearly half of all children on the island suffer from chronic malnutrition, according to UNICEF. Over 20,000 of them are acutely malnourished, which means their bodies are breaking down muscle and fat to survive, putting their immune systems at risk and causing stunting. If another severe drought hits the region, famine is not far away.[40]

What was new about the reporting in 2017 was the direct link drawn between drought and global climate change. The *New York Times*, for instance, reported that the immediate cause of droughts then appearing in southern Africa was an extremely warm El Nino event, which came on top of a larger drying trend in the last few decades in parts of Africa. The American Meteorological Society similarly concluded that human-caused climate change exacerbated El Nino's intensity and significantly reduced rainfall in parts of Ethiopia and southern Africa. They also found that human contributions to global warming reduced water runoff in southern Africa by 48% and concluded that these human impacts "have contributed to substantial food crises."

The international attention focused on Madagascar in 2017 represented a point of departure in another important respect.

Report after dismal report highlighted the impact that decades of massive emissions from the West (and now China) are having on large swathes of the developing world. The United States accounts for more than one-quarter of the world's CO2 emission over the last 150 years, more than twice as much as any other country. The basic injustice, as Nicholas Kristof of the *New York Times* has pointed out, is that rich countries produced the carbon that is devastating impoverished people from Madagascar to Cambodia. The effects are everywhere. Wells in those countries are running dry, forcing poor villagers to walk even further in search of water. The price of cattle has been falling in recent years, in Madagascar and other countries, because so many herders are selling their stock to buy food. The point is that these villagers and farmers are not only blameless for their own plight; they are helpless in combating it.

The consequences for children are particularly severe. Children who don't receive adequate nutrition in their first 1,000 days often can't catch up, so they end up physically stunted and never reach their full mental potential. Fewer children in Madagascar attend school when drought hits and their caloric intake plummets, while more young girls are married off by parents eager to offload the responsibility of feeding them. Aid efforts in Madagascar are admirable, saving tens of thousands of lives each year by providing food, drought-resistant seeds and new technologies to increase the water supply, but as Kristof wrote at the time "the people on the island are caught between their own corrupt, ineffective government, which denies the scale of the crisis, and overseas governments that don't want to curb carbon emissions."[41]

The rising threat of famine in the Great South represents a stunning reversal from recent conventional wisdom. Just a decade or so ago hunger was thought to be on its way out as an international scourge. Famines have thankfully declined over time, as have hunger and malnourishment (though not as quickly). The decline in malnourishment, for example, has now met the UN's Millennium Development Goal, although not the 1996 World Food Summit's target to reduce the number of undernourished people by 50% by 2015.[42] But as climate change intensifies, populations continue to grow and drought worsens in much of the southern half of the globe, the specter of recurrent food crises, if not outright famines, continues to linger. As we'll see, those on the ground in the south of Madagascar almost unanimously agree that famine is a real possibility in the near future, if not a likely occurrence.

The growing scarcity of food relative to the population is of course the most obvious cause for concern in the face of drought, but the effect on food prices is equally distressing for the world's poor. In 2008, food prices spiked to unprecedented levels, increasing the cost of basic sustenance for people in poor countries by 40%. This came as a surprise to most development experts, and, according to David Rieff, should serve as a warning to the optimism prevailing in development circles today. The causes of the rise in prices are only partly clear, but are undoubtedly caused in part by global warming, drought, overpopulation, and the diversion of food crops to ethanol and of farmland to livestock pastures. With all of these factors present in southern Madagascar, the island is susceptible to another sharp rise in food prices as production declines.[43]

How to cope with such crises is the responsibility of both the national government and international relief agencies. As El Nino wreaked havoc on the south, the UN's World Food Program stepped in with a somewhat novel solution that has been gaining traction in much of the developing world: unconditional cash transfers. The World Food Program concluded that in many crisis areas around the world, handing out cash is the quickest and most effective way to help large numbers of suffering people, who can then immediately buy corn, manioc and rice, their staple foods. The agency is now supporting hundreds of thousands of people in two southern districts this way. Each family receives about $20 per month for five months during the dry season. The UN agency has also managed to join forces with the national social protection system with the twin goals of reaching even more people and avoiding any duplication of efforts. They hope to increase support, over time, from 500,000 people to almost 850,000 beneficiaries in areas afflicted by severe drought. The cash families receive is meant to provide them with half of the food they need each month, with the expectation that they can provide the other half by themselves. The challenge remains enormous, however: the region's staple crop production in 2018 was still down by a massive 60 percent from normal years, and the impact hit children the worst. Sadly, nearly half of Madagascar's children are now stunted, according to UNICEF.[44]

Madagascar's government monitors the food crisis in the south on a commune-by-commune basis and appeals for more foreign aid when droughts become severe, but its own interventions have been modest. Perhaps this is to be expected from a government with so little of its own revenue to distribute, but the perception of its indifference to the Great South has historically been widespread. This began to change in 2016, when Madagascar's government embarked upon a somewhat novel program to help those most in need. An unconditional cash transfer program called Fiavota and mimicking the WFP's initiative was launched to give about $10 per month to households in extreme poverty. The program in its first years reached just 5% of those in extreme poverty across the South from 2016-19, but supported nearly 70% of those facing urgent situations like those in the small city of Beloha. The goal now is to triple the program's reach over the next five years to support 15% of populations in the Androy and Anosy regions living in extreme poverty.[45]

The idea of unconditional transfers of cash is a novel solution to a seemingly intractable problem. The question in Madagascar is whether the government, even with international aid, has enough resources to make a real difference. Full funding for the Fiavota program would only reach 15% of those in extreme poverty, and support them only to a level of bare subsistence, so it's hard to see how this initiative, however well intentioned, will help Madagascar find a solution to the worsening droughts that will inevitably come almost every year for the foreseeable future.

After witnessing near-famine conditions in 2017, the Great South finally had a normal rainy season in 2019. The first in five years, the rains were greeted with joy and celebration across the region, with parties and thanks given to everyone from village leaders to the heavens above. But the reaction was in many ways a recognition that predictable rainfall had become an increasingly rare occurrence in the face of unassailable climate change. As many people told me, a bountiful rainy season is nice, but the dry season is the harsh one, and during those months millions of people in the South are reduced to hope that their food supplies will last long enough to see them through to the next period of regular rainfall.

In October 2019, however, in the midst of such celebration, UNICEF produced a major new study entitled *The Situation of Children In The World 2019 – Food and Nutrition*. Focused on the undernutrition and malnutrition of children around the world, it reached the alarming conclusion that one of every three kids under age 5 around the world suffer from undernourishment or are overweight, meaning over 200 million worldwide are malnourished. The consequences of such conditions range from stunted growth to the alteration of cognitive development. Just a few of the chilling statistics: 149 million children suffer from stunted growth or are too small for their age; 50 million are emaciated or too thin for their height; 340 million, or one in two, don't get enough essential vitamins and nutrients; two out of three kids between the ages of six months and two years don't eat enough to support the growth in their bodies and brains.

Poverty, the report found, is a root cause for all of these woes. Only one child in five between the ages of six months and two years in poor regions of the world gets enough to eat to be considered healthy. Another related reason is the lack of variety in their diets: nearly 45% of kids between the ages of six months and two years don't eat fruits and vegetables and nearly 60% don't eat eggs, dairy products, fish or meat. Drought, of course, exacerbates all of these problems, and the report found drought to be 80% responsible for recent losses in the agricultural sector. These losses have further reduced the food options available to children, as well as their quality and price.[46]

This report struck home in Madagascar, a country in which two million (42%) of children are stunted and 270,000 (6%) are emaciated (too thin for their height). Hundreds of thousands of women and children suffer from a lack of vitamins and essential nutrients. Less than 25% of children eat a balanced diet (fruits, vegetables, dairy, protein) that would adequately support their physical and mental development. In the wake of this study Patrice Rabe wrote a perceptive editorial in *Midi Madagasikara* on the crisis, especially as it pertains to the South:

Prioritize The Fight Against Food Insecurity

It's truly a disaster that's occurring now in the Great South of the Big Island and we're not focused enough on it. The population is suffering from severe malnutrition that enfeebles adults but especially children. The recent statistics revealed by international organizations are frightening. Close to one million children less than five years old are innocent victims of this scourge and suffer from stunting that will mark them forever. Madagascar and the Central African Republic are the two countries on the African continent whose cases are the most dramatic. The urgency of the situation has already been reported and Malagasy officials have said that the fight against malnutrition is one of their priorities, but no positive results have been shown.

In 2017, UNICEF Madagascar reported that more than 50% of Malagasy children under five suffered from chronic malnutrition and from stunted growth. This provided a wake-up call to everyone and the Malagasy leaders initiated a series of meetings with their technical partners on how to combat this scourge. Major funds have been allocated to do so. [New organizations] have been created. But two years later, one has the sense that these efforts aren't enough. The situation has gotten even worse. The population in the South suffer from hunger and children are the most vulnerable. The cause of the desolation in this region is obviously climate change. Because of drought, the people are still reduced to eating cactus. Apparently, the government doesn't seem to care about this humanitarian catastrophe taking place here. The Princess of Jordan, Sarah Zeid, on a visit to Madagascar in March 2019, declared herself shocked by the food insecurity and the general health situation in the South. Her comments drew no response from Malagasy officials. Maybe it's time to make this fight against food insecurity a national emergency. This should be one of the most important priorities for our country at the present time.[47]

Even if droughts in the past few years have not been as bad as those during the El Nino phenomenon in 2017, they still happen. In early 2019, Madagascar's nutritional surveillance system, a task force set up by the Ministry of Public Health in partnership with UNICEF, reported that 73 out of the 154 communes in the south were in a nutritional state of emergency, with another 24 communes in a state of alert. The districts of Avombombe, Ampanihy, Bekily and Betioky were the most severely affected, according to the report, with women and children in those districts disproportionately suffering from acute malnutrition.[48]

The news that nearly half of the districts in the south were in a state of emergency came on the heels of another disappointing crop yield in 2018, when lower than average rainfall and the infestation of crops by the armyworm led to a loss of nearly 60% of agricultural production in eight southern districts (Amboasary, Ambovombe, Ampanihy, Bekily, Beloha, Betioky, Taolagnaro and Tsihombe). The government responded by putting these districts on a state of alert, meaning they risk falling back into near-famine conditions when droughts worsen again, which they inevitably will.

So it is no overstatement to say that Madagascar's future remains blighted by the climate change catastrophes that surely await it and the rest of the world. The question is whether anything can be done to change course. According to the International Energy Agency, which published its annual World Energy Outlook in November 2019, cleaner energy may be the solution. At first, glance, green alternatives don't look promising. While clean energy options like solar panels and electric vehicles are spreading far more rapidly than experts predicted, the trend is not nearly enough to offset humanity's rising greenhouse gas emissions and reverse the inexorable trend toward a warmer planet. Analysts estimate that if current energy policies around the world continue, global greenhouse gas emissions could continue rising for the next 20 years. That's because the world's appetite for energy keeps surging, and the rise in renewables hasn't been fast enough to satisfy all the extra demand.

The next surge in demand will come from Africa, and indeed, the report found that what happens in Africa is crucial: the continent is expected to urbanize at a faster rate than China did in the 1990s and 2000s, and that will mean an explosion in its energy needs. If Africa follows the same fossil-fuel heavy path to development that China did during its rise, emissions could rise considerably. But consider the alternative: the continent has about 40% of the world's potential for solar energy but less than 1% of the world's solar panels, meaning cleaner options are available, and if they could only be implemented, the continent could become an enormous generator, rather than simply a consumer, of clean energy.[49] Part of the responsibility to find a cleaner path for Africa lies with the West and China. Currently, 60% of international public aid for energy projects in Africa is spent on fossil fuels – principally through investments in oil and gas infrastructure – with only 18% directed to renewable sources such as wind and solar energy. Perhaps unwittingly, as developed countries and China turn to clean energy for themselves, they may be dooming Africa to a future of rising emissions.[50]

In the end, the strongest momentum for reducing carbon emissions may come as a result of the loss of economic growth that will inevitably follow in its wake. A 2019 study by the National Academy of Sciences found that in most low income countries, higher temperatures are more than 90% likely to have curbed economic output, with climate change already responsible for a 20% reduction in the per capita GDPs of Burkina Faso, Niger, and Sudan.[51] The general rule of thumb for already-warm countries is that every degree Celsius of warming reduces economic growth, on average, by about one percentage point, and experts believe four degrees of warming could reduce yields of cereal crops by 50 percent. Madagascar will simply not be able to withstand either the stunting of economic growth or the loss of food production predicted by these models. Perhaps someday its government and that of other hotter areas of the globe will find a way to force larger, developed countries to take more serious action. Until then, however, the island's future depends on the rest of the world's ability to limit global emissions, which, as we've seen, has to this point been deplorable. Madagascar and the rest of the developing world will only continue to suffer, despite the widespread knowledge of practical, currently available solutions to fight climate change. As David Wallace Wells has written, "If this strikes you as tragic, which it should, consider that we have all the tools we need, today, to stop it all: a carbon tax and the political apparatus to aggressively phase out dirty energy; a new approach to agricultural practices and a shift away from beef and dairy in the global diet; and public investment in green energy and carbon capture."[52]

* * *

Herve Anognona is the Regional Director of the Malagasy government's Ministry of Agriculture in Tulear, a bustling city on the southwestern coast. A member of the Mahafaly tribe from Betioky, deeper into the Great South, Anognona was representative of the new generation of government officials across Madagascar. I had heard that Rajoelina preferred younger cohorts to the old guard that had ruled under Ravalomanana, and young men in their late 30s and 40s were commonplace across the Great South. When we met, Anognona began by describing the huge drop in rainfall he had witnessed across the South in just his lifetime.[53] "When I was in school I used to go home from Tulear to Betioky for two-three months on vacation during the drought season. I've seen an enormous difference between then and now, both in vegetation and in precipitation. The drought was much shorter then, and you could still eat things like corn and manioc. The drought season has gone from two-three months to six months. Then the zebu all survived and could produce milk on a regular basis, even during drought." The rains still come, he said, but they are so much more intense now. The region used to get 400 mm of rain in three months, but now 500 mm in one week is not unusual, often followed by nothing for several months. Plants drown from the deluge and sometimes can't recover, to say nothing of their ability to withstand the periods of no rain.

Anognona confirmed what everyone else had told me: the effects of climate change on agriculture were now the biggest challenge to development in the Great South. "It's becoming a problem of food security," he told me. "We must find a strategy to adapt our way of life to become resilient to climate change. That starts by mobilizing all of our technicians, including foreign experts, to find solutions to the threats posed by climate change." He listed several methods the government was studying to conserve more water and projects funded by wealthier nations to improve the situation. "The Japanese are financing the construction of a new pipeline from Marolinta to Ambovombe that will support a few others we have. The African Development Bank also has projects to improve our irrigation infrastructure. In my opinion it will not be enough to keep the region self-sufficient, but we are determined to find ways to access all available water sources."

He eventually got around to desalinization of ocean water, calling it the long term solution to the desertification of the south. He said Madagascar much embrace desalinization to the same extent Israel has done. "We've started doing this in the southwest but only on a very small scale," he said. There are several nations I heard mentioned as models for Madagascar: China, because of its incredible record of poverty reduction; Rwanda, owing to its newfound fame as an African success story; and Israel, mostly because of its record of development in one of the driest regions on Earth. But desalination on a large scale, as we saw earlier, is extraordinarily expensive for a country like Madagascar, making it a questionable basis for hope.

I asked Anognona if famine was a real possibility for the South if droughts got worse over time.

The fears of famine that arose during 2016 and 2017 have disappeared for now. But climate change means famine is always a possibility because drought has become so severe here. The ground in the south is still fertile if it gets enough rain. But after three more droughts? (Shakes his head) I'm not so sure it will still be able to grow anything. With the new climate you just never know. It poured here last week, in the middle of summer! That would have been unimaginable ten years ago. The seasons are all mixed up now, more unpredictable than ever. That's the new reality in Madagascar. And drought, when it comes now, is much worse than before.

So no, the government is not ready for the next major drought. But no government could be, because droughts now are just overwhelming and millions of people suffer. There's nothing we can really do when it comes. We can develop a strategy and procure sufficient materials to mitigate the worst effects. We can improve our water infrastructure, build up our desalinization facilities, and improve our methods of retaining the rainfall we do get and pumping out more groundwater from under the soil. But can we ensure that every village will have enough food the next time a major drought hits? There's no way.

Like others I met, Anognona lamented the large-scale emigration taking place out of rural areas in the South affected by drought. Most people leaving head for the regional hub of Tulear, but some go even further, sometimes all the way to the capital. There they look for work and take whatever jobs they can find. "Have you seen all the cyclo-pousses here?" he asked me one day out of the blue. "They are a direct result of the migration of young men to the city looking for work. But there is not enough work here for those who arrive, which leads some to turn to crime just to survive."

His reference to the swarm of cyclo-pousses now cruising the streets of Tulear rang true to me. I didn't remember any of them from previous trips and now they were everywhere. A cyclo-pousse is basically an oversized tricycle serving as a taxi, with a young man riding the bike and his fare sitting behind him on a small bench with a canopy overhead to shield him or her from the sun. You couldn't walk through the center of town without hearing "Pousse?" shouted at you every five seconds. Two things I had noticed about the cyclo-pousses: first, this is hard physical labor, and on more than one occasion when we were traveling uphill or I had luggage with me the young man had to walk the bike until he caught his breath. Second, supply had far exceeded demand, and for every pousse with a passenger there were five parked on the street, their owners asleep or playing cards. Something had caused the recent oversupply, and it wasn't the salary. I caught up with a young man named Christophe, age 18, the next time I was in Tulear, to ask him why.

Christophe, who uses only one name, hails from Tsihombe and arrived in Tulear four months ago. He came with two friends to look for work, after hearing from several people from home who were already working in Tulear. "There's nothing for me in Tsihombe," he told me. The droughts there are just too difficult now. "If I stayed, I'd spend all day searching for food, and hopefully end up with a few scraps. I'd probably also drive a pair of zebu for my family, but that doesn't earn anything. So my family actually gave me their blessing and knew it was best for me to leave. Here I can make 5,000 Ariary a day [about $1.75], which isn't much but at least I can eat enough to live. I don't like the work, it's hard work and long hours every day, but life in Tsihombe was even harder. Did you know people there are eating cactus now when there's no rain?"

He appreciates the opportunity to earn a meager living in Tulear, but misses his family and the simple life of Tsihombe.

He saw more teenagers come into the city now, some as young as 15, to ride a cyclo-pousse. "But there are too many pousses here now, so if you get more than three rides a day you are lucky. But I have no choice. I can't do anything else here and I can't go back. So I will keep working like this for many years."[54]

* * *

Whenever I told people I was planning to travel through the Great South, they all told me I had to go to Faux Cap, a small coastal village near the southern tip of Madagascar. "That place used to be a beautiful village on the coast, but now…" and their voices would trail off. I spent three days riding the buses from Tulear to Faux Cap every two or three weeks as I crisscrossed the region. Its howling winds, ocean spray and relative isolation from any other village worthy of the name gives it an end-of-the-earth feel that only increases the longer you stay. I once spent ten days at a small hotel a stone's throw from the beach whose owner, Juliette, has lived in Faux Cap her whole life. Like most residents, she has no desire to leave, even as climate change is turning her once scenic village on the coast into a desert.

Faux Cap is a small village but serves as a microcosm of the food crisis in Madagascar. One day Juliette introduced me to Claude Rafandmezantsoa, the President of Faux Cap and the man who, like many local officials across the island, has the daunting task of helping his people cope with the onslaught of droughts and storms. A youthful man of fifty, Claude often rides the 30 kilometers and back to Tsihombe on his mountain bike to attend meetings. His laid-back demeanor belies a steely resolve to keep his village a safe place to live. Juliette told me that after a spate of thefts in the village a few years ago, Claude convened a meeting of all the adults in the village. Anyone caught stealing, abusing his wife, or otherwise causing trouble would be fined a penalty of one zebu, three goats, and the equivalent of fourteen dollars. Thievery stopped overnight.[55]

Claude presides over 610 people in Faux Cap. He's been president for five years and he loves his job. But drought is probably his biggest worry. "It's very sad," he said ruefully. He told me that when food production starts to plummet he sends urgent requests for aid to the regional and national governments, and then to foreign aid agencies. Luckily the village is by the sea, so people can fish when crops fail. But sometimes the sea is as unkind as the land; in any event, it can't feed everyone. The droughts have gotten worse, he told me. In the 1980s and 1990s, a food crisis occurred once a decade, but since 2015 it comes almost every year (though when I visited in 2019 the situation was stable). And not coincidentally, since 2015 people have started leaving the village in small numbers.

When I asked him if I could meet a few farmers to hear their stories his face brightened immediately. "Why don't I invite all of them," he said. The next day he convened a meeting of 40 people in a barn in the middle of Faux Cap, men and women both, all of whom made their living from subsistence agriculture. They grew everything from manioc, corn, beans and sweet potatoes. "Anything that will grow," they told me. During the summer, when temperatures are highest and the soil hardens almost into rock, it's become hard to grow anything; but in the winter people can generally feed themselves and even sell a small surplus at the market. "Generally the village has become too dry, and we can't grow anything," said Valamana, a middle-aged man who has spent his life here. Some aid gets through, he told me, but not enough. Part of the problem is that, depressingly, a good portion of it is siphoned off by regional chiefs who control its distribution and then sell it instead of giving it away. Valamana also told me that, without enough money to afford pesticides, they have nothing to combat the pests that eat their crops.

From 2016 to 2018, several people in the village died of

hunger each year, and the villagers have become skeptical of their own government's response. "The World Food Program helps us," according to Tsiroahy, another farmer who like many people here uses only one name. "But the central government doesn't do much. If they sent more money, we could send our children to school and hopefully they will have a better life than we have." But only 40% of the children in the village currently attend school because most of their parents can't afford the mandatory fees. And most villagers have 6-10 children, based on an informal survey I took that day. They readily acknowledged that such high birth rates only compounded their financial plight.

Everyone who has spent a decade or more in Faux Cap agreed that droughts are worse now than when they were growing up, though there was some disagreement on exactly when things really got bad. Now they have to eat cactus at times just to stay alive. Or they're forced to eat just once a day (at night), as opposed to their customary habit of eating at noon and night. When I broached the subject of leaving Faux Cap for more fertile regions of the country, they weren't interested. They didn't express any great love for Faux Cap, but, according to one woman who was too bashful to give her name, "This is where we live, this is our home, so we don't have a choice. We must have courage and stay in our village." When I asked them about the United States they all knew of it as a powerful and respected country, but none of them had ever heard of Donald Trump.

Not surprisingly, the intensifying droughts have led not only to a food shortage but to a water crisis as well. There's not enough water in the village well during the dry season, the farmers told me. They eat uncooked corn and manioc when that happens. When it does rain they use simple math to estimate how long their water will hold out: one rain is good for three days of water and cultivation. But now we only have one day of rain a month, a man told me. "How can we live like that?"

On my last day in Faux Cap I went for a long run on the beach. When I started out it was a gorgeous day, full of late afternoon sunshine and little wind. As I turned around at my halfway point dark clouds had gathered offshore, and less than ten minutes later the skies opened up and a deluge ensued. By the time I reached the hotel I was sopping wet, my shoes squishing with every step and my shirt laden with water and sticking to my body. A group of Italian tourists had arrived at the hotel just as the rain began, and they were now under the covered patio, pointing up at the blackening sky. It was exciting for a moment, watching a storm roll in with a group of strangers, but then the wind exploded around us and blew a flat screen TV off the wall. Glasses began to shatter around the bar and the tourists quickly huddled in a small pantry off the kitchen, the door pulled tightly behind them. I dove for cover behind the bar and pulled a blanket over my head – why it was behind the bar I never did figure out.

Eventually the rain stopped and the wind fell to a whisper. The Italians came out from their refuge and Juliette emerged from her bungalow up the hill. As she entered the restaurant she took in the scene with a gasp and put her hands up to her face, unable to move or speak for a few moments. "I've lived here my whole life," she said. "Faux Cap has never seen anything like this before." We comforted her, and each other, but there was something unsettling about her reaction. The hundred year drought, it seemed, had been followed just a few years later by the hundred year storm. That too is how climate change works.

Other than the Italians, who left after one night, I was the only guest at Juliette's hotel for most of my week in Faux Cap. At night there's wasn't much to do other than sit outside and listen to the wind and the surf. Most nights I would sit out on the patio with Juliette after dinner and share a flask of dark Malagasy rum with her. She is by nature a strong and vivacious woman, but the sense of isolation that comes from living in such a windswept outpost has made her as lonely as anyone else at times. We usually talked about Madagascar or Faux Cap or my upcoming travels, but one night we ventured into more personal territory and I made a joke about each of us being single after all these years.

"You too?" she said. "I've been alone here for almost ten years now." Then, after a pause, "Look, you might say I'm crazy, but why don't you stay and live here with me? We could fix the place up into a really nice hotel. And we could take care of each other. It gets so lonely here ... But if you were here I would be happy again, and we could be happy together."

I looked down and an awkward silence followed. "I'm sorry," she said. "It's been a long day and now the rum is making me say things I'll regret. Let's forget we ever talked about this. Ha! I'm such a fool sometimes."

* * *

If Tulear was the regional hub where government policies in response to climate change were planned and carried out, and Faux Cap was a sign of the crisis in miniature, Tsihombe was ground zero in the country's heightening battle with drought. I had come here to see firsthand the situation that had become so dire a few years ago, after reading several reports of its recent suffering. Tsihombe is a major inland town of 10,000 people in the middle of the Androy region, far removed from any water source. If a few people die of starvation in Faux Cap no one pays attention, but when crops fail in Tsihombe it can be potentially catastrophic, so more people take notice. Its dusty, barren streets gave the city an oppressive air, and the open air stalls along the main road stretching down from the Protestant church selling manioc and mostly shriveled fruits and vegetables told me right away that malnourishment was a severe problem. A river just outside of town that served as the primary source of water for almost all residents was shallow enough to be broken up in places by protruding rocks and sandbars. That didn't stop dozens of people from scooping up buckets of water to take home to cook, clean and even drink.

For every well-intentioned government official in Antananarivo developing a plan to save the Great South there is a local official trying to implement it, increasingly against impossible odds. Ralimbisoa Mandova, 66, has been the President of Tsihombe for five years. He's a former schoolteacher and even served as director of schools in Tsihombe for several years. He speaks and walks slowly, carrying a stern expression at all times. If I had been one of his elementary school students I would have been terrified of him. After just a few minutes talking to him, however, you realize that his hard stare is actually his look of concern for others, and that his slow responses were nothing more than a thoughtful man choosing his words carefully. It was easy to see why the people of Tsihombe had chosen him as their leader.[56]

Mandova told me that the South's lack of development could be explained by four factors: drought, of course, but also by the region's culture, the indifference of the national government, and the South's extreme isolation.

First, like every other local official I met, Mandova's greatest worries for his city center on drought. "Rain is so rare here," he told me. "We can't feed ourselves during times of low rain and aid from other provinces doesn't arrive in sufficient quantities. In 2016 and 2017 a lot of people died because of drought." Several aid projects are going on in Tsihombe at any one time, both national and international, with project leaders going door to door to measure the impact of drought in each household. So he knows he's not alone in trying to protect his people even if it feels like it much of the time. He told me that while people in Tsihombe grow manioc, potatoes and corn (with corn being the most dependent on rain), drought forces people to eat cactus. Sometimes when grains won't grow people eat the grain seeds raw. It's not just people who die during droughts, but livestock too. Mothers die at a higher rate because they are too weak to feed themselves and their children. "I've seen a big change just in my lifetime. Before there was no problem with food. Every man had zebu to feed his family. But since about 1980 droughts have gotten much worse. There is much less rain during the growing season now. We have to rely on aid or buy rice, which is very expensive for people here and is not grown locally."

Like others he quickly acknowledged that severe droughts in the region had left the national government and international donors with few options. "When the drought is really bad, there is nothing the government can really do. There is no solution." And the problem is getting worse, not better, he believes. International aid has become so vital, he said, that if it ever stopped flowing more people would emigrate out of the region.

But it is not just climate change that holds the region back. The traditional culture of the South, he believes, also plays a major role. "Zebu have always been a source of wealth here. But the mentality is off: we spend too much on family tombs, even more than on houses! Some for just one person! The people are forced to sell their zebu to build their tombs and to eat. Many girls get married very young and end up having many children. Others prostitute themselves as young as nine years old. A lot of young people roam the streets at night now because they have no homes to sleep in. There are many single mothers now. Girls with no fathers have a hard time finding husbands both for financial and cultural reasons," he said, explaining that fathers often play a large role in selecting spouses for their children. Almost 10% of men in the region have two wives or more. "All of this needs to change," he lamented, "but it is hard to change."

The cultural backwardness of the South also manifests itself in education levels. The people are poorly educated here,

Mandova told me, both because the level of instruction is low and because most students drop out by age 15. Emigration out of the Androy region is also starting to take a toll. "Our city is getting smaller every year because of drought. More people leave us every year looking for a place where crops will grow. But by tradition everyone comes back for funerals of their relatives, or to bring back the remains of family members who die, to be buried with the rest of the family." He remains hopeful that some of those who return from time to time will help the family members who remained.

While culture may account for some of the region's low education levels, neglect from the nation's leaders in Antananarivo also plays a role. Education levels in Madagascar's cities far outpace levels in its rural areas: in 2008, 77% attended secondary school versus just 33% in the countryside, the largest gap of any country with a relatively educated urban population.[57] Mandova did not hold back when I asked him about the central government's response to the crisis. "The Presidents of the country, bothnow and before, have neglected the South. Even those from the South who gain power in Tana neglect the South. They are just there to enrich themselves like everyone else in power." But he holds fond memories of Marc Ravalomanana, in part because he funded a goat farm in Tsihombe on land that Mandova donated to the city. "And corruption is down with the new president [Rajoelina], so I hope things will change."

The last problem he identified was the South's "problem of communication" with the rest of the country, meaning it's too remote from any other region, with insufficient infrastructure. Interestingly, Mandova believes the Great South's isolation is temporary, an artifact of history rather than a geographical fact. He was one of the few who viewed it not as a region off on its own but as an integral part of the nation. "Development in the South is linked to development of the nation," he told me. "If Madagascar develops, the South will too. And even if droughts continue, we will overcome it."

* * *

Not surprisingly, farmers are just as concerned about the future as village leaders. Noel Sonjomana has been a farmer in Tsihombe for over 50 years, growing everything from cassava, peanuts, corn, black eyed peas, beans, watermelon and squash. He met me one day with his wife and son in the back of a food shop in Tsihombe on a cloudy day in November. He considered himself a success story in this struggling town, having learned how to prosper in the good years and ride out the lean ones. His relatively large house and educated children bore testimony to his success.

"The drought has been much worse over the last seven years," he told me. "We've seen a lot of famine over the last seven years, a lot of people have died. Famine is much worse now. Before it was once a decade (in 1971 and 1986, for example), but now it's seven years out of eight. This has driven a lot of people out of the region, and for the ones who stay, you see more beggars on the street than before. The months of the rainy season have also changed, starting later than in the past and lasting fewer months."

Foreign aid is helpful but not all the people get it, especially poor people, he told me. The distribution of aid is riddled with corruption, with village leaders sometimes selling it or just giving it to their allies. But he believes President Rajoelina is trying his best for the region.

When I met with him in 2019, rain had been more than sufficient for Tsihiombe's harvest, but rather than celebrate it, Sonjomana worried it would only raise expectation unrealistically. "People here worry about the future during the bad years but then a year like this one comes along and they think everything will be OK. But in my opinion children here will have to leave the region if they want a better future."

His son, Randrianasolo Brinot, 27, chimed in at this statement, saying there is still enough opportunity here for young people who want to stay. "But most still want to leave, not necessarily because of the droughts but because there is no university here and they want to continue their studies. This might cause even more emigration than the water crisis, but young people here worry a lot about that too."

Bruno Ibramdjee, 45, the District Chief for Ampanihy, also named drought as his main concern. Originally from Tulear, Ibramdjee was another young official in his mid-forties, and in his green short-sleeved polo shirt he reminded me of Anognona, the government official I had met at the start of my journey through the region, except that he was much more cautious, asking me to repeat my questions and revising his statements as I tried to write them down. We met in his darkening office late one afternoon, where the conversation quickly turned to water.[58]

Ampanihy is a large town in the heart of Mahafaly country. There are a few main roads, one good hotel and a large market on the edge of town where meat, fruits and vegetables are sold. The culture is centered around zebu and the family tomb, which can cost $20,000 or more for a large or elaborate one. The biggest problem here is the lack of water. "Zebu and agriculture dominate life here, and both require a lot of water, which is slowly drying up." The El Nino phenomenon from 2014-17 was the worst drought he had ever seen in the region. And where once the rainy seasons were as predictable as the moon, now the rainfall varied from month to month.

He was one of the few people I met who emphasized the importance of technology (other than desalinization plants) in combatting climate change. He would like to see the country and the region find a way to use meteorological tracking systems and computer models to base the region's agricultural practices on the new weather patterns, rather than relying on the outdated concept of "seasons" that have always guided planting dates. Unfortunately, places like Ampanihy don't have that technology yet, so farmers cultivate the soil whenever the first rain comes, taking that date as their cue for the start of the planting season. The problem is that now sometimes they have to wait weeks or even months before the next rain comes. Like others he vouched for the fertility of the soil provided it received enough rain.

Ibramdjee praised the national government's commitment to developing the South, and it sounded a little forced. "The South is the poorest region in Madagascar because of drought. Poverty has caused many people from the region, Androy and Mahafaly, to emigrate to places like Tulear. Tana is aware of the problem and is working on solutions. The President said development of the country must start with the South. His first trip as President was to Ampanihy and he's now been there three times in his first year. But it's a question of initiative, vision, prioritization. This president has made the south a bigger priority than past presidents." He acknowledged, though, that during times of severe drought the region would still need international aid to avoid famine.

Like Mandova, the village leader of Tsihombe, Ibramdjee pointed to the south's traditional culture as a persistent barrier to faster development. "Culture contributes to poverty here," he told me. People live in very basic houses but construct very elaborate tombs, stunting development of the region. He said that people were not always interested in development and actually preferred many of the traditional practices to newer forms of living. He lamented the fact that poverty causes child marriage, which has become prevalent in the region, because many young girls are forced to seek financial protection to survive. "So we must leave parts of the culture behind little by little. I've seen it start to happen over the past 20-30 years, and it needs to continue."

He ended our interview with an eloquent statement on the future of the island before turning, inevitably, to the beacon of Rwanda. "Madagascar is not destined for poverty. Political will is what needs to change in the country for it to develop. Leaders must lead. The new president is a good one, and his zero tolerance policy for corruption is a great initiative, since that's our biggest problem. We have hope in our leaders now. If they can change their mentality and govern in the interests of all the people, I am confident that Madagascar will leave poverty behind. Internationally, we must change the inequity in the earnings from natural resources: foreign partners see much greater profits than their Malagasy counterparts for things like mining, vanilla, coffee. We should look at Rwanda as a model for how to develop; they have been a great success under President Kagame."

As we ended I noticed dusk was falling outside, and with no lights on in the building I could barely see my notes, let alone the young man sitting across from me. I surmised that Ibramdjee was conserving electricity, and as we stood up to say goodbye I thought, this man is an impressive public servant; this man knows how to set an example for his country. Or perhaps, I thought, there is a power outage in Ampanihy and he simply has no choice. Better not ask him, I thought, he might be embarrassed. Then he walked over to the light switch, flicked it on, and said, "Oh, I probably should have done that an hour ago. I didn't realize it had gotten so dark. Sorry."

* * *

The Malagasy government's budget for development aid to the Great South is extremely limited, and food and water crises in the region would be much more severe without the many international aid agencies operating in all of the major towns.

The World Food Program is one of the largest international donors in Madagascar, with a budget in the tens of millions of dollars, and their aid is targeted specifically at food insecurity. I spoke by phone with Vital Batubilema, who since 2017 has served as the Chief of the WFP's Sub-Bureau for the Ampanihy and Bekily Region, to get his thoughts on the crisis. We set up at least two meetings at his office but he had to cancel each time because of urgent calls he received to visit various regions of the South.

Like others, he was greatly relieved by the amount of rain in Ampanihy District and the resultant improvement in food security in 2019. Only four communes out of 19 were classified as "Phase 4" food insecure, a designation signaling extreme stress, and he believes this reflects the urgent response Ampanihy received after a dire report in 2018. But the statistics he provided remained exceedingly grim. Ninety-two percent of the island's people live below the poverty threshold of $1.90 a day, while 42% of its children under five suffer from chronic malnutrition. Madagascar is among the ten countries most vulnerable to natural disasters and is the most cyclone-exposed country in Africa. One study he sent me, put together by multiple organizations working in southern Madagascar and distributed by the country's Bureau of Risks and Catastrophes, showed 20% of the population of the Great South and Great Southeast (730,000 people) facing severe acute food insecurity in early 2020.

Batubilema confirmed what was obvious to everyone traveling through the Great South: Madagascar is extremely reliant on international humanitarian assistance, first and foremost because it is so poor. The total number of people who don't consistently get enough to eat across the island is staggering. But the problem varies by region. "In the South you have drought and the North you have cyclones. Each of them is hard to rectify permanently because as soon as you start to fix the problem, disaster strikes again and wipes out whatever improvements the country has made."

He agreed with everyone else I spoke to that droughts in the South are getting worse. But he expressed an optimism that I hadn't heard from Malagasy leaders on the front lines. "2015 was really the year things here became a crisis attracting global attention. This is when climate change struck for real, that's when it started to show its horrific effects here. But after being here for a few years I truly believe famine is avoidable. If the government and the international community really commit themselves not just to providing a solution to the water crisis here but also to the lack of infrastructure – because they are undoubtedly linked – we can find a solution. I firmly believe that."

Batubilema was an interesting guy, a deep thinker who grew up in the Democratic Republic of Congo, where conditions are even worse than in Madagascar. He offered an opinion on population growth that was wholly different from anything I had heard before, one that struck me as equal parts brilliant and idealistic. Rapid population growth is both a growing problem and a potential solution to the droughts plaguing the Great South, he told me. Obviously, the need for food increases as the number of people rises, and this has the potential to create a huge problem. But if young people throughout the South are mobilized and engaged through new development programs that lift up the region, they will eventually become part of the solution. "The manpower and the young minds are already here to make a positive impact, they just need to be engaged to a greater extent and given an opportunity to improve their country."

In the last analysis, he remained skeptical of the government's competence over the long term. "I don't think the Malagasy government has shown itself fully ready to combat the next severe drought in the South. I haven't felt the urgency coming from Tana that I think is warranted give the potential crisis developing. I've seen it from them on other things like preparing for cyclones, so they have the ability to plan for things, I just haven't seen it yet when it comes to drought."

* * *

Each of these men – and they were all men; I met no women leaders in the conservative cultures of this region – said it in their own way, but their message of gathering peril in the Great South was the same. It occurred to me that all of them carried an air of fatigue, or perhaps resignation, with them as they went on with their duties in the service of a state that was failing them. And how could they not? Every day they persist in their Sisyphean task of trying to prevent a humanitarian crisis of the first order, one that will undoubtedly kill tens of thousands of people. The only question is whether the tragedy will unfold over many years or all at once.

As for me, whenever I think back to the Great South I always think first of the windswept village of Faux Cap, perched above the ocean on a plateau where nothing will grow, its dozens of farmers praying for rain and trying to eke out enough of a living to send at least some of their children to school. It's hard to see how the desert encroaching further each year onto previously fertile land around Faux Cap is anything but a harbinger for the entire region. As climate change takes its horrific toll, more people in the Great South will suffer and migrate. When the next severe drought hits, it will put an area the size of Washington State at risk of famine. No one believes the Malagasy government is prepared for that eventuality; some believe it doesn't even care. International aid agencies will do everything they can to prevent a catastrophe when it comes, but leaders in Antananarivo have a choice to make: invest now in the development of the South, find a permanent solution to the water crisis, or watch the bottom third of the island wither away.

Epilogue

The state is not failing in Madagascar. We aren't looking at the next Somalia. It is, however, unraveling.
Professor Richard Marcus, 2013 Interview

In *Why Nations Fail,* their magisterial book on why some nations never fully develop, the Harvard political scientists Daron Acemoglu and James Robinson distilled the success and failures of various countries around the world into a simple historical explanation. Nations that foster inclusive economic and political institutions over time, they argue, prosper more than those that have extractive institutions. Inclusive economic institutions reinforce inclusive political institutions – those that distribute power widely and establish law and order, secure property rights and a market economy. Extractive institutions, on the other hand, can generate growth when power is centralized, but such growth can never be sustained. Most societies throughout history, they write, have unfortunately been extractive, funneling all economic gains to a very narrow elite. The synergies between inclusive (or extractive) economic and political institutions create a virtuous (or vicious) circle which, once in place, tends to persist. But transitions to inclusiveness do occur, and they are driven almost exclusively by major events that disrupt the existing political and economic balance of a nation and allow for the possibility of fundamental change in the social order. The Black Death, the opening of Atlantic trade routes, and the Industrial Revolution are all examples of these types of transformational shifts. The result, in their telling, is that all development results are historically contingent, and Peru could have ended up richer than Europe or the U.S.[1]

Madagascar is a perfect example of a nation whose weak institutions have left most of its people on the outside looking in. For centuries the island's dynastic rulers showed little interest in building a society that benefited the masses, and the results from its dysfunctional democracy are to this point not much better. As we'll see below, the country is still controlled by a narrow elite that often collaborates to prevent any wide distribution of what limited economic gains there are on the island. But elites and the masses alike are united in their belief that political institutions are failing them both. Both groups rank poor political leadership as the greatest obstacle to Madagascar's development.[2] Moreover, favorability marks for the army, police and justice system have been falling steadily since 2005.[3] With public confidence in the island's institutions on the wane, it came as a shock to no one when the nation's next crisis took a horrific toll.

* * *

Nothing exposed the weakness of Madagascar's institutions more than the onset of a pandemic in 2020. Reports of Covid-19 spreading from China caused widespread fears in Madagascar and especially in Antananarivo, where the government suspended trading with Beijing in early 2020. President Rajoelina then closed the borders to all non-residents soon thereafter. When three Malagasy women on a flight from Paris tested positive for Covid upon arrival in Tana, the news that the pandemic had arrived began to sink in. President Rajoelina delivered a solemn live TV address to the nation confirming the first cases, and alternating notes of panic and insouciance were heard in various quarters of the country. Several friends texted me to ask what they should do, thinking I had better information than they did. How fast does it spread, they asked, how many of us will die? All expressed horror at the possible impact on a nation so poorly prepared from a political and medical perspective to grapple with something so deadly in their midst. Expecting the virus to enter Madagascar from a Chinese visitor, there was some surprise when people heard it had been brought back by one of their own citizens. Rajoelina announced no lockdown at first, although large public gatherings and sporting events were quickly prohibited. Business activity, on the other hand, was not restricted. "It's the responsibility of the state and the government to watch over the health of the health of the Malagasy people," he said. He also appealed for calm: "It's time to stop the provocations and the spread of fake news to spread panic in society." The leading newspaper in Antananarivo urged citizens to take the danger seriously: "The ball is now in the government's court to be vigilant and closely monitor people at risk…The country is now on a war footing. We just need to be vigilant and pay attention."[4]

When Rajoelina finally ordered a nationwide lockdown, many Tananariviens chose to ignore the President's stay-at-home mandate, partly out of desperation. The downtown city streets remained thriving areas of activity until one day military vehicles cruised the streets and ordered everyone home. This display of force worked for a while, until the president shocked everyone in April 2020 by announcing that Madagascar had come up with an herbal remedy for the virus, which he called Covid-Organics. He even appeared to tout it as a vaccine. The remedy was derived from artemisia – a plant with proven anti-malarial properties – as a homegrown cure for Covid-19 – and the drink was distributed not only in Madagascar but also in several other countries, mainly in Africa. Within days the National Academy of Medicine had thrown cold water on the idea, saying it was not a medicine at all and that more research needed to be done to determine its effectiveness against the virus. But that didn't stop the President from trying to advance it as a cure. Thinking the worst was over, he ended the nationwide lockdown after a few months.

After learning of Madagascar's claims of a cure, the UN's

World Health Organization cautioned that no published scientific studies had been published to validate the medicinal benefits of the drink, while dozens of scientists pointed out the potential risks from taking it as a potential cure. The Malagasy people, who have often turned to herbal teas for a variety of ailments, mostly accepted the president's claims, at least at first. But after cases continued to rise after widespread use of the drink, suspicion began to mount, especially when the government appeared to blame them for its poor results. "Positive Covid-19 cases did not take [Covid-Organics] or only took it sporadically, without following the prescribed dosage," they averred. The backlash against the government only intensified when Education Minister Rijasoa Andriamanana was fired after announcing a plan to spend $2.2 million on candy and lollipops for children to ease the "bitter taste" of the drink.[5] The government's efforts to combat the pandemic quickly became haphazard.

New leaders around the world grew frustrated at Covid-19's power to usurp all of their carefully prepared plans to develop their countries, so Rajoelina's premature attempt to declare the health crisis over is understandable to a certain degree. But his own health minister undercut him by requesting international help to cope with a surge in Covid cases. The ministry listed several urgent needs in their requests: hundreds of oxygen bottles, 337 ventilators, 2.3 million face masks, 697,000 pairs of gloves and 533,000 medical blouses. This sparked a harsh rebuke from the President's office: "The government would like to express its dismay at the discovery of a letter signed by the minister of public health urgently requesting support in the fight against the Covid-19 pandemic," government spokeswoman Lalatiana Rakotozafy said in a statement. She called the minister's appeal a "personal initiative" taken without consulting either the president or other government ministries. "It is clear that many crucial points in the management of this health crisis have escaped the vigilance of the minister of public health," she said.[6] Madagascar had recorded over 18,000 cases by the end of 2020, a rise in numbers that the government attributed to increased testing.

It was hard to say in mid-2020 whether the Coronavirus would lead to catastrophe or turn into a non-event in Madagascar. Researchers are still puzzling over why the virus attacks some geographical areas with a fury while leaving others largely unscathed. While North America, China and Europe got pummeled, Africa had relatively few cases. Madagascar had less than 20,000 recorded cases and, miraculously, very few deaths. It could simply be a lack of testing. It could be the overwhelmingly young population of Madagascar. Or, more ominously, it could be that the virus simply hasn't arrived in full force yet. Africa saw just a tiny fraction of its 1.3 billion people contract the virus, maybe because 60 percent of its population is under 25.[7]

If it's simply a matter of time before Covid-19 strikes Africa, countries like Madagascar are in trouble. As of May 2020, fewer than 2,000 working ventilators were in place to serve hundreds of millions of people in hospitals across 41 African countries, compared with more than 170,000 in the U.S. Madagascar had just six ventilators, or one for roughly every 4.5 million people.[8] Even when a vaccine was developed in the West, government leaders I talked to in the capital were still in a panic, with no idea where the money would come from to vaccinate all of their citizens and fearful of new variants of the virus that threatened to bring more misery and death to the island. Another nationwide lockdown was imminent at the time of writing.

* * *

Madagascar will still need help from international partners willing to provide both aid and trade. There is constant debate on the island regarding who its natural trading partners should be. The other Indian Ocean nations surrounding it are dismissed as too small and insignificant to form an economic base for future development. The nations of East Africa and Southern Africa are frequently mentioned as well as potential partners in a free trade bloc, but Madagascar has never really considered itself an African nation and wants to forge closer links with the major economies of the world. Its largest trading partners are still France and the United States, with China a distant third. But while America grows indifferent to places like Madagascar and France struggles to retain its influence over its erstwhile colony, one country has rushed to fill the void. In the middle of 2019, China had more than 20 infrastructure projects in process on the island at one time, including major improvements to the nation's highway system, a Sports Palace at Mahamasina, an international conference center at Ivato and a hospital at Anosiana.

China, that Asian behemoth who rose from a poor, agrarian society into a capitalist, export-driven economic miracle in the space of a generation, offers an interesting alternative for Madagascar. Beijing's investments across Africa and much of the developing world, culminating recently in the Belt and Road Initiative, are well documented. Its focus was slow to turn to Madagascar, however, and just ten years ago there was very little visible sign of its presence. That has begun to change rapidly, and Malagasy and Chinese officials were, pre-Covid, practically tripping over each other as official delegations traveled from one country to the other seemingly every other week to collaborate on development ideas that will bring large-scale projects to Madagascar while supplying China with the raw materials it needs to continue fueling its rise.

The Chinese ambassador to the island used the occasion of the 70th anniversary of the PRC's founding in 2019 to highlight the burgeoning economic partnership between the two countries, stating that China had now become the primary economic partner of Madagascar over the last few years, financing $28 million in new infrastructure projects alone. China is now the largest source of imported goods to Madagascar and receives the fourth largest amount of exports from the island. The impressive stadium at Mahamasina in Antananarivo, she said, stands as a shining example of its power and largesse.[9] She emphasized that ongoing cooperation between China and Madagascar had already produced new partnerships in politics, economics, health, education, culture, sports and security. In addition, the rehabilitation of two national highways and other major roads are well under way. But her comments on poverty reduction may have been the most salient, and were not lost on a desperately poor nation looking for a path forward. In just 70 years, she noted, nearly 800 million people in China had emerged from poverty and more than 400 million had joined the ranks of the middle class. By 2020, she claimed, China will have achieved all of its goals relative to poverty reduction, which "will stand as a miracle in humanity's long fight against poverty."[10]

Madagascar's relations with China have been close ever since Antananarivo severed relations with Taiwan and established relations with the PRC in 1972. But when Deng Xiaoping returned to power the focus of their ties changed from revolutionary brotherhood to trade and economic cooperation. Bilateral relations began to blossom under Ravalomanana, when China broke ground on numerous projects after the Malagasy president took several trips to China and convinced Chinese companies to invest in the island. Trade between the two reached $24.4 million in 2011, $297.6 million in 2016 and $1.25 billion in 2017, of which only $176.4 million consisted of exports from Madagascar to China; the vast majority go in the other direction. Relations grew even closer during Rajaonarimampianina's presidency, when he traveled to Beijing in 2017 and signed a document with the Chinese government to solidify Madagascar's place in China's new Belt and Road Initiative.

That initiative, known as the BRI, was launched by Xi in 2013 to connect China to Europe through Central Asia, the Mediterranean through the Persian Gulf, and South Asia via the Indian Ocean, and is perhaps the most ambitious development strategy in world history by one country. The BRI encompasses 70 countries, including Madagascar, and estimates of China's investment in its new trade system range from $1 trillion to $8 trillion. If fully implemented, it may establish China as the dominant power in the Indian Ocean; but China's interests are bound to collide with other Indian Ocean powers. The central question is what China's true motives are with respect to the BRI. Is it a strategic plan to dominate the developing world and become a first-rate world power, or is it simply a way to secure reliable routes for the massive energy imports China will need to sustain its sky-high economic growth rates?

The problem may be that regardless of its intentions, China will likely need to construct a string of ports and naval stations to protect its new commercial interests, and that chain of infrastructure will inevitably be seen as offensive in nature, an attempt to tilt the balance of power in the region in its favor.[11] This is precisely what happened when China signed a pact with Djibouti for its first overseas military outpost; many analysts saw it as just a harbinger of things to come in the region, with defense treaties with Myanmar, Sri Lanka, Pakistan, Bangladesh, Seychelles and the Maldives the next logical steps.

In any event, China is not spending billions of dollars in poor countries simply because it wants to see them prosper. Some analysts like Bertil Lintner have gone so far as to call China's recent steps in the Indian Ocean its third revolution: the first was in 1949 with the Communist takeover and the country's emancipation from foreign powers, the second was under Deng

Xiaoping when China became an economic powerhouse, and the third is taking place now as President Xi tries to cement China's status as a world power through the BRI.[12] Meanwhile, a new, informal alliance has been formed among the US, India, Australia, France, and even Japan, to counter China's global influence, including in the Indian Ocean. China's intentions for Madagascar in its master plan for the region remain unclear, but the island may soon become embroiled in great power politics once again. After China embedded almost all of the smaller island nations in the Indian Ocean like Comoros and the Seychelles into the BRI, some experts now believe its chief interest is in fact the untapped potential of Madagascar. The big island's huge reserves of ilmenite (titanium ore), its recently-discovered oil fields, as well its significant deposits of metals and precious stones make it an attractive target for a country devouring resources as fast as China.[13]

This was the backdrop when President Rajaonarimampianina traveled to China in 2017 to sign the Memorandum of Understanding affirming Madagascar's intention to join the BRI. Chinese President Xi Jinping said at the time that China "supports Madagascar playing a role as a bridge between the Belt and Road and the African Continent." It's obvious that China is in Madagascar to stay, not just because of their growing economic ties but because Madagascar has Africa's second largest population of Chinese nationals (100,000), trailing only South Africa. The emigrants from China arrived in small numbers at the turn of the 20th century to build the island's first national railroad and then a highway to Tamatave. More arrived after independence, especially with the establishment of diplomatic relations in 1972. Their presence led to the sprouting of Chinese civil society organizations on the island: Antananarivo has had its own Confucius Institute since 2009, an obvious form of soft power for China, and a Chinese trade association now organizes events for more than 90 businesses in Madagascar.

But with a per capita income of under $1,000, Madagascar remains a desperately poor country. It may be easy prey for a country like China given the island's obvious need for foreign investment, but Madagascar's chronic instability still represents a major risk for any country trying to do business there. China's integration of Madagascar into the BRI also risks courting a cultural backlash: periodic outbreaks in protest of Chinese ownership of certain businesses have already occurred, and in late 2016 the Singaporean daily Straits Times reported after one such protest that "across the country, Madagascans have openly expressed their hostility towards the growing presence of China, the country's largest trading partner."[14] Many developing countries like Madagascar are now placing their hopes on the BRI. But in 2018, IMF Director Christine Lagarde offered a grim warning to those countries: rather than faster development, she said, the real legacy of the BRI may end up being its heavier debt burdens loaded onto countries already struggling to keep up with their current payments to lenders.

China's influence in Madagascar will only grow over the next decade, and the big question will be whether it confines itself to an economic partnership or attempts to leverage its outsize role into greater influence in the island's politics. If the latter, Madagascar will be changed considerably. Many experts now believe the Chinese will be a greater ideological threat to the US-led liberal order than the Soviet-Union ever was, and that its sedulous courting of developing nations across the globe risks a serious confrontation between democracy and authoritarianism, or something in between. With Malagasy democracy showing such shallow roots, it could fall under the sway of a resurgent China looking to expand its global influence. And yet the Malagasy people, having once been colonized, having suffered such dramatic political upheaval since independence, and now expressing admiration for the United States and its freedoms, will only take so much. The most likely outcome is that

Madagascar, like many countries its size, will try to retain close links with both centers of power.

* * *

When it emerges Covid-19 Madagascar, like every other country, will be scarred by the lockdowns, confinements and the devastating death toll wrought by the recent pandemic. How and whether the island will be a different place post-Covid is unclear, but one thing about the island is sure to remain unchanged: it will still be desperately poor, and the debate over the reasons for its continual misfortune will resume. A team of development scholars recently put forth one of the more intriguing explanations for the perpetuation of poverty in Madagascar and the country's chronic instability. Political and economic power on the island, they found, have been almost entirely captured by the country's elites, who remain determined not to give up such power to the millions of struggling citizens beneath them. Elites are defined broadly under their theory to include any person with power and/or influence over the decisions and running of society in Madagascar. Perhaps unsurprisingly, this group comprises a cohort that is 80% male, 96% graduated from college and overwhelmingly from the highland tribes. For example, members of the Merina tribe make up 76% of elites in the economic sphere.[15]

Under this theory, the power-brokers ruling over Madagascar have simply become indifferent to the pursuit of the common good, perpetuating a deeply unequal society that often manifests itself in a growing divide between urban and rural worlds. Rural citizens, "overlooked if not despised by the ruling elites," have little choice but to accept authority figures as legitimate and put up with their lot.[16] Elites have come to inhabit an extremely airtight world largely disconnected from the vast majority of the population, a world they guard jealously using strategies designed to limit and control any new group's access to power. Meanwhile, the system perpetuates itself unmercifully as the descendants of elites enjoy easier access to power and influence as they grow up, in a family-based reproduction process that goes on for generations. This has obviously disturbing repercussions for a society trying to develop functioning institutions. As the authors write, "Preserving privilege in this way is at odds with meritocracy and equal opportunity on which modern democratic societies are founded.[17]

And this control over the island has real consequences for the vast majority of its citizens, in large part because the worldviews of elites and the masses are starkly different. First, elites have a weaker attachment to democracy than the rest of the population, with just 55% preferring democracy to any other form of government.[18] This is hardly surprising given the Merina's fears of displacement from what they see as the angry hordes living far from the central plateau. But the main point of disagreement between elites and the population concerns their political priorities, whether in a democratic system or otherwise. Elites prize order and stability above all else, and are only half as likely as the general public (28% to 52%) to place poverty reduction at the top of the political agenda.[19] And they obviously have more influence over which priorities are addressed. "So by maintaining the social order's status quo, the elites have basically protected their status since the colonial period, if not the kingdoms, irrespective of the interests of the vast majority of the population."[20]

The vice-like grip on society by the island's elites has had a noticeably sclerotic effect on the nation's development. Since independence in 1960, the country has witnessed two armed conflicts (1971 and 2002), several political crises and a full-blown Marxist revolution. These upheavals are becoming almost cyclical, for each time the country begins to make economic progress an unexpected crisis explodes and brings it to a halt.

The curious aspect to this phenomenon is that organization by the elites themselves appears to be cyclical as well, occurring only as necessary to prevent one person or group from becoming too powerful, then dissolving until the next uprising forces them to join forces again. For the most part elites on the island are thus content to watch the country drift, so long as their perch atop the social order remains undisturbed. In this view, Madagascar's chronic political instability results from the inability or unwillingness of elites to create durable institutions or coalitions that would stabilize the country, preferring to live with the status quo even as the masses suffer.[21]

By installing and perpetuating a system of control over the years that keeps them in control, elites have therefore created political and economic institutions that work for them and them alone. But as the population grows and dysfunction sets in, they risk merely reaping the whirlwind. The crises and uprisings of recent decades, all of which have taken them by surprise and led to some unpredictable political transition, are proof enough that their power over the island is tenuous and, perhaps in the decade ahead, ripe for reversal. For as the team of development experts found, "the social order is not set in stone." As new centers of power emerge and various political theologies once thought to entrenched in Malagasy society start to decline – for instance, the taboo on violence, the respect for authority, the centuries-old social hierarchies – societal decay could produce even greater dysfunction and even higher rates of poverty. "An already fragile state could become a state of chaos."[22]

As perhaps the last barrier to this chaos stands Andry Rajoelina and his overworked staff. It would be hard to overstate the importance of the current presidential regime to the future of Madagascar. After leading a coup that caused economic devastation and international isolation, then stepping down for a few years to appease the international community, then resurfacing and vanquishing his longtime nemesis in the

2018 election, Rajoelina now has the legitimacy both at home and abroad to carry out the multitude of reforms the island so desperately needs. His party controls an outright majority in Parliament, and international donors have returned with bundles of cash to bolster his development program. If he succeeds in finally unleashing the economic potential of the country, Madagascar can become one of the burgeoning number of success stories in Africa; but if his administration loses its momentum or, worse, if he replaced or overthrown before his five year term is up, the country will once more be staring into the abyss.

For Madagascar has just in the past few years become a country run mostly by one man. Rajoelina, like dozens of quasi-democratic, quasi-autocratic leaders across the world, has secured more power for himself than any other democratically elected leader in Madagascar's history, and he intends to stamp out whatever opposition remains before the next election in 2023. But Rajoelina may only be courting disaster. The problem with such a centralization of power, in Madagascar and elsewhere, is that it stifles dissent to an unacceptable degree. Opposition to the regime only grows, forcing a leader to choose between repression or accommodation. It also raises the specter of a messy, even violent succession crisis once he or she steps down. Rajoelina has learned to play the illiberal democracy game with aplomb, taking incremental steps to silence the opposition and sidelining the institutions that stand in his way, but if his approach becomes too heavy-handed the freewheeling nature of the island's democracy will inevitably lead to calls from multiple quarters for another uprising; and many will heed it.

The lesson here is that Madagascar's democracy is far too fragile to be entrusted to just one person. This is something the Malagasy people willingly acknowledge. As an editorial in Madagascar's leading newspaper put it during Rajoelina's first year in office, the island's democracy is "still in its infancy":

Madagascar is currently experiencing a peaceful political climate. There is a long history of past turbulence where the opposition sometimes expressed itself violently. But a page seems to have turned after the last presidential election. The regime is firmly established. It has a stable parliamentary majority, although it must still take into account a public opinion that does not hesitate to give its opinion. The President has a course to maintain, but he must act with caution despite the fact that he has all the assets in hand ... Our democracy is still in its infancy. It is still in the making.[23]

Madagascar's fragility mirrors the tentative steps toward democracy taken by other nations across Africa. After decades of being associated with coups and civil wars, the continent is now widely democratic, though the competitive elections held in many countries mask the otherwise shallow nature of their democracies. Incompetent or unpopular regimes are now routinely voted out of office, but the persistence of corruption and weak institutions that plagued them often remain. Of the 49 leaders in power in sub-Saharan Africa at the beginning of 2015, just 22 of them remained in power as of May 2019 – and only two of the new leaders were installed by coups. And yet only 11% of Africans live in countries that Freedom House considers free, showing how far these democracies have to go. Meanwhile, the economic growth that followed in the wake of the region's turn toward democracy has slowed in recent years, and economic stagnation in Africa has become normal again. Overall GDP was forecast to grow by just 3% on the continent in 2019, dragged down by even slower growth rates in Angola, Nigeria and South Africa, all of which have suffered from recent declines in commodity prices.[24] The next year, 2020 was far worse, due largely to the pandemic.

Rajoelina is following the playbook of a rising number of would-be autocrats who use the veneer of elections to hide their corrupt and exclusionary rule. They rely on the tried-and-true tactics of censorship, repression and patronage to perpetuate their hold over society, but they are increasingly turning to more direct and aggressive methods to rig the system in their favor: they go after the courts, intimidate the press, hamper civil society, and use parliamentary majorities to push through new laws and constitutions. As one scholar of the new authoritarian populism gaining ground around the world writes, "If one squints, things look normal: elections take place, people can travel in and out of the country, the cafes are full, and the secret police's dungeons are (nearly) empty. But underneath the surface, checks and balances that had once prevented dictatorship are falling away."[25]

The optimism palpable in Madagascar after Rajoelina's election has already begun to dissipate. With a number of small-scale fiascos in 2019 – the leaking of subjects on the baccalaureate prior to the exam, ongoing crises with gas, water and electricity, and the protests breaking out over the planned new city, Tana-Masoandro, large segments of the population were beginning to wonder if his regime was capable of running the country. Ravalomanana and Rajaonarimampianina have now formed an alliance and the opposition is more unified than at any time in recent memory. An editorial in *Midi* in October 2019 described the shifting public mood after a particularly difficult week for the president:

For the regime, the honeymoon ended a long time ago. Reality won't allow it to continue to delude themselves any longer. They may have thought that the promises made during the campaign would be easy to fulfill, but the reality isn't as rosy as it might have been. The difficulties facing the population have provoked a certain disenchantment lately … Nine months after its inauguration, the regime is no longer assured of the massive public support of which it once boasted. The erosion of public confidence is notable. Divisions are also beginning to appear in the ranks of the majority, and the opposition is beginning to raise its voice. This week, the atmosphere became toxic.[26]

And yet the government still maintained lofty goals for the rest of its term. Prime Minister Christian Ntsay used the occasion of his address to the UN General Assembly meeting in 2019 to announce Madagascar's five-year plan to address three major challenges: the consolidation of democracy, the pursuit of inclusive economic growth, and environmental protection. He announced the island's major goal of achieving "emerging country" status in the next few years to make up for the previous delay in its development.[27] This seemed like an impossible aspiration given the island's low economic growth rates and the raft of unaddressed issues. Then Covid-19 hit, and the uncertain response from Rajoelina led to outright revolt. It seems like Rajoelina's administration will do well just to finish its term with its head above water.

* * *

I spent my last night in Madagascar visiting my friends Dodo and Malo at their burger joint in the hills of Antananarivo. We talked about the future of the island while American hits played on their stereo system and a few customers wandered in and out, looking for a beer and a bite to eat, or simply for a place to relax at the end of the week. I found it ironic that Malo, the French transplant, was decidedly more optimistic about Madagascar's ability to escape its endemic poverty and troubled past than her Malagasy boyfriend, who wasn't so sure. Like many of his countrymen, he retained the wry humor of the native toward his island's predicament, a sort of hope tinged with wariness from all that has gone wrong since Madagascar's independence.

As I left them and walked out into the night and down the hill to my hotel I noticed that the lights had gone out across the city, another of the rolling blackouts that had become the source of so much angst and derision across the capital. Antananarivo had lost much of its charm over the decades, but as I took in the unbearable blackness of the sky, its piercing stars, the moon rising over distant hills that I could barely discern, I felt that I would miss the city once I got home. It started to rain, and through the dark and the rain I could still make out a few people on the street. I saw a neatly dressed older man holding onto his hat to keep from losing it in the wind, felt a child beggar tugging at my sleeve, and laughed with a woman selling rice from a street stall as she threw up her hands in a mix of frustration and amusement at the infernal darkness. As I rounded a corner power was restored, and a small cheer went up throughout the city. In this way, I thought, millions of people go on living across Madagascar, waging the daily struggle to make ends meet, to keep their families healthy and safe, and to preserve some dignity in a land that constantly strips it away.

And so life will go on in this beautiful island much as it has before, the slow march of modernization gradually wearing down the ancient customs and the isolation of remote provinces. But the 21st century will bring a new set of challenges that almost no nation, let alone the fledgling democracy of Madagascar, could withstand. The population will continue to grow. Temperatures will rise, especially in the South, and droughts will intensify. Students will clamor for better education and more jobs when they graduate. Corruption will remain the norm, and people will hope and pray that each national election doesn't bring more chaos, paralysis, or even violence. And Madagascar's disparate regions and eighteen ethnic groups will continue to grapple with the problem of how to move forward as one.

Just before I reached my hotel I saw a group of young women in their early twenties, arms linked and walking confidently through the chilly evening, laughing about something that had happened earlier that day or might happen later. They were headed to a nightclub down the street, already excited about the music and dancing that awaited them. At that moment they weren't concerned about history, or the changing climate, or whether they would have good jobs in five years. They took no heed of me as I passed, walking alone through the night with my collar turned up against the cold. But as I watched them I suddenly envied their blissful ignorance and their shimmering conviction that life would hold something magical for them. They were members of that irrepressible tribe found the world over who believe the future, despite all its daunting challenges, should always be better than the past.

Endnotes

Introductory Chapter

1 *Enlightenment Now,* Steven Pinker, Viking Press, 2018, pgs. 51-52

2 Id., pgs. 322-24

3 Id., pgs. 322-24

4 Id., pgs. 4-6

5 *The Great Surge,* Steven Radelet, Simon & Schuster, 2015, pgs. 27-31

6 Id., pgs. 5-11

7 Id., pgs. 16-19

8 *Evidence For Hope: Making Human Rights Work In The 21ˢᵗ Century,* Kathryn Sikkink, Princeton University Press, 2017, pgs. 7-13

9 Id., pgs. 33-35

10 Nicholas Kristof, 2017, 2018 and 2019 articles. *"This Has Been The Best Year Ever (Again)",* NY Times, December 29, 2019

11 *"The Pandemic Depression: The Global Economy Will Never Be The Same,"* Carmen Reinhart and Vincent Reinhart, Foreign Affairs (September/October 2020 Issue)

2 *"Millions Had Risen Out of Poverty. Coronavirus Is Pulling Them Back,"* NY Times, April 30, 2020

13 *Coronavirus Is Battering Africa's Middle Class,"* NY Times, June 29, 2020

14 *"Slowing the Coronavirus is Speeding the Spread of Other Diseases,"* NY Times, June 14, 2020

15 *"The Uninhabitable Earth,"* David Wallace-Wells, pgs. 197-98

16 Id., pgs. 200-01

17 Rieff, pgs. 254-58

18 World Bank *"Face of Poverty Report: Madagascar,"* March 2014

19 US State Department 2019 Country Report; Euronews, March 28, 2019

20 *"Puzzle and Paradox: The Political Economy of Madagascar,"* by Mireille Razafindrakoto, Francois Roubaud and Jean-Michel Wachsberger, Cambridge University Press, 2020, pg. 14.

21 Id., pgs. 8-10

22 Id., pgs. 1-14

Chapter 1

1   *A History of Madagascar,* Mervyn Brown, Markus Wiener Publishers, 1995, pgs. 20-21

2   Brown, pgs. 30-31

3   Brown, pg. 31

4   Brown, pgs. 44-47

5   Brown, pgs. 48-49

6   *"Madagascar: A Short History,"* Randrianja and Ellis, The University of Chicago Press, 2009, pgs. 99-101

7   Brown, pgs. 92-93

8   Brown, pg. 98

9   Randrianja and Ellis, "Madagascar: A Short History," pg. 70.

10 Brown, pg. 102

11 Randrianja and Ellis, "Madagascar: A Short History," pgs. 117-119

12 Brown, pgs. 108-110

13 Brown, pg. 73

14 Brown, pgs. 84-85

15 Brown, pgs. 114-23

16 Brown, pg. 122

17 Brown, pgs. 126-31

18 Brown, pgs. 141-43

19 Brown, pgs. 144-46

20 Brown, pg. 147

21 Brown, pgs. 153-56
22 Brown, pgs. 157-59
23 Brown, pgs. 163-65
24 Brown, pg. 188
25 Brown, pgs. 192-93
26 Brown, pgs. 197-99
27 Brown, pgs. 202-03
28 Brown, pgs. 207-08
29 Brown, pgs. 215-16
30 Brown, pg. 218
31 Brown, pgs. 223-24
32 Brown, pgs. 231-33
33 Brown, pgs. 237-39
34 Brown, pg. 240
35 Brown, pgs. 241-42
36 Brown, pgs. 250-52
37 Brown, pgs. 264-68
38 *Vietnam: An Epic Tragedy, 1945-1975*, Max Hastings, HarperCollins (2018), pg. 16
39 Brown, pgs. 284-92
40 Brown, pgs. 292-94

Chapter 2
1 Mervyn Brown, *A History of Madagascar*, pg. 295
2 *Madagascar: Conflicts of Authority in the Great Island*, Philip M. Allen, Westview Press, 1995, pg. 223
3 Brown, pgs. 304-06
4 Allen, pgs. 224-25
5 Brown, pgs. 307-08
6 Allen, pg. 224
7 Brown, pgs. 313-21
8 Brown, pgs. 327-28
9 Brown, pgs. 329-31
10 Brown, pgs. 334-36

11 Brown, pgs. 339-40

12 Allen, pgs. 230-31

13 Brown, pgs. 354-55

14 *Puzzle and Paradox: A Political Economy of Madagascar*, by Mireille Razafindrakoto, Francois Roubaud, and Jean-Michel Wachsberger, Cambridge University Press (2020), pg. 96

15 "*The Political Crisis of March 2009 In Madagascar*," Adrien M. Ratsimbaharison, Rowman & Littlefield (2017), pgs. 16-22

16 *Puzzle and Paradox*, pgs. 93-94

17 "*The Political Crisis of March 2009 In Madagascar*," Adrien M. Ratsimbaharison, Rowman & Littlefield (2017), pgs. 16-22

18 Ratsimbaharison, pgs. 39-40

19 Id., pg. 42

20 Id., pg. 3

21 Id., pg. 42

22 Id., pg. 58

23 Id., pg. 59

24 Id, pg. 60

25 *Puzzle and Paradox*, pg. 99

26 Id.

27 Id., pg. 38

28 Id., pg. 93

29 Id., pg. 104

30 Id, pg. 80

31 Id., pgs. 48, 62

32 Ratsimbarharison, pg. 35

33 *Puzzle and Paradox*, pg. 97

34 Ratsimbaharison, pg. 62

35 Id., pg. 64

36 Id., pgs. 45, 80

37 Id., pg. 81

38 Puzzle and Paradox, pgs. 112-13

39 Id., pg 78

40 Id., pg. 129, 131
41 Id., pgs. 120-21
42 *"Bolivia Crisis Shows the Blurry Line Between Coup and Uprising,"* NY Times, November 12, 2019
43 Ratsimbaharison, pg. 131
44 Ratsimbaharison, pgs. 14-18
45 Midi Madagasikara, March 3, 2020
46 *Puzzle and Paradox,* pg. 100
47 Id., pgs. 108, 199
48 Thisisafrica.me, May 7, 2018

Chapter 3

1   The Economist, May 10, 2018
2   Opinion in AllAfrica.com, July 21, 2018
3   Interview with Jean-Eric Rakotoarisoa, November 25, 2019
4   Reuters, November 6, 2018
5   Reuters, November 28, 2018
6   Reuters, December 1 and December 12, 2018
7   Reuters, December 28, 2018
8   Puzzle and Paradox: A Political Economy of Madagascar, by Mireille Razafindrakoto, Francois Roubaud and Jean-Michel Wachsberger, Cambridge University Press, 2020, pg. 240
9   *"How Russia Meddles Abroad For Profit: Cash, Trolls and a Cult Leader,"* The New York Times, November 11, 2019
10 Id.
11 The Economist, April 24, 2019
12 *"Fourth Republic: Back to a Strong Presidential Regime,"* July 29, 2019
13 *"The Dictators' Last Stand,"* Yascha Mounk, Foreign Affairs (September/October 2019 Issue)
14 Id.
15 *"Democracy Demotion,"* Larry Diamond, Foreign Affairs, July/August 2019 Issue

16 *"The Vigilante President,"* Sheila S. Coronel, Foreign Affairs, September/October 2019 Issue

17 *"The Dictators' Last Stand,"* Yascha Mounk, Foreign Affairs (September/October 2019 Issue)

18 Le Tribune Madagscar, May 28, 2019

19 Midi Madagaskar, May 18, 2019

20 See "How Autocrats Compete," Yonatan Morse, Cambridge University Press, 2018, and "Africa's Totalitarian Temptation," Dave Peterson, Lynne Rienner Press, 2020

21 Freedom House "Freedom In The World 2019 &202" Rankings

22 Economist Intelligence Unit's "Democracy Index 2019"

23 *"Close to 65% of Malagasy Victims of Corruption In The Health Sector,"* Madagascar Tribune, October 1, 2019

24 *"Why Ethnic Majorities Lash Out Over False Fears,"* The New York Times, May 1, 2019

25 Randrianja and Ellis, "Madagascar: A Short History," pgs. 226-28.

26 *Le Tribune Madagascar*, August 14, 2019

27 *The Opposition Creates the RMDM Political Alliance,* The Tribune August 17, 2019

28 *Marc Ravalomanana Saisit Le SADC,* Madagascar Tribune, August 19, 2019

29 *"The Despot's Accomplice: How The West Is Aiding and Abetting the Decline of Democracy,"* Brian Klaas, Oxford University Press, 2016, pgs. 6-9

30 Klaas, *The Despot's Accomplice,* pgs. 88-90

31 Klaas, "Labeling Elections Good Enough Lets African Leaders Get Away With Fraud;" Foreign Policy Magazine, February 14, 2019.

32 *"Kagame, Le Fantasme de Rajoelina?* Le Tribune Madagascar, June 21, 2019

33 *Puzzle and Paradox*, pg. 114

34 Id., pg. 166

35 Id., pgs. 132-34
36 Id., pg. 143

Chapter 4

1 Interview with Gladonia Razaiarizafy, July 23, 2019
2 Radelet, *The Great Surge,* pgs. 27-31
3 Id., pgs. 48-49
4 Sachs, *The Age of Sustainable Development,* pgs. 104-07
5 Id., pgs. 139-42
6 Rieff, *The Reproach of Hunger,* pgs. 254-58
7 "*How Poverty Ends,*" Abhijit Banerjee and Esther Duflo, Foreign Affairs, January/ February 2020 Issue
8 "*Trials and Tribulations,*" Jeffrey D. Sachs, Foreign Affairs, May/June 2020 Issue
9 World Bank, *The Face of Poverty in Madagascar,* March 2014
10 Id.
11 Id.
12 Razafindrakoto, Roubaud and Wachsberger, "*Puzzle and Paradox: A Political Economy of Madagascar,*" (2020) pgs. 17-22
13 World Bank, *The Face of Poverty In Madagascar,* March 2014
14 Id.
15 Id.
16 Id.
17 Id.
18 Id.
19 Allen, pgs. 232-33
20 *Puzzle and Paradox,* pgs.181-83
21 Reuters, March 2019
22 *Midi Madagasikara,* October 10 and October 28, 2019
23 *Puzzle and Paradox,* pg. 37.
24 Roger Thurow, *Africa, The Fertile Continent,*" Foreign Affairs, November/December 2010
25 *Loss of Fertile Land Fuels Looming Crisis Across Africa,* New

York Times, July 30, 2017

26 *Millennials Make Farming Sexy In Africa*, New York Times, May 27, 2019

27 *The Globalization of Inequality,* Francois Bourguignon *(2015)*, pgs. 186-89

28 Id., pg. 128

29 *Capital In The 21st Century,* Thomas Piketty *(2014),* pgs. 126-29

30 Id., pgs. 571-73

31 *The Great Leveler: Violence and the History of Inequality,* Walter Scheidel *(2017),* pgs. 6-9

32 Id., pgs. 442-44

33 World Bank, 2014 *Face of Poverty Report*

34 *Puzzle and Paradox*, pg. 173-74

35 Interview with Aime Jaony, June 12, 2019

36 Interview with McGordon Ranaivo Arivezo, July 11, 2019

37 Interview with Ismaya Said, July 20, July 27 & August 3, 2019

38 *Puzzle and Paradox*, pg. 178

39 Interview with Nasser Said Amany, July 13, 2019

40 Interview with Justin Sanamo, July 19, 2019

41 Interview with Olin Serazaka, July 17, 2019

42 Interview with Marie Rose Rasoavololona, July 17, 2019

43 Interview with Anissa Volatiana Mahazatsakila, July 29, 2019

44 Interview with Dodo Razafindrakoto, May 9, 2020

Chapter 5

1 *The End of Plenty,* Joel K. Bourne Jr., (W.W. Norton & Company, 2015), pgs. 35-37

2 *The Globe is Graying Fast, U.N. Says In New Forecast*, NY Times, June 17, 2019

3 *The Globe Is Graying Fast,* NY Times June 15, 2019

4 *The Globe Is Graying Fast,* NY Times June 15, 2019

5   Eugene Linden, *Remember The Population Bomb? It's Still Ticking*, NYT June 15, 2017

6   *Overpopulated and Underfed: Countries Near A Breaking Point*, Bill Marsh, NYT, June 15, 2017

7   *Overpopulated and Underfed: Countries Near A Breaking Point*, Bill Marsh, NYT, June 15, 2017

8   *"Instead of Coronavirus, The Hunger Will Kill Us,"* New York Times, April 22, 2020

9   *Countdown,* Alan Weisman, 2013, pgs. 39-40; 91-94

10   Id., pgs. 113-15

11   Id., pgs. 424-27

13   Bourne, *The End of Plenty*, pgs. 5, 56

14   Id., pgs. 146-48

15   Id., pgs. 148-52

16   Id., pgs. 307-13 and 274-77;

17   Id., pgs. 295-97

18   *The Reproach of Hunger*, David Rieff, Introduction

19   Id., pgs. 82-83

20   Id., pgs. 13-18

21   Id., pgs. 40-54

22   Id., pgs. 136-39

23   Id., pgs. 175-80

24   Id., pgs. 273-75

25   *The Age of Sustainable Development,* Jeffrey Sachs (2015), pgs. 194-99

26   Id., pgs. 317-25

27   Id., pgs. 208-14

28   Id., pgs. 54-55; pgs. 360-65

29   *How Population Change Will Transform Our World,* Sarah Harper (2016); pgs. 10-13

30   Id., pg. 1

31   Id., pg. 2

32   Id., pgs. 10-13; pgs. 53-54

33   Id., pgs. 120-24

34 Id., pgs. 134-41

35 David Wallace-Wells, *The Uninhabitable Earth,* pgs. 48-50

36 Id., pgs.88-92.

37 *"There's No More Water,"* NY Times, April 16, 2020

38 Ruchir Sharma, *The Demographics of Stagnation,* Foreign Affairs, March/April 2016

39 Id.

40 Id.

41 Id.

42 Id.

43 Randrianja and Ellis, *A Short History of Madagascar,* p.12

44 Randrianja ad Ellis, pgs. 187-88, citing Iliffe, *Africans,* p.2.

45 *The Population Bust: Demographic Decline and the End of Capitalism as We Know It;* Zachary Karabell, Foreign Affairs, September/October 2019

46 Id.

47 *Puzzle and Paradox, pg. 151*

48 *Overpopulated and Underfed: Countries Near A Breaking Point,* Bill Marsh, NYT, June 15, 2017

49 CIA World Factbook - Madagascar

50 *Early Pregnancy Affects 48% of Girls,* Madagascar Tribune, August 24, 2019

51 *59 Enfants Malgaches Meurent Avant de 5 Ans,* Madagascar Tribune, October 25, 2019

52 *"As Egypt's Population Hits 100 Million, Celebration Is Muted,"* NY Times, February 11, 2020

53 *Population Census: Limiting Births Is Becoming Imperative,* L'Express de Madagascar, August 7, 2019

54 *Madagascar Compte 25,680,642 Habitants,* Le Tribune Madagascar, August 7, 2019

55 *The Danger of A Galloping Population,* Midi Madagascar, August 10, 2019

56 *Overpopulated and Underfed: Countries Near A Breaking Point,* Bill Marsh, NYT, June 15, 2017

57 *La Ville des Mille Devenue La Ville du Million,* Midi Madigasikara, June 7, 2019

58 Id.

59 Wallace-Wells, *The Uninhabitable Earth,* pgs. 101, 104

60 William Laurance, *Al Jazeera,* December 17, 2018

61 *We Are Planting Trees Everywhere,* Mongabay.com, July 17, 2019

62 *Changement Climatique: L'Agriculture Responable de 75% de la Deforestation Mondiale,* Midi Madagasikara, August 17, 2019

63. *Reforestation de Madagascar: Les défis de l'auto-appropriation des Malgaches,* Midi Madagasikara, July 4, 2019

64 Interview with Anja Hobiniaina Ratovomamonjy, October 25, 2019

65 Interview with Isabella, August 8, 2019

66. Interview with Zaramany, August 8, 2019

67 Interview with Giselle, age 32, August 23, 2019

68 Interview with Elizabeth Soa, August 23, 2019

69 Interviews with Rano Ben Florentin and Rano Lazal, Faux Cap, September 28, 2019

Chapter 6

1 *"Losing Earth,"* Nathaniel Rich, The New York Times Magazine, August 5, 2018 (Prologue)

2 *"Carbon Dioxide Emissions Hit a Record in 2019, Even as Coal Fades,"* NY Times, December 3, 2019

3 *The Uninhabitable Earth* (2019), David Wallace-Wells, pgs. 44-48

4 *"How Much Will The Planet Warm If Carbon Dioxide Levels Double?"* NY Times, July 22, 2020

5 *"Greenhouse Gas Emissions Accelerate 'Like A Speeding Freight Train' in 2018,"* NY Times, December 5, 2018

6 *"The Climate Debt,"* Mohamed Adow, Foreign Affairs (May/June 2020 Issue)

7 *"Climate Change: What Everyone Needs to Know,"* Joseph

Romm, 2016, pgs. 73-75

8 *"Less Than Zero,"* by Fred Krupp, Nathaniel Keohane and Eric Pooley, Foreign Affairs, March/April 2019 Issue

9 *"How To Understand The UN's Dire New Climate Report,"* The Atlantic, October 10, 2018

10 United Nations IPCC Press Release, October 8, 2018

11 *"How To Understand The UN's Dire New Climate Report,"* The Atlantic, October 10, 2018

12 Id., pgs. 154-58

13 Wallace-Wells, pgs. 179-80

14 Id., pgs. 247-49

15 "Bleak UN Report on a Planet in Peril Looms Over New Climate Talks," NY Times, November 26, 2019

16 *"Warming Earth: Why Climate Change Matters More Than Anything Else,"* Joshua Busby, Foreign Affairs, July/August 2018 Issue

17 *"How Scientists Got Climate Change So Wrong,"* NY Times, November 8, 2019

18 *"Climate Change Poses Threat To Children's Health Worldwide,"* NY Times, November 13, 2019

19 Id., Epilogue

20 "UN Climate Talks End with Few Commitments and a Lost Opportunity," NY Times, December 15, 2019

21 The New York Times, August 6, 2019

22 Bourne, *The End of Plenty,* pgs. 208-10.

23 *"India's Terrifying Water Crisis,"* The New York Times, July 15, 2019

24 *"In Zimbabwe, The Water Taps Run Dry, and Worsen a Nightmare,* The New York Times, August 2, 2019

25 *"Warming World: Why Climate Change Matters More than Anything Else,"* Joshua Busby, Foreign Affairs, July/August 2018 Issue

26 *"The World Can Make More Water From the Sea, But at What Cost?"* The NY Times, October 22, 2019

27 Bourne, *The End of Plenty*, pgs. 156-58

28 Bourne, *The End of Plenty*, pgs. 14-21

29 Id.

30 *Can We Grow More Food On Less Land? We'll Have to, A New Study Finds;* NY Times, December 5, 2018

31 *Climate Change Threatens the World's Food Supply, UN Warns;* NY Times, August 8, 2019

32 Id., pgs. 123-27; pgs.131-35

33 *"Billions Could Live In Extreme Heat Zones Within Decades,"* NY Times, May 4, 2020

34 Wallace-Wells, pgs. 24, 28.

35 *"A Quarter of Bangladesh Is Flooded. Millions Have Lost Everything,"* NY Times, July 30, 2020

36 *Global Wealth Gap Would Be Smaller Today Without Climate Change,"* NY Times, April 22, 2019

37 Wallace-Wells, pg. 165-66

38 Marsh, *Overpopulated and Underfed*

39 Nicholas Kristof, New York Times, January 6, 2017

40 *Warding Off Famine In Drought Prone Madagascar With EU Aid,* Euronews.com, March 28, 2019

41 *"As Donald Trump Denies Climate Change, These Kids Die of It,"* New York Times, January 6, 2017

42 Kathryn Sikkink, *Evidence For Hope,* pgs. 145-153

43 Rieff, *The Reproach of Hunger,* Introduction

44 Id.

45 Midi Magasikara, July 18, 2019

46 *"Denutrition, Carences Alimentaires et Surpoids,"* Midi Madagasikara, October 17, 2019

47 *"Prioritize The Fight Against Food Insecurity,"* Patrice Rabe, Midi Madagasikara, October 18, 2019

48 *73 Communes of the Great South In State of Nutritional Emergency,* Madagascar Tribune, May 21, 2019

49 *"Five Global Trends Shaping Our Climate Future,"* NY Times, November 12, 2019

50 *"The Climate Debt,"* Mohamed Adow, Foreign Affairs (May/June 2020 Issue)

51 Id.

52 Wallace Wells, pgs. 117, 226-27

53 Interview with Herve Anognona, Regional Director of MAEP, 9/6/19, Tulear.

54 Interview with Christophe, 10/10/10, Tulear

55 Interview with Claude Rafandmezantsoa, September 16, 2019

56 Interview with Ralimbisoa Mandova, 9/30/19, Tsihombe

57 *Puzzle and Paradox*, pg. 161

58 Interview with Bruno Ibramdjee, Ampanihy, 9/10/19

Epilogue

1   *Why Nations Fail: The Origins of Power, Prosperity and Power,"* Daron Acemoglu and James Robinson, (Crown Business, 2012), pgs. 429-34.

2   *"Puzzle and Paradox: A Political Economy of Madagascar,"* by Mireille Razafindrakoto, Francois Roubaud and Jean-Michel Wachsberger, Cambridge University Press, 2020, pgs. 219, 222.

3   Id., pgs. 184-85

4   Patrice Rabe, Midi Madagasikara, March 21, 2020

5   Id.

6   *"Minister's Coronavirus Appeal Leaves Madagascar Government Split,"* Agence France Press, July 22, 2020

7   *"The Covid-19 Riddle,"* The New York Times, May 3, 2020

8   *"Ten African Countries Have No Ventilators,"* New York Times, April 18, 2020

9   *"China: Principal Economic Partner of Madagascar,"* Madagascar Tribune, October 1, 2019

10 *"Chine: Plus de 20 Projets d'Infrastructure a Madagascar,"* Midi Madagascar, August 9, 2019

11 *The Costliest Pearl: China's Struggle for India's Ocean,* Bertil

Lintner, (Hurst, 2019), p. 21

12 Id., pgs. 217-220

13 Id., pgs. 128-29

14 Id., p. 137-4015

15 *"Puzzle and Paradox: A Political Economy of Madagascar,"* by Mireille Razafindrakoto, Francois Roubaud and Jean-Michel Wachsberger, Cambridge University Press, 2020, pgs. 195-202.

16 Id., pgs. 184

17 Id., pgs. 209-10, 217

18 Id., pgs. 218-19.

19 Id., pgs. 226-27

20 Id., pg. 232

21 Id., pgs. 190-91

22 Id., pgs. 235, 238-240

23 *"A Democracy In the Making,"* Patrice Rabe, Midi Madagasikara, August 2, 2019

24 *"Africa's Democratic Moment?"* Foreign Affairs, July/August 2019 Edition

25 *"Paths to Power: The Rise and Fall of Dictators,"* Anna Grzymala-Busse, Foreign Affairs, January/February 2020 Issue

26 *"Une Atmosphere Qui Commence A Devenir Deletere"*, Patrice Rabe, Midi Madagasikara, October 19, 2019

27 *"Madagascar Tries to Reach Emerging Country Status,"* Madagascar Tribune, October 1, 2019

Author Biography

Nathaniel Adams is an attorney in the United States who has traveled to over 25 developing countries, both for business reasons and out of personal curiosity. He holds degrees from Georgetown University's School of Foreign Service and the University of Virginia School of Law. This book, his first, is based on eight months of travel and research in Madagascar in 2019. He would welcome any inquiries or feedback at nathanieladams44@gmail.com.

Index

stunted growth of, 327

undernutrition and malnutrition
of, 328–329

Chile, 267

China, 19, 83, 259, 266–267, 306,
307–308, 310, 358–362

Christanity/Christians

hostility towards, 51–52

in Madagascar, 56–57

support for, 49–50

Churchill, Winston, 69

civil society organizations, 136,
217

climate change

and food insecurity, 319–321

and food production, 263–264

global warming and droughts,
319–322

and human progress, 21–22

and land use, 285

coastal–highland divide. see
distrust between ethnic groups

coastal tribes, 39–40, 73, 79, 82,
161, 168, 169, 236

college education, 217–229

Collier, Paul, 192

Colorado River, 306

Comoros, 59, 265

Confucius Institute, 361

Conseil Superieure, 134

constitution

1972 amendment, 83–85

1992 amendment, 88–89

1998 amendment, 89–90

2002 amendment, 92

2010 amendment, 124, 141

constitutional crises, 13

Convention on International
Trade in Endangered Species
of Wild Flora and Fauna
(CITES), 284–285

Copernicus Climate Change
Service, 306

Coronel, Sheila, 146

corruption, 161–167, 209–210, 225

Countdown (Weisman), 254

coup (2009), 96–97

CAPSAT's role in, 103–107

circumstances leading to, 108–
112

declining economy after, 194–195

French involvement in, 104

General's narrative of, 5–11

international condemnation of,
107

and new constitution, 83

Ravalomanana's version of,
119–122

coup d'etat, 111, 116, 123, 241

Covid-19 crisis in Madagascar,
20–21, 253–254, 354–357

Covid-Organics, 355

crime and vanilla cultivation,
215–216

cultural barriers, 225

in education, 224

in production of new goods, 244

cultural shift, 56–57, 275

economic inequality in, 207–208
elites and the population, 363–365
emigration, 335
English missionaries in, 49
European settlers in, 34–38
export crops, 214
family planning programs in, 287–288, 290–291
food aid, 202–203, 323
foreign aid dependency, 199, 201, 259, 289
foreign policy post independence, 80
French attempt to colonize, 60–66
French influence post independence, 79–82
French settlements and trading posts in, 43–47
geographic isolation and poverty, 198
Gini coefficient, 207
ideological beliefs, lack of, 139, 147, 151
independence, 71–73
internal migration, 335–337
job prospects in, 229–242
living conditions, 183–190
mining sector, 200
natural resources in, 12, 79, 125, 139, 194–195, 198–199, 208, 214, 240, 286, 300, 348
out-of-school children in, 24–25
overpopulation problem in, 288

people's trust in the administration, 181
per capita GDP in, 23–24, 81, 191–192
political freedom, lack of, 160–161
political participation by the electorate, 160–161
population growth crisis, 261, 272–274, 277–281
presidential election of 2001, 91–92
public opinion surveys, 207–208
Radama, reign of, 45–50
Radama II, reign of, 55
Rainilaiarivony's policies, 56–62
Ranavalona I, reign of, 50–52
Ranavalona II, reign of, 56–58
Rasoherina, reign of, 55–56
Ratsiraka's rule, 83–90
Ravalomanana's rule, 92–93
revolutionary socialism in, 84–85
rise of indigenous kingdoms, 38–43
sanctions on, 107–108, 123, 125–126
staple crops, 323
and Taiwan, 359
Tsiranana's rule, 79–81
university education in, 217–229
urbanization in, 212–215
urban poverty, 299–300
World War II, impact of, 68–69
youth unemployment in, 216

CHRONOS
BOOKS

HISTORY

Chronos Books is an historical non-fiction imprint. Chronos
publishes real history for real people; bringing to life people,
places and events in an imaginative, easy-to-digest and
accessible way - histories that pass on their stories to a
generation of new readers.
If you have enjoyed this book, why not tell other readers by
posting a review on your preferred book site.

Recent bestsellers from Chronos Books are:

Lady Katherine Knollys
The Unacknowledged Daughter of King Henry VIII
Sarah-Beth Watkins
A comprehensive account of Katherine Knollys' questionable
paternity, her previously unexplored life in the Tudor court
and her intriguing relationship with Elizabeth I.
Paperback: 978-1-78279-585-8 ebook: 978-1-78279-584-1

Cromwell was Framed
Ireland 1649
Tom Reilly
Revealed: The definitive research that proves the Irish nation
owes Oliver Cromwell a huge posthumous apology for
wrongly convicting him of civilian atrocities in 1649.
Paperback: 978-1-78279-516-2 ebook: 978-1-78279-515-5

Why The CIA Killed JFK and Malcolm X
The Secret Drug Trade in Laos
John Koerner
A new groundbreaking work presenting evidence that the CIA
silenced JFK to protect its secret drug trade in Laos.
Paperback: 978-1-78279-701-2 ebook: 978-1-78279-700-5

The Disappearing Ninth Legion
A Popular History
Mark Olly
The Disappearing Ninth Legion examines hard evidence for the
foundation, development, mysterious disappearance, or possi-
ble continuation of Rome's lost Legion.
Paperback: 978-1-84694-559-5 ebook: 978-1-84694-931-9

Beaten But Not Defeated
Siegfried Moos - A German anti-Nazi who settled in Britain
Merilyn Moos
Siegi Moos, an anti-Nazi and active member of the German
Communist Party, escaped Germany in 1933 and, exiled in
Britain, sought another route to the transformation
of capitalism.
Paperback: 978-1-78279-677-0 ebook: 978-1-78279-676-3

A Schoolboy's Wartime Letters
An evacuee's life in WWII — A Personal Memoir
Geoffrey Iley
A boy writes home during WWII, revealing his own fascinating
story, full of zest for life, information and humour.
Paperback: 978-1-78279-504-9 ebook: 978-1-78279-503-2

The Life & Times of the Real Robyn Hoode
Mark Olly
A journey of discovery. The chronicles of the genuine historical
character, Robyn Hoode, and how he became one of England's
greatest legends.
Paperback: 978-1-78535-059-7 ebook: 978-1-78535-060-3

Readers of ebooks can buy or view any of these bestsellers by
clicking on the live link in the title. Most titles are published in
paperback and as an ebook. Paperbacks are available in
traditional bookshops. Both print and ebook formats are
available online.

Find more titles and sign up to our readers' newsletter at
http://www.johnhuntpublishing.com/history-home

Follow us on Facebook at
https://www.facebook.com/ChronosBooks

and Twitter at https://twitter.com/ChronosBooks